The Subject of Philosophy

Theory and History of Literature
Edited by Wlad Godzich and Jochen Schulte-Sasse

For other books in the series, see p. 203

The Subject of Philosophy

Philippe Lacoue-Labarthe

Edited and with a Foreword by Thomas Trezise

Translated by Thomas Trezise, Hugh J. Silverman,
Gary M. Cole, Timothy D. Bent,
Karen McPherson, and Claudette Sartiliot

Linda M. Brooks, Editorial Consultant

Theory and History of Literature, Volume 83

University of Minnesota Press
Minneapolis
London

Chapters 1, 2, 3, 4, and 5 originally appeared in *Le Sujet de la philosophie*. Copyright Aubier-Flammarion, Paris, 1979. Chapter 6 originally appeared as "L'Imprésentable" in *Poétique* 21 (1975).

Published by the University of Minnesota Press
2037 University Avenue Southeast, Minneapolis, MN 55455-3092
Printed in the United States of America on acid-free paper

Library of Congress Cataloging-in-Publication Data

Lacoue-Labarthe, Philippe.
   [Sujet de la philosophie. English]
   The subject of philosophy / Philippe Lacoue-Labarthe ; edited and with a foreword by
Thomas Trezise ; translated by Thomas Trezise . . . [et al.].
     p. cm. — (Theory and history of literature ; v. 83)
   Includes bibliographical references and index.
   ISBN 0-8166-1697-3 (alk. paper).
   ISBN 0-8166-1698-1 (pbk. : alk. paper)
   1. Philosophy—Miscellanea. I. Trezise, Thomas, 1953–
II. Title. III. Series.
B68.L3213 1993
100—dc20   92-29837
                                                CIP

In memory of
EUGENIO U. DONATO
1937–1983

Contents

Memorial Note

There could be no more apt a place for a tribute to Eugenio Donato than in a book by Philippe Lacoue-Labarthe. In the mid 1970s, Donato was among the first to grasp the seminal character of Lacoue-Labarthe's work. He also initiated the dissemination of Lacoue-Labarthe's *œuvre* in English, discussing a project with him in 1981 and commissioning translations shortly thereafter. When Donato's project was cut short by his death in 1983, I asked Lacoue-Labarthe's permission to continue it in his memory. Two volumes have resulted: *Typography* (1989), and now *The Subject of Philosophy*. Because both volumes are emblems of Donato's deep commitment to Lacoue-Labarthe's work, the memorial celebration of Donato here is as much a celebration of Lacoue-Labarthe, of their similar probings of romantic philosophy, of their shared love of music, of poetry—a celebration of all the things that Donato's intense consciousness brought to a new light.

The project's memorial character springs almost entirely from the participation of Donato's friends and colleagues—from their advice and support throughout the slow progress of the project; from their translations of Lacoue-Labarthe's essays, albeit painstakingly reworked in *Typography* by Christopher Fynsk and now in *The Subject of Philosophy* by Thomas Trezise; from their willingness to write introductions, Jacques Derrida for *Typography*, Louis Marin and, subsequently, Thomas Trezise for *The Subject of Philosophy*; and from Lacoue-Labarthe's generous consent.

In addition to these, I would like to thank, for their fidelity and responsiveness, Eduardo Cadava, Alain Cohen, Tom Conley, Rodolphe Gasché, Josué Harari, Barbara Harlow, Judd Hubert, Marie-Hélène Huet, Richard Macksey, Kerry McKeever, Kishin Moorjani, Sam Weber, and Ningkun Wu.

It remains only for me to express my deep gratitude to Thomas Trezise for the superb job he has done, and to both Thomas and Philippe for their gentle acceptance of this memorial impulse.

Linda Marie Brooks

Editor's Preface

The publication of this volume originated with Eugenio Donato's desire to make the work of Philippe Lacoue-Labarthe available in English. It is not entirely certain how Donato himself would have organized the various essays of which he commissioned translations; indeed, it is not even certain how many volumes he had in mind. Based on Lacoue-Labarthe's own recollection of Donato's plans, however, a first volume has been published with "Typography" as its "centerpiece," and including "The Echo of the Subject" (originally the last chapter of *Le Sujet de la philosophie*) as well as essays on Hölderlin, Diderot, and Heidegger from *L'Imitation des modernes*.[1] This second volume—*The Subject of Philosophy*—includes the first five chapters of *Le Sujet de la philosophie*, all of which figure among Lacoue-Labarthe's earliest philosophical publications, as well as the previously uncollected essay "The Unpresentable," the translation of which was commissioned and at least partially edited by Donato in 1982 (for further information, see "A Note on Sources," this volume).

To those already familiar with *Typography*, the publication of *The Subject of Philosophy* may appear somewhat "untimely": with the exception of "The Unpresentable," all of the texts gathered here predate "Typography," and hence portray belatedly or *après coup* the genesis of a thought whose extraordinary force is now widely associated with the "deconstruction" of mimesis. It should immediately be stressed, however, that even if, as Lacoue-Labarthe himself has pointed out, the trajectory traced in *Le Sujet de la philosophie* subsequently underwent considerable alteration—leading, instead of to a second book entitled *L'Avortement de la littérature*, to what became *L'Imitation des modernes*[2]—there remains between these two "moments" of his career an undeniable continuity: not only are the seeds of his later thinking of mimesis clearly perceptible in the early essays, but his concern with such questions as subjectivity and representation has lost none of its urgency or acuity in the later work. One could add that the appearance of *both* of these volumes in translation is untimely in another, more important sense; for precisely when the purveyors of critical fashion and ideological reaction would have us move "beyond deconstruction," Lacoue-Labarthe (who, incidentally, makes rather sparing use of the term and whose work is in any case irreducible to what is commonly [mis]understood by it) reminds us, in his radically defamiliarizing way, that the questions it raises—aesthetic, ethical, political, social, historical, and of course philosophical—will by their very nature persist regardless of anyone's desire to "have done" with them, or, which amounts to the same, that the "economy" in which it involves us admits of no simple "beyond." But I shall reserve further substantive comment for the Foreword.

As editor of this volume, I have naturally tried, while respecting the work of each translator, to insure a certain uniform fidelity to Lacoue-Labarthe's text, and this especially in the way of lexical continuity and the reproduction (to the extent that this is possible in English) of his singular syntax—a syntax emblematic of his extraordinary attentiveness to the rhythm of language and of the no less extraordinary prudence and rigor of his thought. And while I assume ultimate responsibility in the matter, I would like to thank, in addition to the translators themselves, all those who have contributed in one way or another to the long-awaited realization of this project. To begin with: Layla Ahsan, Nancy Davies, Pamela DeRuiter-Prach, Christopher Fynsk, Mary Jean Green, Josué Harari, François Rigolot, Ted Ruel, Steven Scher, and Andrzej Warminski. I am especially indebted to Patricia Carter and Marianne Hraibi of the Interlibrary Loan Office at Dartmouth College, whose efficiency and grace enormously facilitated my task in its final stages; and to my friends, Alain Toumayan and Kimball Lockhart, whose critical reading of the Foreword has, I trust, helped me to make it more intelligible and useful to Lacoue-Labarthe's readers.

I would also like to express my gratitude to Linda Brooks, for inviting me to undertake this project; to Biodun Iginla, for his expertise, patience, and supportive cooperation over the years; to Philippe Lacoue-Labarthe, for—among other things—responding so graciously to my numerous and insistent queries; to the Committee on Research in the Humanities and Social Sciences of Princeton University, for financial support; and to the University itself for leave time that enabled me to complete my work.

Lastly, to Susan Brison, especially now, I owe much more than gratitude.

T. T.
Lyme, New Hampshire
January 1992

Foreword
Persistence

Thomas Trezise

The introduction of a thinker as forceful and productive as Philippe Lacoue-Labarthe would doubtless prove an impossible task were its scope not clearly restricted from the outset. I shall accordingly focus on this volume alone, in an effort to explain its importance both for philosophy per se and for the relation between philosophy and literature or art in general. To this end, I am inclined to argue first of all that Lacoue-Labarthe's thought moves essentially within the "space" opened by the ambiguity of a title such as *The Subject of Philosophy*. But everything depends, of course, on the definition of this space and of the subject pertaining to it.

Since we must begin somewhere, we might as well do so by saying that the ambiguous subject of philosophy is at least double: it is both the matter and the form of philosophy, its "what" and its "how," that about which there is philosophizing—its *object*—and the philosophizing itself as an activity identified, especially since Descartes, with a thinking self or philosophical agent—its *subject*. So far, so good, or so it would seem: are we not already on what Hegel called, precisely in reference to the philosophy of Descartes, "solid ground"?[1] In fact, we have unwittingly decided the nature of the space just mentioned, no less than of the subject(s) of philosophy, before even allowing it to emerge as a genuine question. For to invoke the modern distinction between subject and object is immediately, and despite the best of intentions, to construe this same "between" in a certain way, namely, as a relation grounded in the separation of self-identical terms. It is to assume the very *interval* constitutive of the modern metaphysics of subjectivity, in which a subject entirely present to itself confronts an object present or op-posed to that subject. To the extent, moreover, that it is through and *as* this interval that the subject defines itself, to the extent that this metaphysics depends on the initiative of the subject, the opposition of subject and object necessarily implies a hierarchy. Indeed, as Lacoue-Labarthe himself will not fail to point out, any such opposition or negation, in which each term is self-identical if only by virtue of its *not* being the other, involves a fundamental dissymmetry that renders the opposition itself reducible to unity: in the case at hand, that is, in the philosophical era extending from Descartes to Hegel, subjectivity ultimately negates its own negation, sublates its other as or into itself. Needless to say, this is only possible if the other in question is initially conceived in conformity with subjectivity *as* negation. In other words, only if the other of negation is originally understood as but another negation, if alterity is made in the image of identity, will it eventually lend itself to the *Aufhebung* or sublation in which it is reappropriated by the Subject. It is to this apparent circularity that Hegel alludes when, in the preface to the *Phenomenology of Spirit*, he characterizes the truth of subjectivity as "the process of its own becoming, the circle that presupposes its end as its goal, having its end also as its beginning."[2] Thus, the space of *this* subject turns out to be the projection of an absolute closure. But since it is not so much this subject of philosophy, since it is not so much this closure or totalization as its *failure* that interests Lacoue-Labarthe, the properly interrogative movement of his own thought inevitably describes, relative to Hegel and the tradition culminating in him, a radical eccentricity. In order to follow Lacoue-Labarthe, then, we have to start over.

To be sure, such a repetition, wherein the ostensible focus of a critical discourse serves as the starting point of its own displacement, characterizes to a considerable degree the very deconstructive strategy of which Lacoue-Labarthe himself is one of the most rigorous and least apologetic practitioners. But it would be a mistake to think that on its basis we can know what comes next, any more than we can know this in the precursors of deconstruction on whom Lacoue-Labarthe chooses to focus, namely, Nietzsche, Freud, and Heidegger. For the failure to which I have just alluded and whose "advent" in the history of philosophy is attested by—among other things—the unthought in Heidegger, the unconscious or the late doctrine of drives in Freud, and the Nietzschean affirmation "God is dead," undermines precisely this kind of certainty by suggesting that the meaning of subjectivity (or, for that matter, meaning in general) does not lie in a *principium*, such as the principle of negation or identity, by which one could assure in advance the closure of interpretation. Indeed, it is the nature of discourse itself and the way in which it makes sense—assuming it still makes sense, and this is perhaps the whole question—that change: given that "in no case is the beginning the end and [that] if the Absolute *defers* its manifestation, it does so indefinitely, because it is not here and never could be,"[3] those who would articulate this failure are inevitably impelled toward something other than the other that the Absolute, the traditional subject of philosophy, has always purported to en-close within its own circle of meaning, something other than another identity. As Lacoue-Labarthe says concerning Nietzsche's own efforts to elaborate such a lan-guage: "It must above all be other by virtue of an alterity that is itself other than dialectical alterity."[4] The deconstructive displacement of the subject does not therefore merely reverse an oppositional dissymmetry while leaving the opposi-tion and its terms intact (as it is often said of Marx relative to Hegel, or, less credi-bly still, of Nietzsche relative to Plato); rather, it seeks to articulate a relation other than that of opposition itself, a relation of differential intrication in which the involvement of terms with each other constitutes their only identity or quid-dity. Whatever name one may wish to give this relation—"difference" in Heideg-ger, "writing" in Derrida, or, as we shall see, "literature" in Lacoue-Labarthe—we end up with a double discursive economy that accounts in large part for the strategic complexity of deconstructive criticism. We end up, to borrow Bataille's vocabulary, with a "restricted" economy in which meaning is founded still on the principle of identity, in which, to simplify, language "means what it says," and a "general" economy in which, as a differential or *contextual relation* whereby every term is fundamentally non-self-identical or "outside" itself, meaning ex-ceeds the closure of the restricted economy—and does so precisely to the extent that it informs this economy in the first place. As this excess over closure, this failure of closure, meaning or sense in the general economy is always *à venir*, yet to come, indefinitely deferred—which is to say that it is *essentially* a question, an indecision, or, indeed, an ambiguity.

Now one may very well ask what these ostensibly digressive remarks have to do with the "space" of Lacoue-Labarthe's thought and with his understanding of the subject of philosophy. Although this question cannot be answered in a simple way, we can at least say the following: this metaphorical space is certainly not the (other) one invoked by Hegel when he says, in the passage already cited, that with Descartes we are philosophically *zu Hause*. It is not the interval whereby, distinguishing itself from what it is not, subjectivity is "at home" with itself. In fact, as the very failure of this interval, as the defection of the distinction between a "here" and a "there" or an inside and an outside, such a space cannot be ade-quately designated by any single *unequivocal* term or metaphor. This may well include even the ambiguous Heideggerian *Ent-fernung* or *é-loignement* examined in "Obliteration," which seems less than satisfactory in Lacoue-Labarthe's case as it is indissociable from the "step back" through which, in spite of everything, the claims of a certain phenomenology appear to be reaffirmed.[5] So we might do better to look again to Nietzsche, who says, in a late fragment: "*Wir hören auf zu denken, wenn wir es nicht in dem sprachlichen Zwange tun wollen*, wir langen gerade noch bei dem Zweifel an, hier eine Grenze als Grenze zu sehen."[6] While one can hardly dispute the translation of *Zwang* as "constraint," it seems to me that we miss the full tenor of the italicized proposition if we fail to keep in mind that *Zwang* can also mean *compulsion*. The first sense of the word conveys claustration, that is, a confinement or enclosure obviously different from that of a "being at home"; but it does this so clearly only because the second sense conveys an irresistible inclination to exceed the limits of that enclosure. It is as though the constraint of language were simultaneously the compulsion to break, in language, the barrier of silence, as though this imperative were indistinguishable from an incapacity, as though, in short, the obligation for thought to speak were also and at once its *inability not* to do so. In this fragment, *Zwang* may therefore be understood to designate an interiority *engendered* by the necessity of its own transgression, much as the restricted economy is produced by the force of a general economy that exceeds it. As for the second part of the passage, it is certainly no less important than the first, since it indicates the most basic corollary of language so conceived, to wit, that the limit we are both compelled to transgress and unable to abolish does not lie at a phenomenal distance from us, such that it might become an object of knowledge, but rather constitutes an *internal* breach, at once too near and hence too far to be grasped, and giving rise to doubt about itself—about whether language is a prison or a desert, about whether it even makes sense to ask what difference there is between the subject(s) of philosophy. It is the space of this indecision, this question, that the ambiguity in *The Subject of Philosophy*, to which I alluded at the beginning, may be said to create. The space, so to speak, of Lacoue-Labarthe's thought.

We can thus begin to gauge the significance of this work. For in addition to the extraordinarily patient, rigorous, and even surprising readings it offers not only of Nietzsche, Freud, and Heidegger, but also of Hegel and German romanticism, *The Subject of Philosophy* presents a convincing portrait of Lacoue-Labarthe himself as one of the very few philosophers of our or any day for whom the alternatives of knowledge and its frustration, or power and its frustration, do not form the ultimate horizon of thinking—one of the few who *affirm* the "failure" of philosophy as the very possibility of thought.

But there is more. For what, again, of the subject(s) of philosophy? Can we continue to speak of it or them in terms of subject and object, "how" and "what," form and matter, that is, in the very language of that metaphysics—which in fact is not just modern but post-Socratic—whose undoing is at issue? On the other hand, what alternative do we have? And why should the thinking of the subject(s) of philosophy necessarily lead to the question concerning philosophy and *literature*? One thing seems certain: in Lacoue-Labarthe's readings of Nietzsche, Freud, and Heidegger—indeed, even in his reading of Hegel[7]—the uncanny sense of being outside so-called Western metaphysics while remaining somehow enclosed by it is of a piece with the equally uncanny sense of a historical belatedness motivating a kind of return to origins—in Freudian terminology, a sense of the *Nachträglichkeit* inseparable from that other compulsion, the *Wiederholungszwang*. I am thinking, of course, of the influence exercised on these three thinkers by Greece, especially of the pre-Socratic era, which not only is crucial to an understanding of their work but, as it is broached here in *The Subject of Philosophy*, already foreshadows Lacoue-Labarthe's subsequent and incomparable meditation of mimesis as both an aesthetic and a political problem. Why this return, then, particularly to myth, if the problem of meaning in the post-Hegelian age does not recall something through whose exclusion or denial philosophy has, since Socrates — "he who does not write" — and to a great extent because of him, defined itself? How can meaning even *be* (again) a problem or a question, that is, an indefinite futurity, unless it repeats the forgotten or immemorial past of what makes philosophy possible in the first place? And what is this condition of possibility, if not the very form of philosophy, if not its literary representation? Fiction in "The Fable," rhetoric in "The Detour," style or literary genre in "Apocryphal Nietzsche," authorial subject and the work in "Obliteration," theatrical representation in "The Scene Is Primal," the whole domain of the aesthetic in "The Unpresentable" — these are so many angles from which Lacoue-Labarthe foregrounds the formal dimensions of a discourse perennially driven by a will to transparency. But here we must be careful not to jump to the conclusion that if form and matter are not opposed to each other, they must be identical; to say, without further qualification, that philosophy simply *is* literature. The nature and the difficulty of the problem do not allow of such facile solutions. If Lacoue-Labarthe speaks of "displacing the bar that symbolically separates literature and philosophy (literature/philosophy) in such a way that on each side literature and philosophy are both crossed out and cancel each other in communicating,"[8] it is because their relation does not conform to a logic of (non)contradiction, whose only modalities are separation and union, because the identity of each is strictly a function of their communication. And if, furthermore, Lacoue-Labarthe is more concerned here with the literariness of philosophy than with the philosophical dimension of literature, it is because, historically and in keeping with what was earlier said regarding the dissymmetry intrinsic to every opposition (a dissymmetry determined, in this case, by the relative values of truth and fiction), the relation between philosophy and literature or art in general has been weighted by philosophy in favor of philosophy itself. So that, in short, what happens in this displacement of the bar is that the (literary) *form* of philosophy — from Socratic dialogue to Nietzschean dithyramb, and not excluding Hegel's *Phenomenology of Spirit* — becomes the *matter* of philosophical reflection. This much, it seems, is clear. But then, a new problem immediately arises. For how is this reflection to be distinguished from the *Aufhebung*, from the *relève* or *reprise*, from the dialectical sublation of the very discourse it supposedly calls into question? If the reflection on the literary form of philosophy is itself of a philosophical nature, has anything really changed? Do we not mystify ourselves and others even further by making form the matter of philosophy, by making an object of its subject(ivity) and hence diverting attention from the very subject(ivity) responsible for this transformation?

Of course, Lacoue-Labarthe is perfectly aware of this problem. And the question just asked is already raised, albeit in a different context and form, when he studies Heidegger's relation to Hegel, in which it appears that "the more thinking distances itself from the philosophical, the more it resembles it."[9] This is, in a nutshell, the double bind of mimesis, and it points to the figure that, in Lacoue-Labarthe's work, will supersede the "solid ground" of Cartesianism, namely, the figure of the abyss. But to return to our question, now reformulated: How can one articulate a thinking of the subject of philosophy that is not sublatable by philosophy? A knowing that is not a knowledge? A force irreducible to power? Does the abyss itself represent anything more than a suspended Hegelianism? Where does Lacoue-Labarthe "himself" stand in all of this?

It is certainly not Lacoue-Labarthe's *intention* to elaborate a metaphilosophy. But neither was it Nietzsche's or Heidegger's, as he points out in the polemic against Granier.[10] If nevertheless the deconstruction of the traditional subject of philosophy cannot avoid claiming for itself the very truth it purports to undo, is not every thinker condemned to take a position, to enunciate a thesis, and so to succumb to philosophy's redoubtable power of enclosure? Or is it rather the unavoidability, the ineluctability itself that is at issue? Something like a powerlessness corresponding, in the order of thought, to that which, in the order of discourse or language, I earlier called the inability not to speak? Imagining the abyssal structure in which the Absolute indefinitely defers its manifestation, one cannot help but see each successive position, at once container and contained, enframing and enframed, as the *effect* of the deferral itself. In other words, what is absolute or unconditional in the structure of the abyss is precisely that which both produces and exceeds the order of manifestation, just as the general produces the meaning or meanings of the restricted economy but is not itself, strictly speaking, meaningful. The abyss is therefore indeed the figure of something other than an arrested Hegelianism, since it does not admit of the Absolute as a future presence, or, in Heidegger's words, as "the Not-yet of the god that is coming";[11] nor, for that very reason, does it allow one to construe its "principle" or "ground"—let us call it here, for the sake of convenience, difference—as merely a negativity in abeyance. The figure of the abyss or *Abgrund* is only possible if the ground gives way, if the principle of negation "fails" in such a way that the power and knowledge it founds as predicates of subjectivity respectively become an im-possibility in the etymological sense of the word, that is, a powerlessness, and a *non-savoir*. But let us be precise: this *non-savoir*, this nonknowledge is not a mere lack of knowledge or of consciousness, any more than powerlessness is a mere absence of force. The failure of the negative describes the intrication of subjectivity with an exteriority that cannot indeed be known as an object, since this very intrication precludes the separation required for such knowledge; but it also defines this exteriority as something that cannot *but* be known, as that which is at once strangest and most familiar to us, in a word, as *unheimlich*, since the force with which it invests subjectivity impels the repetition whereby the sameness or identity of the subject *as* difference first achieves awareness. Such "knowing," which is both more and less than a knowledge, thus proves to be, for the subject, not just an impossibility but also a compulsion, an obligation to think and an inability not to think that condition all philosophical power.

Of course, one could say that this too is only another position, all the more pretentious as it purports to account for the possibility of position taking in general. Perhaps. Yet, unlike a philosophical thesis, it is not primarily concerned to distinguish itself from other theses, whether in order to confirm or to contradict them; that is, it does not concern itself with distinction per se, since this pertains to the philosophical. Thus, unlike Heidegger, for example, Lacoue-Labarthe systematically refrains from ascribing a doctrine to Nietzsche in order then to distinguish his own thinking from said doctrine. However, if this were all there was to it, he would obviously fall headlong into the mimetic trap, since such non-ascription would serve precisely to distinguish his own thinking from Heidegger's. Accordingly, rather than succumb to the temptation to reify Heidegger, Lacoue-Labarthe sets himself the task of doing justice in his reading of Heidegger to the tensions informing Heidegger's reading of Nietzsche. In the process, he shows how Heidegger's efforts to obliterate or erase the "literary" in Nietzsche (understood here as an alterity that is not of a philosophical order, as "that *other* of thought which would not be thought itself or would not be – like the unthought that must be written un-*thought* – of the order of thought"[12]) have as their paradoxical effect an entirely different kind of obliteration, an "interminable surcharge or . . . superimposition."[13] So it is that "the erasure of the text engenders its proliferation";[14] like signification in the strange structure of the supplement,[15] "literature" here designates for Lacoue-Labarthe the general economy in which the philosophical repression of a nonphilosophical alterity takes – despite itself, and this is precisely the point – the form of literature or writing in the conventional sense.

Does this apparently descriptive or diagnostic account of obliteration imply that Lacoue-Labarthe "himself" somehow eludes all mimesis? Of course not. For again – and as I suggested just a moment ago – nothing is more clearly symptomatic of mimetic entrapment than the claim to escape the mimetic. But this does not mean that the *experience* of the abyss remains invariable from one thinker to the next. In fact, I will readily go so far as to say that no thinker is more acutely aware than Lacoue-Labarthe of the semantic affinity between the words "abyss" and "experience." As he notes elsewhere,[16] appealing to the Latin etymology of the term, "experience" is for him to be construed as "la traversée d'un danger," as the crossing or passing through of a danger or peril – the peril being, in this case, the abyss itself. Yet, the challenge for Lacoue-Labarthe is not to get through or out of the abyss, but precisely to stay in it, to seek the difference that invests and exceeds all pursuit, "to be faithful to what tolerates only infidelity."[17] The challenge, in other words—the "task of thinking"—is not to step back, to think the *un*thought as the un*thought* or difference as Being to be thought, but rather to think the unthought as the other of thought and to think difference "itself" outside of onotology, as—in Lévinas's expression—an *autrement qu'être*. In short, the task of thinking is to "desist," in the special sense that Lacoue-Labarthe gives to this word:[18] it is to remain impossibly faithful to the very deconstitution of a subject that lends itself neither to truth as *aletheia* nor, a fortiori, to truth as *homoïosis*, to maintain what Beckett once called a "fidelity to failure," and this even or perhaps especially at the unassignable limit of sense and nonsense. One begins to see why Lacoue-Labarthe returns so often to the themes of madness and of tragedy. And one begins to see why, as Derrida has suggested,[19] Lacoue-Labarthe's desistance does not desist in the conventional sense of the word, that is, does not cease. On the contrary: the impossibility of thinking that has to do with the desistance of the subject is inseparable from a force or exigency that compels its persistence. In Lacoue-Labarthe's work, desistance persists.

Chapter 1
The Fable
(Literature and Philosophy)

We would like to inquire here into the "form" of philosophy; or more precisely, to cast upon it this suspicion: What if, after all, philosophy were nothing but literature? We know how insistent philosophy—metaphysics—has generally been in defining itself against what we call literature. We also know to what extent, particularly since Nietzsche, the struggle against metaphysics has been coupled with, or has even identified itself with, a specifically literary effort. We would like to ask, then, whether the dream, the desire that philosophy has entertained since its "beginning" for a *pure saying* [*dire pur*] (a speech, a discourse purely transparent to what it should immediately signify: truth, being, the absolute, etc.), has not always been compromised by the necessity of going through a text, through a process of writing, and whether, for this reason, philosophy has not always been obliged to use modes of exposition (dialogue or narrative, for example) that are not exclusively its own and that it is most often powerless to control or even reflect upon. In other words, it is a matter of questioning this more or less obscure and silent obsession with the *text*, which is perhaps one of the deepest obsessions of metaphysics and which reveals in any case one of its most primal limits.

To speak in this way requires, however, a few remarks:

1. First of all, it is obvious what this inquiry owes to Derrida's thought, and we cannot avoid, at the outset, a brief explanation. To the extent, indeed, that the desire for a pure saying is linked to the repression of writing and therefore to the thinking of being as presence, the suspicion we cast upon metaphysics is the very one cast upon it by Derrida. As a consequence, metaphysics so determined is obviously no longer quite the same as in Heidegger's sense, or rather, Heidegger

himself may very well be inscribed within it. But to the extent that writing "as such" is not directly at issue, the question is not exactly the same. Everything depends, in fact, on what we mean by *literature*. Do we mean the letter (*gramma*, trace, mark, inscription . . . writing), or do we mean *only* literature, in the most conventional, the most decried sense (which is, moreover, a belated sense), as, for example, when someone says, "And everything else is literature"? In this banal and somewhat pejorative but nonetheless revealing sense, *literature* signifies above all what has for a long time been conventionally called *fiction*.

2. We therefore assign ourselves here a relatively simple task. Drawing upon a distinction for which metaphysics itself is responsible, we must ask to what extent one can level against it the accusation it has always brought against any discourse that it did not absolutely master or that was not absolutely its own; and we must do so in such a way as ultimately to show that its own discourse is not radically different from that of literature. We will thus refer, furthermore, to Nietzsche rather than Derrida, that is, to a debate that is apparently more limited (in that metaphysics is supposedly reduced to Platonism) and more superficial (in that only the question of appearance is presumably raised) — but that threatens to become more crucial if, as Derrida himself has clearly shown, to adopt a metaphysical concept in order to turn it back against metaphysics (in metaphysics; one would even have to say, if one could, *between* it) is to deny oneself in advance the possibility of breaking out of any closure and to doom oneself more obstinately and more desperately to the "wasteland," to the desert that "ensues" and has perhaps never ceased to "ensue."

3. This means that the question asked is also that of the "completion" of metaphysics. A difficult, even an inevitably impossible question, for one cannot ask philosophy about literature as though it were a question raised "from the outside," any more than one can pursue this question to the very end, unfold it in its entirety. First of all, there would have to be an *outside*. Then, if a means of access were perchance imaginable, the outside would have to allow of unfolding, that is, exposition, properly metaphysical *Darstellung*: presentation, unveiling. The discourse of truth, in other words. Exposing would therefore be a way of not posing the question; posing the question prohibits exposing, for by necessity it is impossible to expose the question of exposition itself. It is not a matter of giving excuses in advance for the necessary discontinuity of what follows, nor for the difficulty of a *commentary* linked very precisely to exposition, nor even for the predicament of having to use the language of philosophy (even though it is also this discourse that despairs of being able to efface itself, to disappear, to let quite simply be what it designates). Rather, it is a matter of indicating that one cannot traverse the whole question, and especially that one cannot reverse it. Rigorously speaking, however, this is indeed what would have to be done. But could one keep this operation from becoming dialectical if one ventured to suspect literature (does literature exist, moreover, for anything but metaphysics?) of having always

been traversed by the desire to go beyond the process of writing toward thought conceived according to the model of metaphysics—if one ventured, in other words, to consider literature as an *ideology*?[1]

4. Finally, for all these reasons, it should be clear that it is not only impossible to "treat" such a question; it is also impossible to inquire whether it can *legitimately* be asked. One can only become involved in it to see what it involves. It is, in other words, a kind of "preliminary work," provided, however, that we dissociate this from remarks of the "transcendental" type concerning the conditions of possibility of such an undertaking.

Practically speaking, the only text that will be "commented upon" here is a well-known one by Nietzsche, a note from the year 1888 that can now be found in the collection entitled *The Will to Power*. Nietzsche writes the following: "Parmenides said, 'one cannot think of what is not';—we are at the other extreme, and say 'what can be thought of must certainly be a fiction.' "[2] *One cannot think of what is not*. Although formulated in a negative manner, this is clearly the *to gar auto noein est in te kai einai* of Parmenides: thinking and being are, in effect, the same. Nietzsche translates it as: that which is—is thinkable, or, more precisely, one only thinks that which is and there is no thought of that which is not. Nietzsche considers this to be a text of the beginning, as it were, an inaugural text: *we are situated at the other extreme*. Perhaps he even considers it to be *the* Text of the beginning, that is, the *whole* text of philosophy, of metaphysics, which, at the conclusion, "at the other end" (*am andern Ende*) of a history that might very well be History, must be reversed and canceled. In other words, from Parmenides to Hegel (to whom else could this end allude?), all of metaphysics would be a commentary on this proposition. Which means two things (since "we" are at the end and since the end is the cancellation of this text, history ceases when this text becomes obsolete): not only is history the history of this text, but history has taken place because this text needed to be commented upon, unfolded, taken up again, critiqued, reaffirmed, etc. It *required* this.

Nietzsche is therefore suggesting an *interpretation* of history. One can at least venture to decipher it: the identity of being and thinking was only affirmed, that is, desired, by Parmenides; and history is the history of the pursuit of this desire. In other words, in the "beginning" is the rift, the gap, the difference that troubles Identity. History is therefore the history of the Same, which is not the Identical. It is the history of lack, of withdrawal, of the repetition of alterity.

All of this could be taken for Hegelian thinking. At least we can see how difficult it is to remain thus on the fringes of Hegelian discourse. In reality, the whole problem is a matter of knowing whether Nietzsche in fact designates an *end* when he uses the equivocal words "am andern Ende" and whether he thus refers to an *origin* of history, be it faint or divided. For we know that history is completed precisely at the moment when the originary difference no longer functions, that is, when a (self-)conscious labor has surmounted the initial split and when identity can be reaffirmed in spite of (thanks to) difference: the identity of identity and difference. The end of history is desire satiated, the Same enslaved to the Identical, difference finally thought as determined negativity. History completes itself dialectically in Absolute Knowledge.

But not in its disavowal. Nietzsche wants, therefore, indeed to speak another language. But this other language must not be a "ruse." It must above all be other by virtue of an alterity that is itself other than dialectical alterity. It is therefore necessary:

1. That there be no question of origin and end.
2. That, consequently, the *we* that makes itself heard not be the Hegelian *we*, for example, the *for-us* of *The Phenomenology of Spirit*.
3. That the cancellation of Parmenidean (therefore Hegelian) identity be neither its reversal nor its *Aufhebung*—that in the text, in other words, the play of negativity not be the simple play of *negativity* or the *work* of negativity.
4. That the "concept" of *fiction* escape conceptuality itself, that is, not be included in the discourse of truth.

These four conditions are indissociable. However, we cannot examine all of them here. We will restrict ourselves to a consideration of the last, since it brings fiction into play and hence touches immediately on the question of literature.[3]

It is therefore fiction that must be questioned. In principle, the fictional is that which is not true, that is, in the language of metaphysics, that which is not real: that which *is* not. According to Parmenides, there is no thought except of that which is; there is no thought except true thought. We are at the other extreme and we say that the thinkable and the thought (being, reality, truth) are fictional, *are* not (real, true . . .). What metaphysics designates as being, namely, thought itself, is pure fiction. At the very least, metaphysics is not the discourse of truth but a fictional language. But it is clear that fiction is not something capable of cohering on its own, of being spoken and affirmed otherwise than in reference to truth. To invoke fiction, as Nietzsche perpetually does—especially from *Human, All Too Human* on[4]—is still to speak the language of truth, to admit that there is no other. Moreover, the other texts that Nietzsche wrote at the same time and that revolve around the same question are, at least upon first reading, unambiguous. This is particularly true of *Twilight of the Idols*. For Nietzsche, fiction—being as fiction—refers back to the thought of Heraclitus as if, in sum, it were simply a matter of opposing Parmenides to Heraclitus and of destroying the official (Parmenidean, Platonic, Hegelian) version of (the history of) philosophy by reviving a previously repressed Heracliteanism. The question of fiction is, finally, the question of *appearance*, as witnessed by this text from *Twilight of the Idols*: "Insofar as the senses show becoming, passing away, and change, they do not lie. But Heraclitus will remain eternally right with his assertion that being is an empty fiction. The 'apparent' world is the only one: the 'true' world is merely added by a lie."[5] In other words, Nietzsche calls fiction the lie that is truth and calls into question the essentially Platonic, metaphysical break between appearance and reality as well as the whole system of oppositions it engenders and by which it is accompanied: opinion/science, becoming/eternity, etc. The theme is well known: Nietzsche is the reversal of Platonism and hence still a Platonism — and ultimately the accomplishment of metaphysics itself. And it is true that a text such as this one, among many others (and without even taking into account all that is said about the concept of *will*), justifies an interpretation of this kind. In the same chapter of the same book, for example, the four theses of section 6 say approximately the same thing.

However, the text that comes immediately after makes use of a completely different language. And perhaps it allows us to sketch out an interpretation that is not as simple. This text is a famous one, narrating in six theses the history of metaphysics from its dawn to noon when (the decline of) Zarathustra begins. It is entitled "How the 'True World' Finally Became a Fable (The History of an Error)." The sixth thesis indicates the properly Nietzschean moment:

> 6. The true world—we have abolished. What world has remained? The apparent one perhaps? But no! *With the true world we have also abolished the apparent one.*
> (Noon; moment of the briefest shadow; end of the longest error; high point of humanity; INCIPIT ZARATHUSTRA.)[6]

This Nietzschean moment, inasmuch as it is confused with Zarathustra's departure, is therefore indeed an end (the end of the longest error), but not the Hegelian end. In any case, it is not evening but the furtive and culminating noontime at which decline begins (again), that is, the course of an identical (and yet not identical) trajectory toward midnight, that other noon, perhaps the *same*—assuming, at least, that the *difference* between the dazzling brightness of full day and the absolute darkness of night (which is no less dazzling) is not that which separates the illumination of *parousia* from the famous night in which all cows are black. What might have remained "naïvely" anti-Platonic in the preceding texts has disappeared here.[7] To think fiction is not to oppose appearance and reality, since appearance is nothing other than the product of reality. To think fiction is precisely to think without recourse to this opposition, *outside* this opposition; to think the world as a fable.[8] Is this possible?

We must refer here to Klossowski's interpretation,[9] which links together the play of fable and event (of the repetition of the difference between appearance and reality) and the play of fable and *fatum*, in which therefore the essence of the *Eternal Return of the Same* begins to define itself. From this commentary, we will retain especially Klossowski's analysis of the move outside history. The six moments of Nietzsche's text correspond to the six days required for the true world to become fable again. Similarly, the apparent world was created in six days "as the divine fable drew to a close." History is "completed" in this inverted Genesis, which Klossowski calls the *refabulization of the world*: "The refabulization of the world means as well that the world departs from historical time and reenters mythical time, that is, eternity."[10] Klossowski remarks that only the experience of *forgetting* allows of such a departure.[11] And it is clear that we must understand the precise relationship that Nietzsche's forgetting maintains, on the one hand, with metaphysical forgetting (for example, that of the *Phaedo*, or of Saint Augustine's *Confessions*, Books X and XI, or even that of natural consciousness in the *Phenomenology of Spirit*), and on the other hand, with what Heidegger designates as *oblivion of being*—and, finally, with what we are trying nowadays to think under the name of the unconscious. But the opposition to which one must appeal here is that of history and myth. This opposition should lead to a language that is no longer the language of truth, assuming that history is ultimately nothing other than the history of Logos.

We must therefore take up the question once more. The world has become a fable (again). Creation is canceled. This is as much as to say that God is dead, and not only the metaphysical God. Nevertheless, one can say that what was designated by the concept of being in the discourse of truth is now revealed as fictional. This discourse was itself a fable: the world becomes a fable again because it already was one; or, to be more precise, because the discourse that constituted it as such was already a fable. Fable: *fabula, muthos*. The discourse of truth, *logos*, is nothing other than *muthos*, that is, the very thing against which it has always claimed to constitute itself.

From the preceding opposition between appearance (fiction) and reality (truth), we move on to another opposition (*muthos/logos*), which is unfortunately the same. This hardly allows us to make any progress. Commenting on Nietzsche, Heidegger says, it is true, that *muthos* and *logos* are not originally opposed to each other. It remains to be seen, however, under what aegis, and how, this can be said. Here, moreover, is the text in question, which we must quote in its entirety:

> Myth means the telling word. For the Greeks, to tell is to lay bare and make appear—both the appearing and that which has its essence in the appearing, its Epiphany. *Mythos* [sic] is what has its essence in its

telling—what is apparent in the unconcealedness of its appeal. . . .
M]ythos and logos are not, as our current historians of philosophy
claim, placed into opposition by philosophy as such; on the contrary,
the early Greek thinkers (Parmenides, fragment 8) are precisely the
ones to use mythos and logos in the same sense. Mythos and logos become separated and opposed only at the point where neither mythos nor
logos can keep to its original nature. In Plato's work, this separation
has already taken place. Historians and philologists, by virtue of a prej-
udice which modern rationalism adopted from Platonism, imagine that
mythos was destroyed by logos. But nothing religious is ever destroyed
by logic; it is destroyed only by the god's withdrawal.[12]

We are well aware of precisely what is metaphysical here, as paradoxical as
it may seem. Metaphysical in what sense? As the last lines of this text attest
("nothing religious is ever destroyed by logic"), the stakes of this question are
serious since it controls in fact the whole interpretation of Nietzsche. Moreover,
to a certain extent, the belief in a pre-Platonic and pure Greek origin, the indictment of historians and philologists, the "mysticism" of the disappearance of the
divine,[13] and even the ennoblement of appearance as appearing,[14] a certain vener-
ation of presence—all of this has indeed a Nietzschean resonance. But this
Nietzsche undeniably belongs to metaphysics qua metaphysics of presence. This
is the Nietzsche for whom, precisely, appearance and muthos are to rehabilitated,
not the one for whom they are both abolished. Nietzsche tries indeed to state the
identity of muthos and logos, but certainly not as Heidegger does. The identity
that Nietzsche suspects does not in fact hide a profoundly dialectical identification
in which logos is the truth of muthos (as true saying), but in which muthos authen-
ticates the ontological originarity of logos, its purity prior to their separation and
opposition.[15] Muthos and logos are the same thing, but neither is more true (or
more false, deceptive, fictional, etc.) than the other; they are neither true nor
false; both are the same fable. The world has in effect become a fable. So therefore has what is said about it (fabula, fari), as well as what is thought about it.
Being and saying, being and thinking are the same thing. The "becoming-logos"
of the world in the metaphysics that is accomplished in Hegelian logic is nothing
other than its "becoming-muthos," inasmuch as truth is not opposed to anything,
is not tied to anything, does not refer to anything, and as the history of the (re)con-
stitution of truth is always at the same time the history of its corruption. For as
true thought creates the appearance it requires as its only guarantee, appearance
itself, by definition, continually abolishes itself (which clearly refers us to the
whole problematic of origin and beginning). To abolish appearance, that is, to
let appearance abolish itself, and to risk this vertigo, to thus renounce presence
and refuse to repatriate it as an appearance promoted to the level of appearing
or epiphany—this is doubtless the decisive "leap" attempted by Nietzsche. Not a
very spectacular leap, in fact, one whose space is in any case short enough so that,

on either side, the ground is ultimately (more or less) the same. There is only a brief and, so to speak, unapparent difference. It is somewhat, as in Bataille, the "experience" of a transgression: the intangible limit one exceeds and does not exceed is the limit that separates and does not separate one from unreason, from madness [*l'insensé*]. It thus "begins" to be no longer a question of truth, or, if it is still necessarily a question of truth, it is no longer quite in the same way. Apparently nothing, or almost nothing, has changed. In any case, and despite what a certain Nietzschean violence allows one to think (a violence that is indispensable but doubtless falls far short of this insidious perversion), there is no radical upheaval. If the use of metaphor is inevitable here, one could say that, with thought in effect repeating itself, beginning (again), but emptily and without henceforth referring back to anything or *believing* that it can do so, it is as though one were "penetrating" into an unlimited space that is the same as the space one has (not) just left, but in which the ground gives way, in which the distinct opposition between shadow and light, whereby the whole adventure of *aletheia* is clearly produced, has been effaced. Therein reigns a uniform, blinding whiteness that the eyes cannot endure.

Thus, the world is what is said about it. In its own way, metaphysics itself continues to say this—but by tailoring saying to the truth: *muthos/logos*. From the moment that this tailoring is undone, that saying is not a true as opposed to a fictional saying, but rather a saying pure and simple, from the moment, then, that truth is no longer transcendent, no longer a "beyond saying," be it a negative one, there remains nothing outside of saying—and nothing, to begin with, from which saying would have begun. Neither true saying, nor the other. There is no origin and no end, but only the same, as it were eternal, fable. Tearing philosophy from mythology, the repression of mythology, and all the divisions accompanying it (opinion/science, poetry/thought, etc.), no longer mean anything. It never began. It is true that·this uneasiness regarding the absence or, at least, the difficulty of the beginning, itself necessarily traverses the whole of metaphysics. But henceforth it cannot be appeased, either through violence (a certain Plato, for example) or even through deceit (the symbolism of the circle must not mislead us: in no case is the beginning the end and if the Absolute *defers* its manifestation, it does so indefinitely, because it is not here and never could be). In short, it is clear that the *error* whose history this text retraces is the occultation of a difference, but one that is not a difference of *origin* between truth and its other. And it is indeed—however difficult it may be to think this—the ontological difference itself that Nietzsche places in question, insofar as the thinking of this difference according to the problematic of origin is the hallmark of metaphysics: always viewed within the horizon of identity, of ontological "predominance," difference is always missed, and what one can call the ontic reduction (Being thought *as* beings) is always inevitable.[16] The error, in other words, would consist in substituting another referent (truth) for the one previously crossed out (the world). One could even say that the error is substitution or transfer in general, that is, a belief in origins that even the discovery of an "originary difference" would not be able to correct. The history of an error: the history of a language, the history of language itself insofar as it has desired and willed itself[17] as a literal language at the very moment when it functioned essentially and necessarily through figure(s). As though language, as Rousseau claimed, were initially metaphorical. But we would have to cross out this "initially," which allows us to assume a future literality; or else adapt to metaphysics that definition of Goethe's according to which "a poetry without figures is in itself an immense trope."[18] Or better yet, to avoid speaking of metaphors at all. For fable is the language with respect to which (and in which) these differences—which are not differences—no longer obtain: literal and figurative, transparency and transfer, reality and simulacrum, presence and representation, *muthos* and *logos*, logic and poetry, philosophy and literature, etc. Is such a language thinkable except as a kind of "eternal repetition" ["ressassement éternel"] in the course of which the same play of the same desire and of the same disappointment would indefinitely repeat itself? Perhaps this is a way of saying the *Eternal Return*—unless something has already moved and the circle never entirely closes upon itself. That which has never really begun would begin forever again: INCIPIT ZARATHUSTRA. We know from the last aphorism of *The Gay Science*, Book IV, that, for Nietzsche, this meant: *Incipit tragoedia*. So: *Incipit parodia*.

It is on this basis that we would like now to inquire into the relation between literature and philosophy. We can see at least that there may be a way of wresting literature from the domination of metaphysics and of breaking the circle in which we found ourselves at the outset. But it is obviously no longer a question of "literature." Fiction, myth, and fable are provisional words. It would doubtless be better to speak of *writing*. But we are not yet there. Or rather, it is clear that if we want to follow this path, we must not take shortcuts. We should in fact distinguish between two tasks:

1. Turning against metaphysics (within metaphysics), under the name of literature, that against which metaphysics itself has turned, that from which it has striven to constitute itself. Fair enough.

2. Undertaking to force the limits of metaphysics, that is, displacing the bar that symbolically separates literature and philosophy (literature/philosophy) in such a way that on each side literature and philosophy are both crossed out and cancel each other in communicating. Hence we would have: literature philosophy. This would mean approaching fable *at the same time*[19] as what metaphysics hereafter sees (but has perhaps often seen) of itself in a kind of mirror that it does not present to itself from the outside and that must be thought by repetition (even at the inevitable price of intensifying the meaning of Heideggerian *Wiederholung*), with-

out recourse to metaphysical reflection or self-consciousness, *and* as the play of what today we call the text.

We must note that Nietzsche thought about at least the first of these tasks from the beginning, in the texts preparatory to *The Birth of Tragedy* and in *The Birth of Tragedy* itself. Moreover, this is not by accident. *The Birth of Tragedy* is doubtless not entirely, as is often said and as Nietzsche himself—but not unequivocally—let it be understood,[20] a "youthful" text, falling far "short" of the others. In fact, it is hardly likely that a naïve historical (vertical) "break" could have taken place in Nietzsche's thought. If there was a break, it occurred as of *The Birth of Tragedy*, so that one must read in it, while keeping them rigorously separate, at least two languages: one in which the greater part of post-Hegelian metaphysics and of metaphysics plain and simple is confirmed; and another (but quite often it is the same one in the process of coming undone) in which "deconstruction" is already under way. We cannot establish this here; but let us reread chapter 14 of *The Birth of Tragedy*, which begins: "Let us now imagine the one great Cyclops eye of Socrates fixed on tragedy, an eye in which the fair frenzy of artistic enthusiasm had never glowed."[21] Here Nietzsche shows that in the matter of poetry, Socrates hardly likes anything except Aesopian fable—and even then . . . Tragedy is irrational, deceitful, dangerous. The result was that "the youthful tragic poet Plato first burned his poems that he might become a student of Socrates."[22] Socratism, which at this time Nietzsche considered to be the beginning of metaphysics, is the "*repression*" of tragedy, that is—and this is an inevitable consequence of repression—the shameful and more or less disfigured resurgence of tragedy:

> Plato, who in condemning tragedy and art in general certainly did not lag behind the naïve cynicism of his master . . . was nevertheless constrained by sheer artistic necessity to create an art form that was related to those forms of art which he repudiated. Plato's main objection to the older art—that it is the imitation of a phantom and hence belongs to a sphere even lower than the empirical world—could certainly not be directed against the new art; and so we find Plato endeavoring to transcend reality and to represent the idea which underlies this pseudo-reality. Thus Plato, the thinker, arrived by a detour where he had always been at home as a poet—at the point from which Sophocles and the older art protested solemnly against that objection. If tragedy had absorbed into itself all the earlier types of art, the same might also be said in an eccentric sense of the Platonic dialogue which, a mixture of all extant styles and forms, hovers midway between narrative, lyric, and drama, between prose and poetry, and so has also broken the strict old law of the unity of linguistic form. . . .
>
> Indeed, Plato has given to all posterity the model of a new art form, the model of the *novel*—which may be described as an infinitely enhanced Aesopian fable, in which poetry holds the same rank in relation

to dialectical philosophy as this same philosophy held for many centuries in relation to theology: namely, the rank of *ancilla*. This was the new position into which Plato, under the pressure of the demonic Socrates, forced poetry.[23]

This text would require an exhaustive commentary. But the questions it raises, particularly that of the repression of art in general, are too vast. However, we can retain from it the genealogy of the philosophical text.[24] The *novel* is the genre of Platonism and might well be the genre of metaphysics in general. Yet we would have rigorously to determine its essence. Nietzsche alludes at once to the mode of exposition (the "mixture of all extant styles and forms") and to the genre (the novel). We could therefore take up the modern analyses of narrative, for example, Genette's distinction between narrative and discourse, or the general relation he establishes between narrative and representation.[25] One could even attempt a structural analysis of "philosophical narrative" to the extent that narrative analysis can be achieved without exorbitant presuppositions. Finally, one could have recourse to the Hegelian tradition from Lukács to Girard, that is, to the analysis of the dialectic of desire, of the conflict between the pure and the impure, of idolatry.[26] And perhaps it would not be impossible to show that the desire for presence, the belief in origins, the will to truth are necessarily linked to exposition, that is, to narrative—that they must necessarily defer themselves as *text*.

In any case, we must come to the text. We must repeat it, not without running the risk of being unable to "exceed" dialectical discourse. For if it is true that there is not and never was such a thing as literature except for philosophy, if it is true that philosophy has raised itself up against this "other" language which it so constituted while debasing it (to the point where literature could never speak of itself except by borrowing, more or less shamefully, the language of philosophy), if, in short, the relation that unites and divides philosophy and literature is a *master-slave* relation (and one of them has indeed feared death), what discourse can one employ about philosophy that is not already the discourse of philosophy itself—the one that always precludes in advance the possibility of being turned back against itself and of being questioned about what it has constituted itself against, even though it also denies, without allowing the question of its own origin to be effaced, the possibility of asking in relation to it another type of question? We have therefore to experience a certain powerlessness that is the paradoxical effect of an excess of power: Logos is absolute mastery and there is nothing outside of it, not even literature, to which it has given a "meaning." Unless perhaps, not writing exactly what we wanted to write, we experience a weakness, a powerlessness that is no longer the effect of an excess of power but rather like the obscure work of a force that is foreign to what we say, to the consciousness we have of it, to the will to say it, a hidden, incessant resistance that is absolutely impossible to control and on which we can barely gain ground at the price of great efforts. We write: we are dispossessed, something is constantly fleeing, outside of us, slowly deteriorating. It could well be that by directing our attention to it, to this strange practical difficulty, we would gradually be obliged to suspect a flaw where we thought we had found infallibility itself. It may have to do, for example, with a certain confusion in thought, with a blurred insufficiency of consciousness, a kind of lethargy. One could also speak of fatigue, of weariness (I'm thinking of Bataille); or of a resistance, a refusal both of language and of the body. It is certainly an *experience*, no matter how dubious the connotative power of this word, and even if it were an ultimately paralyzed and frozen experience, the very failure of experience. If writing has this privilege (writing, the act and the torment of writing, in which something else is also at stake), it is not because—as people say a bit hastily these days, by simply reversing or not at all reversing metaphysical oppositions—we are finally delivered from the world, from presence (and from representation), but rather because writing is first of all that reflection of experience wherein reflection (and hence experience) is constantly undone, because it is the most painful of failures and because, in it, the radical alterity of force "reveals" itself most painfully. We know that there is no language except that of phenomena, of that which has appeared (never of appearing itself), that language and *aletheia* are linked, or, to employ another vocabulary, that Dionysus himself never appears, that he is always already dead, dispersed, and that he is only "visible" when on stage behind the mask of Apollo (*as* Apollo)—invisible therefore, *not being*, and thereby leading to madness [*vertige*].[27] If language is lacking strength [*force*], if language is this lack of strength, it is quite in vain that we would seek in it the strength necessary to "deliver" us from it, that is, in the case at hand, to turn it against itself. Even if it is sufficiently reflective to have always had a nostalgia for strength, or at least to deplore not having any. As such, language "manifests" the decline of strength: language—writing, a degradation of strength that is still, in the extreme, a strength. Can one think this without having recourse to dialectics, if dialectics is the illusion of strength and of the mastery of strength *in* language? Can one think a strength of weakness, a strength born of its own exhaustion, of its own difference? A strength that is by virtue of having no strength?

All of this is to say that one cannot "come to" the text, for the text is precisely without a shore. There is therefore no way to reach it, and if we imagine ourselves able to do so, we must understand that we never disembark except where we have already had a foothold for a long time, according to an almost unthinkable movement, a kind of turning inside out by which we would move to that outside of ourselves which is already our interiority, by which we would no longer be either "outside" or "inside," but would experience our intimacy as that blinding alterity forever beyond us and to which nevertheless we are destined, which we paradoxically inhabit and which perhaps bears that name which is the shortcoming, the signal shortcoming of all names: death. This is as much as to say that we must now accept what cannot be accepted and try to be faithful to what tolerates only infidelity. A test that can no longer even be characterized as the inverse of the preceding one. And perhaps it is simply a question of admitting the *impossible*, which is neither speech nor silence, neither knowledge nor ignorance, neither strength nor impotence, something of which one can say nothing except that it gives us over to an infinite murmur, infinitely disjointed but infinitely renewed, to what Blanchot calls by a name that designates for us what the unjustifiable and necessary enterprise of writing has become, what it has always been: *ressassement éternel*.

As the reader has surely noticed (if only because of the theme of fiction), the question initially raised is not foreign to Borges, among others. It is not surprising that one can say it is not foreign to Cervantes either, at least as we are able to read him today. We could, in the end, reformulate the question in this way: Are we capable of no longer believing what is *in* books or of not being "disappointed" by their "lie"? Or, as Nietzsche would have said, can we cease to be "pious"? Are we capable of atheism?

Translated by Hugh J. Silverman

Chapter 2
The Detour

The figure is modeled on truth and
truth is recognized in the figure.

Pascal, *Pensées*, B. 673

Truth kills—indeed it kills itself.

Nietzsche, *Das Philosophenbuch*, III, §176

Nietzsche was thus concerned with rhetoric: he taught it; he considered devoting a book to it; and, above all, he assumed its vocabulary (at least the major categories of the theory of tropes) in a certain number of philosophical texts that have become well known even though they all remain in the state of outlines or fragments.[1] We know that in "using" rhetoric, Nietzsche sought to question the truth-claims made by the language of philosophy and science, its desire for a pure and simple literality—its will to be proper, so to speak. This is in fact a twofold task: on the one hand, it involved turning against philosophy, as Nietzsche always attempted to do, that against which philosophy claimed to erect itself (myth, poetry, eloquence, any avowedly "doxic" use of language); on the other hand, as an indispensable condition of the first, it involved determining language as originarily figurative, as trope, and in such a way that no true language could escape from this except by forgetting, ignoring, or concealing from itself its own origins. In its inspiration, this enterprise was hardly original. Stretching things a bit (but are we really stretching them?), we could almost venture to say that it arises from a suspicion as old as philosophy itself and necessarily contemporaneous with its "inauguration." It is in any case linked to a certain *era* of modern philosophy and of the "science" of language that this philosophy governs. And at its basis, whatever the brutality or subtlety of its strategic intentions, it is completely subordinated to a whole conceptual apparatus that is metaphysical through and through.[2] One could doubtless not even credit Nietzsche with radicality or systematicity.

But it is not this enterprise in itself that interests us here. This does not mean that it is uninteresting or that we can afford to ignore it. It means that what is essential is perhaps, paradoxically, that Nietzsche did not wish, or was not able, to see it through—that, in any case, he abandoned it. Yet he devoted himself to it with a certain determination during the years immediately following the publication of *The Birth of Tragedy*, from 1872 until at least 1875. He increased his reading and research, accumulated notes and plans, and repeatedly outlined drafts of various books. Of course, rhetoric was not the only focus of his work during this period. But, as we shall see, it is not an exaggeration to say that it is the "center," however concealed. Nevertheless, none of this material was completed, and, at least on the surface, not a trace of it remains in Nietzsche's subsequent work. One still spots, here and there, numerous texts on eloquence, stylistics, the art of reading, the art of speaking or writing, persuasion, etc. One also sees that, despite some changes in terminology, Nietzsche's analyses of language will vary little and that he will almost always stick to the knowledge gained in these first years. Even the constant accusation of ontological or metaphysical responsibility leveled against language and grammar represents a resurgence of this work.[3] But there is nothing, it seems, that would resemble a systematic effort; in any case, there is no declared and sustained recourse to a properly rhetorical vocabulary. As of 1875, rhetoric ceased to be a privileged instrument. It even appears that Nietzsche deprived it of all its rights and that, for all practical purposes, it ceased to be a problem.[4]

It is thus this abandonment that needs to be examined—this passage (or this detour) through rhetoric, which is incomplete and inconclusive and which, for that reason, appears to open a strange breach, rather indistinct but impossible to seal, both in the work and in the philosophy in which the work is supposedly inscribed. For in leaving—perhaps in spite of himself—this task suspended (a task which, for that matter, owes to Nietzsche the place it still occupies more or less in the program of "modernity"), it is quite possible that Nietzsche was ahead of his time and began to undo, almost noiselessly (and almost invisibly), this long turning of philosophy against itself in which, most of the time, it is believed that Nietzsche himself can still be enclosed.

Fatum Libellorum

In order for us to see things a bit more clearly, a whole empirical study—a whole history and investigation—would obviously be necessary. This might not be very exciting, but one wonders what could justify us in excluding it: we would gain little in the way of elegance and certainly lose a great deal by ignoring or neglecting that weight (that resistance) of the empirical of which one occasionally glimpses, even if one does not know very well exactly what status to grant it, how it burdens Nietzsche's thought in decisive fashion and doubtless more than it ever did any other thought. It is indeed *also* in this way that Nietzsche was resolved to break with the past and it is perhaps this exteriority always in the process of being reduced, this joined fracture of life and (the practice of) writing that is designated by the divided word bio-graphy, a word we must learn to *read*.[5] It is not certain, however, that we could carry out this study, that we could fully develop it and give it the complete form of *exposition*. Less because we still lack a complete disclosure of these texts (although this is not unimportant since it touches on the always enigmatic question of Nietzsche's text, that is, of his "work") than for reasons of principle. One does not interrogate with impunity an abandonment, an incompletion; one does not expound with impunity the reasons for it (even if complicating their web for the *purpose* [*cause*] in hand), when what is at issue is precisely a thought's running up against the impossibility of expounding, of assuming the style of *presentation*, and even of maintaining the specific logic of its questioning (and of questioning in general). In this abandonment, in what it leaves behind as unorganized and discontinuous traces, in its barely visible wake, in the work that follows or can no longer, as such, follow — in the failure with which "it" is marked, there very likely dawns something that exceeds, but without surpassing, the possibilities of dialectical recuperation inherent in criticism, in interpretation, in commentary, etc., and that shakes, or more precisely erodes, slyly contaminates, and begins relentlessly to destroy (though neither in its themes nor in its concepts) philosophical assurance. A failure, a catastrophe, especially when they have not yet really taken place and cannot be expressed in the language of mastery. It is not a question of making our relationship to Nietzsche one of pathos (of drama, perhaps, caught in the repetition that always betrays and degrades — but that is another matter). Rather, how can we speak of powerlessness and understand that "what gives food for thought," as they say, is neither an outcome nor even something that truly deserves a question?

With these limitations pointed out, and because one should also avoid exaggerating the fears of the "beginning," we must, in spite of everything, undertake this *history*. Circumstances compel us to be brief; we shall simply make these few external and lacunary observations:

1. The interest Nietzsche shows for rhetoric is, if you will, accidental.[6] It dates very precisely from his reading, at the end of 1872, of Volkmann's *Systematic Exposition of Greek and Roman Rhetoric* and especially of Gerber's *Language as Art*, both of which had just been published. Prior to this, it cannot be said that Nietzsche had been particularly aware of rhetoric as such. His allusions to Greek rhetoric or to the rhetorical use of language, in *The Birth of Tragedy*, for example, and in the texts that accompany it, are rare and vague. The word itself is almost always used in its "modern," that is, in a distinctly pejorative, sense.[7] And in the major projects of 1871–72 concerning a series of *Meditations on Antiquity* and a *Treatise of General Aesthetics* (*Studies in Rhythm*), nothing, it seems, is planned on rhetoric. So rhetoric is a discovery. And Nietzsche immediately found in these

readings the pretext (and the text) for a course given during the winter semester of the same year (1872–73). In the initial notes for *The Book of the Philosopher*, which he is drafting at the same time, the effects of these readings are immediately apparent. Moreover, if we examined closely the order and progression of these notes, we would in fact see colliding with one another the more or less contradictory results of two readings: that of Gerber and the earlier reading of Zöllner's book (*On the Nature of Comets*, 1871), which was implicated in Nietzsche's decision to resume, on a different basis, the "critique" of rationality and philosophy organized in *The Birth of Tragedy*.[8] The reading of Gerber then began to reorient the whole earlier analysis of language (and not only of language) and necessitated a readjustment that appears to have occupied Nietzsche's next few years.

2. Not only did Nietzsche not complete this work (no plan he made could even be construed as definitive), but he wrote practically none of it. During all these years, which were haunted by the desire to attain to "literature," Nietzsche wrote nothing publishable, with the exception of the four *Untimely Meditations*, about which, for all that, much remains to be said.[9] No *book*, in any case. Neither of the two texts he began were pursued to completion: neither the 1872 course on the pre-Socratics written for Cosima Wagner (this was not the first time that a book for Cosima Wagner remained incomplete), nor even the 1873 *Introduction to The Book of the Philosopher*. It was not until 1878 that a new "book" appeared, *Human, All Too Human*, and that was a book of aphorisms. So it was here, no doubt, at the time of this detour (perhaps because of this detour), that the problem of *fragmentation*[10] came into play, a problem that began, moreover, to pursue Nietzsche as did everything having to do with the "destiny of books," the *fatum libellorum*.[11] The fragmentation of Nietzsche's notebooks was obviously not intentional. It followed from the practice of note taking, and, paradoxically, from unbroken note taking. It is odd, nevertheless, that it ended up engendering the form of the "books" to come, as if it had become a constraint and Nietzsche had had to resign himself to "accepting" the very form of his inability to give the desired form to his work. For, in itself, fragmentation certainly testifies first of all to a failure—and very precisely to the failure of a *book*, assuming that *The Book of the Philosopher* is indeed the great book conceived at the time to follow or take the place of *The Birth of Tragedy*. It therefore also testifies to the failure of *the* book, of the one already written (*The Birth of Tragedy*), since it was not self-sufficient, and of the one that Nietzsche, until the end and from "book" to "book," will desperately try to write. But this was not a simple process of decay. In the failure of the book is discovered, with difficulty and not without resistance (did Nietzsche ever really accept this? *can* it even be accepted?), another form of writing, the very one that he had never ceased, and would never cease, to practice: this unremitting writing which does not so much precede the book "in progress" (the "book," although Nietzsche doubtless always *willed* it to be a rigorous organization of fragments, will ultimately prove to be only a more or less ar-

bitrary sampling, and in any case will elude this intention) as it follows all the books of which it is a reading (a copy and an interpretation) and whose empirical discontinuity, despite all of Nietzsche's efforts to justify aphorism (but this is perhaps another form of resistance), poorly conceals their infinite circulation, their uninterrupted course.

3. This barely visible subterranean movement through which Nietzsche's "work" thus began to break up, or, more precisely, to slip slowly outside the proper space of the work and to lose itself in what is nevertheless not the absolute other of the work but its persistent alteration, its endless exhaustion—this *work-lessness* [*désœuvrement*],[12] as Blanchot would call it—was contemporaneous with a certain number of "events" that describe a complex configuration and that, in one way or another, are all tied to the questions exposed by the encounter with rhetoric. To put it schematically, there was the break with philology, which was practically consummated with the publication of *The Birth of Tragedy*, and its inevitable consequence, the way it affected Nietzsche's teaching, since it is difficult, as we know, to withstand a university coalition (year after year, the failure here again is confirmed—although it freed Nietzsche from everything that bound him to the metaphysical persona of the man of science and of the teacher). There was also the beginning of illness: fatigue, weakness, pain, difficulties in working, etc. Finally, there was the break with Wagner, of which it is known that the premature publication of *The Birth of Tragedy* was already an indication. These "events" do not, however, constitute an actual rupture: on the surface, nothing, or almost nothing, is happening. Nietzsche prepares a pamphlet against philologists, for example, but does not finish it; he continues to teach; he already knows full well what is to be thought of Wagner, but writes the fourth *Untimely Meditation*, etc. If all of this comes together, it does so obscurely, without a stir.

The People of Discourse

There is thus, tied to this unforeseen encounter with rhetoric, a bending [*in-fléchissement*]—a weakening [*fléchissement*]—of the "work" that doubtless cannot be subsumed under any of the classical categories of historicity, even (and especially) dialectical historicity. It is neither a pure accident, nor a kind of simple transition, nor a moment, nor a break [*rupture*] (and even less a severance [*coupure*]).[13] It is, rather, a kind of dispersed debacle whose "logic" escapes us. Why, in what way, would rhetoric be implicated here? We must admit that, in spite of all these reasons, nothing seems to allow us to attach or intend to attach so much importance to this encounter. No doubt it would be necessary to attend to it if we wished to follow the transformations of Nietzsche's thinking about language. But, after all, the rhetorical interlude is perhaps not very important in this respect either. It is not surprising that Nietzsche abandoned a question ultimately lacking the importance he thought he could give it (nor that others have used this abandonment as an excuse not to examine the question more closely). For at the moment that it presented itself, rhetoric apparently did not cause much of a disturbance. If it is essentially from Gerber that Nietzsche derives the "concept" of rhetoric (this is the term he uses; see *Rh.*, §1), he is dependent yet again on the romantic tradition to which he already owed not only the determination of the essence of Greek tragedy, but also a whole theory of language. Consequently, the scenery hardly changes. We might suppose, moreover, that Nietzsche would not have suddenly placed such great value on rhetoric if he had not recognized something in it and if he did not believe it possible to insert it without much harm into an already constituted thematic and conceptual chain. Of course, the insertion of a new concept (or a new group of concepts) always imparts a certain disturbance to the system [*dispositif*] that precedes it. But this does not necessarily affect its overall structure. Thus, rhetoric could be rather easily interpreted—and manipulated—within the vocabulary of *The Birth of Tragedy*. The "linguistic" terminology inevitably underwent some changes: "symbol," for example, which was the key word of the years 1870–71, no longer appears. This is hardly negligible, but nothing should prevent us from measuring the effects of these apparently limited transformations and describing the play of disappearances, displacements, or substitutions they produce. For as far as what is decisive is concerned, there seems to be, from the point of view of the general economy, no radical difference between *The Birth of Tragedy* and *The Book of the Philosopher*. Almost like tragedy (myth, music, etc.), and in the same way, rhetoric appears to be integrated into the strategic project already defined in *The Birth of Tragedy*.[14] And this is ultimately what would explain why we have always considered these texts to have been produced in the wake of this first essay—as a pure and simple *reiteration* [*reprise*].

This would perhaps be the case if there were, or if there could be, a concept of rhetoric as such. And an *innocent* concept. But it so happens that there is none, or at least that if Nietzsche actually tried to construct one, it was immediately diverted, erased, carried outside of itself. The reason for this is very simple: rhetoric was only taken into consideration to the extent that it revealed something about the essence of language itself. In other words, there can be no fixed concept of rhetoric when rhetoric is actually the essence of that of which, in principle, it is only a certain usage. Not only does the attention given to rhetoric shift the emphasis from music to language, but, unlike tragedy, whose determination changed nothing (quite the contrary) in the specific nature of its constitutive elements (music, language . . .), rhetoric remains completely inaccessible unless one pays the price of entirely recasting the analysis of language (this is at least a risk taken). None of this is new. There exists, here again, a long tradition—of which Nietzsche was largely unaware, moreover, and to which, therefore, he could not have been faithful. But for Nietzsche himself, this was not to be without its consequences—which is what must now be shown.

For example (the paths taken by Nietzsche are many—to state the obvious—and we have to agree to choose arbitrarily this or that point of departure): it is understood that rhetoric is an *art*, and a *Greek* art. The Greeks are, in fact, the people of discourse. This is the distinctive feature of their *culture*. In the Course on Eloquence, Nietzsche states: "To no task did the Greeks devote such incessant labor as to eloquence; the amount of energy they expended on oratory can perhaps be symbolized by Demosthenes' autodidacticism. Devotion to oratory is the most tenacious element of Greek culture."[15] But the Greeks are also this way *by nature*— whatever the difficulty of determining an origin that would not be an idyllic and naïve state of nature, like Schiller's Homeric Age. If the Greeks are naturally the people of discourse, it is owing to their *language*: "The nation which was educated by means of such a language, the most *speak*able [*die* sprech*barste*] of all languages, spoke insatiably. . . . On the whole the Greeks feel that they are speakers, in contrast with the *aglossoi*, the non-Greeks."[16]

The Greek language lends itself, therefore, to speech. This is why, first of all, speech is the essence of the Greek people, what distinguishes them absolutely and makes all other peoples into peoples deprived of language, neither mute nor voiceless but unintelligible, crying out like animals: "But on the whole the Greeks feel that they are speakers . . . the ones who speak understandably and beautifully (the opposite is *barbaroi*, the "quackers"; cf. *ba-trachoi*)." Speech is, therefore, also what gives the Greeks their power, their political power (thus eloquence is connected to democracy [*Rh.*, §1]) and their destiny, the persistence of Greek culture in spite of its fading away, its actual decline, that is (and this comes as no surprise), in spite of the degradation of living speech into writing where true power is concentrated:

> Hellenic culture and power are gradually concentrated in oratorical skill [*Reden-können*]; it probably also spells their doom . . . devotion to oratory is the most tenacious element of Greek culture. . . . It is communicable, contagious, as can be seen from the Romans and the whole Hellenistic world. . . . The effectiveness of Christian preaching can be traced back to that element: and indirectly the development of the whole modern prose style depends on the Greek orators, directly of course mostly on Cicero. . . . [17] Basically, even today "classical" higher education still preserves a good portion of this antique view, except that it is no longer oral speech but its faded image, writing, that emerges as goal.[18]

But the Greek language is not only conducive to *mastery*, assuming that we can speak of mastery in relation to the Greeks. (The immeasurable strength given them by speech was short-lived, ecstatic, almost lightning. It made them dazzling, but they were also burned by it, and if they exercise a posthumous power, it is an ambiguous one, and rather, in fact, a fascination in which all power is at risk.) The use of speech is not simply political, that is, economic and servile. If the Greek language lends itself better than any other to speech, it is because it lends itself to an *excessive* use of speech. The Greeks are insatiable speakers; they speak too much. Necessity, indigence, distress, and need in no way preside over the creation and the practice of the Greek language—nor those of any other language, for that matter (but it is too soon to say this). The Greek language is not the daughter of poverty but of superabundant wealth. To borrow a "concept" from Nietzsche's most "faithful" reader, let us say that it is the fruit of an unreserved expenditure and that it naturally lends itself to a *sovereign* speech.

> "Reading and Writing," §1.
> Do we actually believe we hear, in the sovereign [*herrlich*] sonority of
> a language, the echo of an indigence that would have given birth to it?
> Is not everything born in joy and exuberance, freely, and under the
> auspices of the depths of the spirit, the contemplative spirit? What
> could an apelike man have to do with our languages? A people who
> have six cases and conjugate their verbs with a hundred forms possess a
> soul that is completely collective and overflowing; and the people capa-
> ble of creating such a language have spread the fullness of their soul to
> all posterity: for in the succeeding ages the same forces, thanks to the
> poets, the musicians, the actors, the orators, and the prophets, flow into
> form. But when they were still in the superabundant fullness of their
> first youth, these same forces begat the creators of language: these were
> the most creative men of all time and they stood for [*aus-zeichnen*]
> what musicians and artists have ever afterward stood for: their soul was
> greater, fuller of love, more collective; it was almost as if it lived in
> everyone rather than in some gloomy and isolated corner. In them, the
> collective soul spoke with itself.[19]

This text (although it does not pertain strictly to the field of rhetoric) says a great deal. Let us simply note, for the moment, that this originarily sovereign language predetermines an artistic use of language. For Nietzsche, excess or super-abundance defines art, the practice of art. If the Greek language is naturally disposed to rhetoric, it is because the Greeks are also, naturally, an "artistic people." What is specifically Greek in the relationship the Greeks maintained with language is art, play. At the beginning of the Course on Rhetoric, Nietzsche quotes the celebrated passage from the *Critique of Judgement* on eloquence and poetry: "The arts of speech are *rhetoric* and *poetry*. *Rhetoric* is the art of transacting a serious business of the understanding as if it were a free play of the imagination; *poetry* that of conducting a free play of the imagination as if it were a serious business of the understanding."[20] He then adds this brief comment: "What is unique to Hellenistic life is thus characterized: to perceive all matters of the intellect, of life's seriousness, of necessities, even of danger, as play."[21] This is why eloquence is more Greek (and therefore more "artistic") than poetry itself.[22] This is why it is not only *a* Greek art, but indeed *the Greek art par excellence*: "*Ars techne* is the theory of the art of *rhetoric* [*Kunstlehre*] *par excellence*, very characteristic among a nation of artists!"[23]

All of this holds together pretty well, but obviously relies on something that has not yet been explicitly stated. It is quite understandable that the Greeks are an artistic people and that what is natural in them is always already "art." But why this privilege granted to their language, that is, to language itself? Why indeed should rhetoric be considered the Greek art par excellence? This can hardly be explained unless (and this is in fact what one can already see in the text of "Reading and Writing") language itself is already the *techne kat exochen*. The Greek language as art, that is, as naturally rhetorical. It follows that the Greeks relentlessly exploited a possibility of their own language, a *natural* possibility of their own language—and, consequently, the very nature of language in general. Because it engendered rhetoric, the Greek language reveals the essence of language itself. This is, moreover, a prerogative proper to the Greeks: they reveal, they always possess, in Nietzsche's eyes, the power to reveal what is essential, provided we "know how to understand them," interpret them, read them as they themselves never did and never could. Thus language is an art. There is an art of language because language is already an art. And precisely *this art*. "Language is rhetoric" (*Rh.*, §3). One might even sum it all up by saying: Language is art par excellence.[24]

Force and Language

In this venture, the "concept of rhetoric" was entirely lost. Or, what amounts to the same: it invaded everything, it disappeared in blending with everything else, in becoming "generalized." Absolutely anterior to itself, rhetoric as such is practically nothing. At most a dim, uncertain, and, above all, an ashamed awareness (imagining itself as ornament) of its primitiveness. The only way to conceive of the rhetorical origin of language is to mobilize the concept of the *unconscious*:

> But, it is not difficult to prove that what is called "rhetorical," as a
> means of conscious art, had been active as a means of unconscious art
> in language and its development, indeed, that *the rhetorical is a further
> development* [*Fortbildung*], guided by the clear light of the understand-
> ing, of *the artistic means which are already found in language*. There is
> obviously no unrhetorical "naturalness" of language to which one could
> appeal; language itself is the result of purely rhetorical arts.[25]

Here Nietzsche faithfully follows Gerber. But he finds himself once again on familiar ground. Indeed, this is not the first time that Nietzsche had recourse to the unconscious in discussing language. In a text of 1871, for example, it had already come up:[26] there Nietzsche unraveled the "enigma" of the origin of language in what is doubtless the most radical fashion – by doing away with it, by asserting that it was "unthinkable." It was, in fact, a question of challenging all the "earlier naïve positions," in particular the opposition of nature and culture bequeathed to us by the Greeks (the Greeks never quite entirely understood that their nature was merely their pure aptitude for *techne*). Nietzsche there thinks language as the product of an *instinct*, and instinct itself was understood, under the influence of the *Critique of Judgement* (read in a certain way) and the third lecture of Schelling's *Philosophy of Mythology*, as a nonconscious finality [*finalité sans conscience*]. Almost everything that the detour through rhetoric opened up was contained in embryo in this text – including the outline of a critique of philosophical and scientific conceptuality already more radical than Schopenhauer's. But curiously, despite the reference to Schelling – or else because of it[27] – it was not yet a question of rhetoric. If rhetoric is the origin of language, however, it is indeed because language is the product of an unconscious (artistic) instinct.

This instinct is a *force*, an "artistic force" – or, more precisely, that force which is called, since Aristotle, rhetorical force. In assuming the Aristotelian definition of rhetoric – *rhetorike dunamis peri hekaston tou theoresai to hendechomenon pithanon* – Nietzsche retains two things: *pithanon*, which is not *peithein*, persuading, but the persuasive in general, and *dunamis*. Rhetoric is "neither *episteme*, nor *techne*, but *dunamis*, which, however, could be elevated to a *techne*."[28] Nietzsche translates *dunamis* as *Kraft*, force. Rhetoric is thus a certain persuasive force, a force intended to persuade. The essence of language, its origin and its end, is this very force – whose primary characteristic is that it is not the force of truth. Just as "by nature, man is not created for knowledge,"[29] originally, language is not created for speaking the truth:

> The power [*Kraft*] to discover and to make operative that which works and impresses, with respect to each thing, a power which Aristotle calls rhetoric, is, at the same time, the essence of language; the latter is based just as little as rhetoric is upon that which is true, upon the essence of things. Language does not desire to instruct, but to convey to others a subjective impulse and its acceptance.[30]

Thus language does not instruct; it conveys no knowledge. "Rhetoric arises among a people who . . . would rather be persuaded than instructed."[31] It contains no reference at all to the being of things: it does not apprehend them, it does not allow them to appear; it does not present them. "It desires to convey only a *doxa*, not an *episteme*."[32] This is because the force that constitutes language resides entirely in what Nietzsche calls transposition – transport or transfer: *die Übertragung*. Originally, language transposes. Or, more exactly, it transposes a "perceptual" transposition: "Man, who forms language, does not perceive things or events, but stimuli [*Reize*]: he does not communicate sensations [*Empfindungen*], but merely copies [*Abbildungen*] of sensations. The sensation, evoked through a nerve stimulus, does not take in the thing itself: this sensation is presented externally through an image."[33] In turn, this image must be represented by a sound-image [*Tonbild*]. Between the "thing in itself" and language (the word), there are consequently three breaks (if we take into account the separation of the thing and the sensation), three "passages" from one "sphere" to another, absolutely heterogeneous one. This destroys any possibility whatever of adequation. Language is founded on an originary and irreducible gap [*écart*], across which it forces its way by identifying the non-identical, by introducing analogy. Language, therefore, posits by imitation (see *Phb.*, I, §§131, 144, 148, etc.) a "subjective" relation to things. This relation is the *pithanon*, which is also translated as the *verisimilar* (*Rh.*, §1): "It is not the things that pass over into consciousness, but the manner in which we stand toward them, the *pithanon*."[34] In the "experience" of *pithanon*, the thing disappears: "in its place" a mark [*Merkmal*] presents itself. For this reason, language designates, but in the sense of noting [*aus-zeichnen, bezeichnen*], of a substitutive mark. It signifies improperly; it connotes rather than denotes. The originary transposition is thus a figure, that is, a trope, a word-figure. *Übertragung* translates for Nietzsche the Greek *metaphora* ("The Greeks first signified the metaphorical use by *metaphora* [Isocrates and Aristotle, for example]. Hermagenes says that the grammarians still called *metaphora* what the rhetoricians called *tropos*").[35] Language is therefore originarily figurative, tropic, that is, originarily metaphorical. The essence of language is the *turn*; and metaphor is the artistic force itself, the mimetic force that traverses, without, however, reducing, the gap of representation. The *Theoretical Introduction* of 1873 summarizes all of this in a few words:

> The various languages, juxtaposed, show that words are never concerned with truth, never with adequate expression; otherwise there would not be so many languages. The "thing-in-itself" (which would be pure, disinterested truth) is also absolutely incomprehensible to the creator of language and not worth seeking. He designates only the relations of things to men, and to express these relations he uses the boldest metaphors. First, he translates a nerve stimulus into an image! That is the first metaphor. Then, the image must be reshaped into a sound. The second metaphor. And each time there is a complete overleaping of spheres—from one sphere to the center of a totally different, new one.[36]

The Rhythm of Language

The analysis we have just outlined obviously remains very schematic. It does not take into account the detail of Nietzsche's operations, nor especially the tangle of attempts, regrets, and hesitations punctuating, for example, the first notebook of *The Book of the Philosopher*.

If we followed attentively the path taken by Nietzsche, if we noted down the variations in his language or the differences introduced between the "models" and the course, and then between the course and *The Book of the Philosopher*, if we took into consideration, without becoming too alarmed by it, Nietzsche's "empiricism" and "materialism," the particular type of physiology he brings into play and in which there is *also* sketched out a whole conception of inscription and trace, we might see that what appears so banal, so "naïve," and so deeply buried in a "suspect" metaphysical ground, is not so to quite the extent that we imagine. It is true that the mobilization of rhetorical conceptuality, the reduction of rhetoric to trope and of trope to metaphor, the notion of an *originary* difference or gap, all indicate an unequivocal affiliation with the metaphysics of identity and presence—even if in the form of its "reversal." It is also incontestable that the way in which Nietzsche wishes to radicalize Kant, his efforts to reduce as it were the a priori to tropes and the transcendental to a fact of language, does not escape, in spite of everything, in spite of a growing distrust of Schopenhauer, the modern determination of metaphysics as a metaphysics of subjectivity and of the will, as Heidegger's interpretation emphasizes. We know, furthermore, what this costs: Nietzsche must first have recourse to a use of the concept of metaphor that is itself metaphorical, which obviously is not enough—quite the contrary—to tear metaphor away from its original ground and cannot fail to expose him to the risk of an infinite regression; next (but this is the same problem), it is necessary—at least it would be necessary—that the charge of "impropriety" brought against the supposedly adequate language of the concept and of truth might not be brought in the name of an "other" literality. There does exist a "solution": the idea, organized at the beginning of the *Introduction* of 1873 (*Phb.*, III), of an originary power or *art* of *dissimulation* (that *Verstellung* which is the very perversion of *Vorstellung*, of representation) by which human beings supplement [*beigeben*] their weakness, their fragility, their ephemerality, by which, in other words, they compensate for their finitude. Dissimulation is in fact defined as a force of illusion, but such that it can deceive itself, and this to the point that it takes itself for the force of truth as such (as if there were a force of truth). It is thus nothing other than the unconscious, the artistic instinct, but this time conceived as the originary *forgetting* inevitably included in the *aesthetic* response to terror (the breakdown of meaning, the absolute indifference of nature, its infinite, repetitive, fatal flux), the unavowal [*inaveu*] of art,[37] that negative tension [*crispation*] and that lack of approval which is already nihilism, whereby the "lie" immediately passes itself off for "truth," metaphor for concept, myth for science, etc., and whereby the process of *wearing away* [*usure*][38] is initiated. But it remains to be seen on the basis of what truth exceeding all truth, on the basis of what "beyond" of truth, truth can acknowledge itself as lie. Is it enough, as indicated by the title of the

1873 *Introduction*, to speak of it "in an extra-moral sense"? Would it be enough if some discourse could transgress the philosophical order of the concept, of proof? After all, it is not by chance that the *Introduction* of 1873 begins with the *narration* of a *fable*. Nor is it by chance that the fable remains unfinished.

But again, it is doubtless not in what these texts say, or even in what they do not succeed in saying, that we must locate the crux of the matter: in this case, the way in which an initial assurance (or at least what could pass for such) becomes frayed or out of tune. Actually, we might as well recognize that everything is played out not in these texts considered in and for themselves (if indeed it is possible to consider them so, in the state they are in) but in their difficult, complex, and disconcerting relation to *The Birth of Tragedy*. It is true that *The Birth of Tragedy* does not constitute, any more than these, a *single* text. It is itself involved in a no less difficult relationship with its own outlines and the already organized drafts that preceded it. The "definitive" text shows the effects of this: there is an intersection and superimposition of discourses that cannot really blend or overlap and whose (fragile) reconciliation requires the deployment of quite a hyperbolic "eloquence"—and/or the resources of a certain dialectic. Nietzsche will only denounce this profound equivocation much later, "at the end."[39] Already, though, contrary to all expectations, it is this equivocation that the texts of the detour through rhetoric are beginning to destroy. This would have to be shown in detail. But it is perhaps not impossible to group things around a few major themes.

In the first place, the theory of language put forth in *The Birth of Tragedy* falls apart when rhetoric enters on the scene. This was hardly a spectacular event; it is even possible that Nietzsche was not very clearly aware of it, to the extent that, in the course of his work on tragedy, from draft to draft (since, in revealing fashion, the question of language would never become the focus of a *definitive* systematic exposition), he had already gradually weakened the original version. And this was possible especially to the extent that, in terms of results, as far as the critique of conceptuality is concerned, the differences between drafts could appear minimal or hardly discernible. This is because, in any event, language had always been conceived as inadequate, abstract, superficial, and unrelated to the essence of things. For example, in a fragment from 1871: "Language suggests through concepts; it is therefore by means of thoughts that sympathy is born. This imposes a limit on it. . . . The word itself only suggests; it is but the surface of a stormy sea that thunders in the depths."[40] And if language has always been this way, it is because it became this way: the disembodiment of language is already the object of a narrative that, like all narrative (and even if the story recapitulated in *The Birth of Tragedy* tangles its web), is the story of an origin and a fall. The history of language is that of an illness, a decline, a mortal agony: a gradual loss of breath and voice, anemia, pallor, enfeeblement. The same metaphors constantly return. Writing inevitably shares the responsibility: in the same fragment, "language suggests through concepts," but "this is only true of objective, written language." We know the plot of this story. It is what makes the whole "first" period of Nietzsche's thought (that which, in Nietzsche, *precedes* Nietzsche and of which he is "himself" the unceasing plagiarist) depend on the *age of Rousseau* as Jacques Derrida has defined it.[41] Nothing is missing — not even a blindness (and future lucidity) on Nietzsche's part necessary to call into question the Rousseauistic idyll of origins.

But the resemblances end here. Even if we take into account a certain break with Schopenhauer along the way (the "decisive step" is taken between 1870 and 1871, between "The Dionysian Worldview" and the last preparatory draft, where the Will is decreed "the most general phenomenal form of something which for us remains otherwise totally undecipherable"),[42] even if we stress this break (which is, however, still quite precarious), we still cannot keep from recognizing the upheaval to which the encounter with rhetoric would give rise. The reason for this is quite simple: when rhetoric is introduced, it tends to eliminate music and take its place.[43] It destroys at least in part that which, in language, was not properly linguistic and would allow the "salvation" of language: its originally musical nature, its sonorous essence, that which, in the exercise of speech, in accentuation, retains an originary force and provides the power of expression. The same fragment, quoted here almost in its entirety, says exactly this:

> Language suggests through concepts; it is therefore by means of thoughts that sympathy is born. This imposes a limit on it.
> But this is only true of objective, written language; oral language is sonorous and the intervals, the rhythms, the pace, the volume, and the accentuation are symbolic of the emotive content to be expressed. All of this also pertains to music.
> But the bulk of feeling is not expressed in speech. And the word itself only suggests; it is but the surface of a stormy sea that thunders in the depths.

But this must be qualified.

In its tropic originarity as well, language expresses and restores an emotive content. Thus, while the rhetorical part of language could not substitute for its musical part, it could coexist with it and, let us say somewhat hastily, could correspond, on the side of the signified, to what sonority, accentuation, etc., represent in the order of the signifier. And this all the more so as, contrary to what is suggested by the text just quoted, there is in principle no longer, in the last texts of the period devoted to tragedy, any adequation possible between language (even in that "subterranean" aspect of sonority [*der Tonuntergrund*]) and the essence of things. We could quite easily assume, then, that the musical symbolism of language is exactly the same thing as the phenomenon of figuration, or that the general symbolic system of *The Birth of Tragedy* is at least the prehistory of the future tropology. All of this would appear perfectly coherent and would ultimately give the impression of a genuine system.

Things would be so—strictly speaking, it is quite possible that Nietzsche thought, at least for a time, that things were this way—if music itself and most of the concepts necessary for its determination were not the site of a persistent ambiguity. First and foremost of these concepts is the concept of symbol itself, on which everything rests. This is all the more serious in that Nietzsche uses indifferently the two terms *Symbol* and *Gleichnis*. *Gleichnis*, as we know, is a polysemic word, difficult to translate. It has the general sense of *resemblance* or *image* (as when we say: in the image of . . .), but it can designate *comparison* and, consequently, *symbol, allegory, parable*, etc. As it is used in rhetoric, it even designates *figure*, indeed *metaphor* itself.[44] Besides, didn't Nietzsche accept the classical definition of metaphor as "a shortened simile [*ein kurzes Gleichnis*]"?[45] There is, accordingly, in the symbol, the same value of transposition (during his study of tragedy, Nietzsche speaks especially of externalization) as in figure or metaphor in the "broad" sense. Moreover, as in the texts on rhetoric, symbol is related to image, copy [*Abbild*], and sometimes it even has the sense of a "quite incomplete and fragmentary image [*Abbild*]," of an "allusive sign [*ein andeutendes Zeichen*] on whose meaning there must be agreement."[46] In another passage from the same text, concerning the actor who "tries to equal his model through the emotion of the sublime or the emotion of laughter," who "goes beyond beauty without necessarily seeking truth" and "remains hovering between the two," the symbol appears already to be inscribed within that intermediate zone of the *verisimilar*, which the Course on Rhetoric (we should not forget the kinship affirmed there between the actor and the orator) would later make the very object of language under the name of *pithanon*: "[The actor] does not seek beautiful appearances . . . nor the truth, but *verisimilitude*. (The symbol, sign of truth.)"[47] Under these conditions, the language of a text such as this would ultimately already be that of *The Book of the Philosopher*:

> The multiplicity of languages demonstrates that the word and the thing do not completely or necessarily coincide, but that the word is a symbol [*Symbol*]. But what does the word symbolize? Unquestionably only representations, either conscious or, more often than not, unconscious. For how could a word-symbol [*Wort-Symbol*] correspond to that inward essence of which we ourselves, and the universe along with us, are but copies [*Abbilder*]? We understand this essence only in the representations we have of it, we are only familiar with its externalization in images.[48]

There is nevertheless a very clear difference: unlike metaphor, which transposes once and for all and which, so to speak, keeps the thing always at the same distance from language, the symbol is *more or less* adequate. It is indeed of the order of representation (in the Schopenhauerian sense), but not all forms of representation are equivalent. The linguistic symbol is not the only symbol. Only the symbol that has been retained and as it were "consigned" to memory [*ein bemerktes Symbol*], that has already (almost) lost all of its symbolic *force*, belongs to language, is ultimately a *concept*. In "The Dionysian Worldview," for example, an entire analysis is worked out (an analysis that will often be repeated and modified) of the relation between language and feeling, that properly Rousseauistic mode of self-presence. In accordance with the Schopenhauerian tradition, feeling is described as "a compound of unconscious representations and states of will."[49] But the will only externalizes itself in the form of pleasure and unpleasure, which have merely quantitative variations. The qualitative distinctions introduced into feeling are due simply to the play of accessory or accompanying representations [*begleitende Vorstellungen*], of which only a portion reaches consciousness. This is, of course, the only part that language—the concept—can translate. Language therefore only expresses what is "reducible" [*der Auflösbar*] in feeling. Which is as much as to say that language practically does not express feeling at all. If feeling can be communicated, it is in the language of gesture and in the language of sound. Still, a distinction is called for: although mimicry is instinctive (unconscious and finalized), it only symbolizes an accessory representation, by authority moreover of that law (which the Course on Rhetoric no longer observes) that "an image can only be symbolized by an image." This is why mimicry (in language, this means the system of consonants and vowels without tone or accent, according to the draft of 1871) expresses only "intermittent forms of the will," that is, "in the symbolism of music, a *rhythmics*." What symbolizes the will itself therefore is *dynamism*, whose essence, at that time, was hidden "without even being able to be expressed in symbols," in *harmony*.[50] It is obviously necessary here to make allowance for Wagnerian metaphysics. All the same, even when the idea of an originary and insurmountable representation was reinforced or simply established for the first time, this idea of a possible reduction of symbolic distance continued to dominate all of Nietzsche's analyses of language.

Actually, in all the work carried out on tragedy, that is, on music, this ambiguity was never dispelled. As long as it was a question of justifying—against the (Italian, Florentine) operatic tradition, which subordinates music to language through a misinterpretation of the essence of Greek tragedy—an original lyricism, the *Lied*, musical drama, as long as it was a question of effecting the romantic (German) reversal and of freeing music from the textual captivity in which, with a few exceptions (Lutheran chorale . . .), it had been kept by theoretical, Alexandrian, "bookish" idolatry, language was always conceived on the basis of its musical essence and the analysis of music was always governed by the dream of, by the desire and the nostalgia for, proximity, immediacy, and presence— even the divine, if, as in a whole metaphysical tradition (which would also include Heidegger),[51] music is properly theology. Doubtless, Nietzsche would not always assert that "through sound" humanity "expresses the most intimate thoughts of nature" and that "the genius of existence in itself [*der Genius des Daseins an sich*], the will, makes itself immediately understood [*macht sich . . . unmittelbar verständlich*]"; nor that the scream, the pure externalization of the rapture of feeling, is the origin of music; nor that "melodic speech [*der Sprechgesang*] is like a return to nature" in which "the symbol weakened by use regains its original force."[52] But one might say that *The Birth of Tragedy* is ultimately nothing but an ambiguous commentary on this single statement by Schopenhauer, never accepted without reservation, but also never truly contested—and which chapter 16 formulates in these terms: "Music [has] a character and an origin different from all the other arts, because, unlike them, it is not a copy of the phenomenon, but an immediate copy [*unmittelbares Abbild*] of the will itself, and therefore complements *everything physical in the world* and every phenomenon by representing *what is metaphysical*, the thing in itself."[53]

Thus, only the passage through rhetoric will allow Nietzsche, if not to decide this ambiguity (will he ever do this?), then at least to reduce it. It is not that, by substituting rhetoric for music in determining the essence of language, Nietzsche no longer wished to recognize the musical aspect of language. On the contrary, he will seek for a long time yet to reconcile the two natures of language. Witness, for example, this project from 1874–75:

> To investigate and prepare: *the rhetorical sentence and its analogue in music*. For example, the interrogative proposition, first derived from vocal music, then, through it, from instrumental music—to be demonstrated—(melodic, rhythmic, harmonic).
> Then the interjection, the exclamation point.
> Then the conditional proposition "if."
> Then the accent of the sentence.
> Then rhetorical figures.[54]

It is clear that in the pursuit of this analogy, and in the form it takes of a deduction of syntax, song is still the origin (it is the form of the primitive question),[55] and rhetorical transposition the end, the outcome. Still, we should take into account, in order better to gauge the fragility of all this, a very clear displacement, relative to the period of tragedy, in the hierarchy or priority of the "syntactical" and the "semantic," since the constitution of the "sentence," of the proposition [*Satz*], which is "an imitation of melody" (draft of 1871), had previously been given as a symptom of the "aging" of music: "Monstrous process of aging in music: all that is symbolic can be imitated and thereby killed: continual development of the 'phrase' ['*Phrase*']. . . . Evolution of the incomprehensible hieroglyph which becomes a phrase."[56] Nevertheless, as a general rule, the attention given rhetoric forces the reduction of the musical aspect of language to *rhythm*, to the detriment of melody and harmony. In *The Birth of Tragedy*, it was stated that in the *Lied* or poetry, "language is strained to its utmost that it may *imitate music*."[57] Music here is essentially melody. In the Course on Rhetoric, where poetry is ultimately devalorized relative to eloquence, if the literature of antiquity "seems 'rhetorical' to us," it is no doubt because "it appeals chiefly to the ear, in order to bribe it"; but this power of seduction is connected to rhythm: "Among the Greeks and Romans, one finds an extraordinary development of the sense of rhythm, as far as listening to the spoken word is concerned. [This was achieved] through an enormously persistent practice."[58] And rhythm is precisely, compared to melody and harmony, the least musical element of music.[59] More often than not, it is only an index that allows one to detect the presence of music wherever it is still captive ("Rhythm in poetry proves that the musical element still exists in captivity").[60] It does not belong exclusively to the veritable, "authentic" essence of music. In a word, it is only the *Apollinian* side, the almost visible or plastic part, the one that, in any case, is articulated with appearance alone, like the language of gesture that constitutes it ("cadence [*Takt*] is the reaction of mimicry to music" [draft of 1871]). Concerning the hypothesis of an eruption of the Dionysian in Homeric Greece, *The Birth of Tragedy* says this:

> If music, as it would seem, had been known *previously as an Apollinian art*, it was so, strictly speaking, only as the wave beat of *rhythm*, whose *formative power* [*bildnerische Kraft, force plastique*] was developed for the representation of Apollinian states. The music of Apollo was Doric architectonics in tones, *but* in tones that were *merely suggestive*, such as those of the cithara. The very element which forms the essence of Dionysian music (and hence of music in general) is carefully excluded as un-Apollinian—namely, the emotional power of the tone, the uniform flow of the melody, and the utterly incomparable world of harmony.[61]

This is indeed what made things difficult in *The Birth of Tragedy*—and even disturbed the narration of this birth. This strange "intermediate being,"[62] over which Nietzsche passes so quickly, which pertains neither to the (plastic) domain of appearance nor to the (musical) domain of presence, of which one can only speak through virtually impossible metaphors, is ultimately what language will be when rhetoric has furnished the means of approaching it for itself and defining it in itself.

Monstrosity

But, as is already obvious, the introduction of rhetoric ultimately does not so much affect the theory of language as it subverts the conception of *art* itself. Or, more precisely: because it foregrounds the question of language, the introduction of rhetoric forces one to conceive of art on the basis of language, and not the reverse—and in this movement, art and language are jointly transformed; neither the one nor the other can remain what it was. The more the idea of an originary transposition is stressed, the more is confirmed the idea that transposition is the essence of art and that language furnishes its very model—and the more the ambiguity of presence tends to be effaced. During the period of *The Birth of Tragedy*, art as such was already transposition. The word itself appears, for example, in a fragment of the draft "Homer as Agonistic Poet" ("Homer als Wettkämpfer," §2), which is contemporaneous with *The Birth of Tragedy*: "all laws of art relate to transposition."[63] Except at moments of extreme vigilance, Nietzsche can nonetheless assert that in Dionysian art, nature speaks with its "true, *undissembled* voice [unverstellte *Stimme*]," when, on the other hand, in Apollinian art, pain is "obliterated . . . from the features of nature" by "lies."[64] What rhetoric breaks apart, at the most decisive and fragile articulation of *The Birth of Tragedy*, is therefore the very distinction between the Dionysian and the Apollinian, or at least what this distinction still contained in the way of opposition and contradiction. What rhetoric averts, in other words, is the inevitable danger that the non-dialectical unity (difference) of the Apollinian and the Dionysian (the always anterior but never primitive splitting up or dispersion of Dionysus behind the mask of Apollo) might open out as a simple difference of presence and its contrary, of which art or tragedy would ultimately be the *Aufhebung*, the *sublation*. It is true, as we have seen, that nothing in this definitive accentuation of the representational gap or distance fundamentally disturbs the mimetics established in *The Birth of Tragedy*. To define the "aesthetic relation" as an "allusive transposition, a stammering translation into a completely foreign tongue,"[65] may dispel an uncertainty, but does not modify the structure of transposition. However, rhetorical analysis reverses its order: the play of transposition that, in *The Birth of Tragedy*, accounted for the genesis of poetry (§5), does not lead from sensory stimulus to image and from image to sound, but from "the copy of this primal unity as music [*das Abbild dieses Ur-Einen als Musik*]" (music was a repetition [*Wiederholung*] and a recast [*ein zweiter Abguß*] of the world) to a "reflection [*Widerschein*] . . . a second mirroring . . . like an analogous [*gleichnisartig*] dream image."[66] The order that will become that of rhetorical transposition was then looked upon as "an upside-down world": "*As if a son could sire his father!*"[67] Music could "give birth" to images, but not the reverse. The *natural* order leads from sound (which, even isolated, is "already Dionysian") to the image, which is Apollinian. Dionysus is the "father." He was always the "father." To be sure, the engendering of his "son" is his death. But he can rise again, be born again. The ambiguity is such that he could even be resuscitated. (What else was celebrated in Greek mysticism, in the mysteries? See *The Birth of Tragedy*, §10.) And in the countenance of the "son," prey to fury (or joy), it was possible to recognize suddenly the features of the "father." Music could always make itself heard again, while language could always be swallowed up in music as in an ocean—and this, moreover, was the whole adventure of modern art since Beethoven's Ninth Symphony, the "return" of Dionysus, the rebirth of tragedy, etc.[68]

Rhetoric is thus a monstrosity. Language is born unnaturally: in language, Apollo comes first, the "son" comes before the "father." This is more than a "reversal." This is an aberration, or even an impossibility.

We would have to say—but would it be sufficient to say?—that the origin is not originary, that representation precedes presence, etc. We could obviously propose something of this kind. For in art as it is now defined, Dionysus has practically disappeared. Or, more correctly, he has become Apollo. There is henceforth no force that is not always already weakened *as* form, that is, as language. Apollo is the *name* of Dionysus ("originary" metaphor). Dionysus can therefore no longer appear: Apollo precedes him, and in preceding him—him whom he represented—he hides his face for good, he eliminates all hope that his true face (the face of truth) might one day reveal itself *as such*. Without manifestation, without epiphany, Dionysus is henceforth without identity. He is no longer and can no longer be a god of presence—a *present* god. It is not in tragedy that the god dies, but in rhetoric. And it is not by chance that tragedy, the representation of his "passion," will later be interpreted as an art of discourse and eloquence, and not as a "musical drama."[69]

Doubtless, we should add that the form of the *as* [*als*, *e*], even, or especially, when it is effaced in metaphor, is, by a kind of absolute privilege, the form of ontological discourse itself. But it will also be noted that what kills Dionysus is not that he might be seen (or might not be seen) behind the features of another. Dionysus is no longer a god of presence, but neither is he a god of absence or a *deus absconditus*—even less a "withdrawn" god. His death is no longer in the realm of appearance, it is no longer connected—it is *less* connected to some necessity of phenomenality, that is, of truth, of unveiling. His death is a fact of language. It is not so much that he dies from being proffered—that language is the death of God, or that the death of God is the birth of language, although this is doubtless part of the story. We must rather imagine a death without disappearance (nor reappearance, of course), a kind of haunting, perhaps, which would explain at once how the "dead" god continues to inhabit the language that has "killed" him (grammar[70] . . .) and how he never stops undoing it, ruining its assurance, faith, and power. But one would finally have to admit that, at the point to which Nietzsche succeeds in bringing this "deconstruction," truth still prevails and the *labor* of truth continues, since we are trying to regain something that has been forgotten, to reveal something unconscious, to find the path of a kind of "reminiscence."

But this is precisely what remains unspoken. What Nietzsche did not say—could not say. And what we cannot read. Indeed, none of these propositions has a meaning outside of *The Birth of Tragedy* itself, that is, outside a certain reading of *The Birth of Tragedy* that one might always be tempted to do in order to "save" Nietzsche from the well-known abusive interpretations, and that Nietzsche himself, for similar reasons, wished to do (what is *The Book of the Philosopher* if not, already, a reading of *The Birth of Tragedy*?). But such a reading is impossible. To read *The Birth of Tragedy* in order to isolate and draw out its meaning, to repeat it in order to make manifest, as that which already disturbed the whole "system," a clearer break in the ontological or theological ambiguity, in order to emphasize, in any case, the difficulty of the relation between Apollo and Dionysus, to *rewrite* it, then — this implies (and it is an absolute paradox) that one change nothing and overthrow everything. This is no doubt the very law of repetition. Rhetoric is precisely that paradoxical element which should be able to confirm everything, but which, once introduced, begins to destroy everything and ends up by compelling the abandonment of everything. For, fundamentally, what rhetoric destroys is the very possibility of continuing to speak the language of *The Birth of Tragedy*. That is, a certain "rhetoric" (of course, unaware of itself as such) does this, a use of language that never ceases to doubt language itself and that assumes it possible to exceed within language the limits of language. It is less a question of *style* (which must not, however, be neglected)[71] than of the status or province of language. What rhetoric destroys is in reality the possibility of returning to *myth*. It reveals that any "return to myth," however vigilant one may be (and whatever may have been, in this case, the distance taken from romanticism, from F. Schlegel or Schelling),[72] is in fact a return to *allegory*, to the philosophical use and interpretation of myths. Therefore, no new mythology is possible, no mythology, in any case, that philosophical discourse could imagine as being *prior* to itself. Let us recall that, in *The Birth of Tragedy*, Nietzsche asserts (with all of "Wagnerianism" hanging in the balance) that myth is born of music and that it cannot "obtain adequate objectification in the spoken word."[73] This is precisely what rhetoric rules out: myth is not originally musical; myth is *rhetorical*. As such, it is caught in the doxic duplicity of language whereby language speaks no truth, but always believes itself to be the language of truth.[74] The border separating philosophy from its *other* thus started to blur. The passage through rhetoric led Nietzsche to the point where it is no longer possible to turn back against philosophy, as though from its pure "outside" (that is, dialectically, from its purest interiority), any originarity (musical, mythic, etc.). Rhetoric ends up contaminating a whole *belief*.

It is probably for this reason that the names Dionysus and Apollo are not pronounced a single time in all these texts (any more than we see there the categories that Nietzsche had forged from them). The only proper names we encounter are historical names. The gods have quit the stage; they are no longer an issue. This is not for the purpose, as Fink, for example, would lead us to believe, of finally realizing, without recourse to metaphor, some "negative" ontology or other.[75] Neither is it a process of "demythification," like the Socratic moment where tragedy culminates in the disappearance of all the gods. The gods are purely and simply absent. And it is not by chance that the only mythological names that still appear, in two related fragments of the first notebook of *The Book of the Philosopher* (85 and 87; Musarion, 6: 35–36), are those of Titan (Prometheus) and Oedipus, the symbol of sacrilege and the symbol of parricide,[76] whom *The Birth of Tragedy* portrayed as Apollinian figures par excellence, the "idols" or the mask of Dionysus, the only true hero of tragedy. Both made tolerable the violent rupture and the terror involved in myth: they conversed in the full light of day and their discourse masked a frightening monstrosity, the dazzling, nocturnal depths of truth.[77] But when truth has foundered, when its lack is no longer dazzling, there remains only an allusive shred of ancient mythology in which they henceforth embody the "last man," "the last philosopher." The first fragment still concerns a scene, the sketch of a scene for a drama, the idea of which would pursue Nietzsche for some years yet:[78] the last philosopher, "in fearful solitude," cries to an absolutely indifferent nature to grant him forgetfulness: "Grant forgetfulness! Forgetfulness! – No, he *bears his suffering like a Titan – until redemption is offered him in the highest tragic art.*" This attitude could still be taken for that of the tragic hero as defined by *The Birth of Tragedy*, assuming, however, that tragic art could be defined not as the pure will to illusion, an artistic response to the failure of truth (see *Phb.*, I, §38; Musarion, 6:12), but as the miraculous equilibrium and "fraternal alliance," the pure dialogue of the Dionysian and the Apollinian, of which the third act of *Tristan* (the *opus metaphysicum* par excellence, as the fourth *Untimely Meditation* puts it) offers the most beautiful example: "Dionysus speaks the language of Apollo; and Apollo, finally, the language of Dionysus."[79] This is why the scene previously sketched is repeated in the *soliloquy* of the last philosopher, in "the *discourse* of the last philosopher with himself." This time, the last philosopher is not *like* Titan, it is Oedipus "himself." He is not blind; he does not cry out; even less does he "sing." And if, in the ultimate solitude in which he finds himself, he yet speaks with an *other*, this other is his own voice, whose echo interminably fades in the murmured lament reverberating at his death:

> Do I still hear you, my voice? Do you whisper a curse? May your malediction burst the bowels of the earth! But it still lives and only fixes me more brilliantly and coldly with its unpitying stars, it lives, as stupid and blind as ever, and man alone dies.
>
> And yet! I still hear you, beloved voice! There is still *someone* dying outside of me, the last man, in this universe: the last sigh, *your* sigh, dies with me, this long Alas! Alas! sighed over me, the last miserable man, Oedipus!

This voice, which haunts the discourse of the last man on (the absence of) truth, which doubles that discourse and echoes its desolation (which defers its death), is perhaps already the one it will be given to "Nietzsche" to make heard. But he will have to persist in the repetition of his first "book" (and its mythology), which will always be too much the book of the "other" (Wagner, in this case, but it is Platonism and Christianity that spoke or "sang" in it). He will, therefore, have to carry through with "rhetoric," to accept the *eloquent* dissolution of myth, the language (which does not teach) of parody and of laughter. The *discourses* of Zarathustra will thus refer again to Dionysus. Already in these years of the detour, the mythic configuration is irreversibly modified. Ariadne appears to be strangely united with another Dionysus, who flees her as one does the Sirens, the fatal magic of music.[80] To conclude with an *illustration*, this is perhaps what Hugo von Hoffmansthal and Richard Strauss understood when, in the final scene of the *hybrid* opera, neither "comic" nor "serious," that is *Ariadne at Naxos*, they gave to the appearance of Dionysus (Bacchus) the air of a nostalgic parody of the second act of *Tristan*. But that is another story.[81]

Translated by Gary M. Cole

Chapter 3
Apocryphal Nietzsche[1]

I would like to begin by simply making two remarks—remarks that are, moreover, complementary. First, what I will say (or rather what I will read) is deliberately inscribed within what others here have already said (that is, written). For this reason, nothing of what I will propose here is "new." At the very most—but this is not so certain—I will combine things a little differently. Be that as it may, this will remain, in the strictest sense of the word, a *contribution*. If, nevertheless, I insist (and here is the second prefatory remark) on returning to certain questions (or even one question), this is neither innocent nor without design. Today it is a question—as I think we all understand—of persevering *despite everything*. But as Nietzsche says in *Ecce Homo*, "nothing decisive is constructed except by building upon a *despite everything*."

"Question of Literature"

This is why I will try in my turn to reintroduce myself into the question we are (nearly) all asking ourselves here and that—in diverse ways, it is true—has constantly animated these debates. Without further precaution, I will formulate this question as follows: *Where does Nietzsche depart from philosophy?* Or, to be more precise: *Where does Nietzsche dissociate himself from philosophy?* And I will not add: *exactly.* . . .

Despite appearances, this is not a Nietzschean question, although Nietzsche is certainly no stranger to it. But that we still ask it today, that we are constrained to maintain it as a question, should indicate in sufficiently clear manner that between Nietzsche himself (assuming the expression "Nietzsche himself" means anything) and us, between the affirmation of philosophy's *Überwindung* and our uncertainty (or our suspicions), something has occurred that henceforth renders problematic our relation to Nietzsche—or, which amounts to the same, to philosophy. This something, as we all now know—if only by denying it—is Heidegger's reading, in which, moreover (this perhaps makes all the difference), "Nietzsche himself" really and truly exists. And as to the question raised above, what indeed are we faced with today, whether or not we like it, if not the Heideggerian *answer*: Nietzsche is the last philosopher; it is in him that metaphysics as a whole reaches its culmination and conclusion?

In one respect—and of this no one can be unaware either—Heidegger's reading is unavoidable, because it is the only one (or one of the few) that actually takes Nietzsche absolutely seriously, meaning to the point of showing that the question of overcoming philosophy is itself a philosophical question. Hence the establishment of this complex relation in which the patient and painstaking work of repetition replaces affirmative derring- do [*coup de force*], where the *Überwindung* (the overcoming) is displaced and degraded into *Verwindung* (distortion)—in short, where the Nietzschean objective is indeed reiterated, but in the process twists back so to speak upon itself, reinforces itself and loses in innocence, which is to say also in weakness, what it gains in implacable rigor. Thus, if Nietzsche is the "last metaphysician," Heidegger is the first post-Nietzschean or at least—since we must not forget Bataille—one of the first to have tried to be.

But if this reading is unavoidable, it has also never been self-evident. To say that the question of overcoming philosophy is itself philosophical is only possible precisely if we turn the overcoming of philosophy into a *question*. Nietzsche himself, in part, refused to do this—or rather, he *also* made it an affirmation. And inasmuch as affirmation can go so far as to become detached from, or move beyond the orbit of, interrogative circularity, and thereby disperse itself in the unending reverberation of all unique and definitive answers, Nietzsche might finally and forever escape philosophy's grasp. At least this is what one is always slightly tempted to oppose to Heideggerian closure, which in its way is even more redoubtable than the Hegelian kind. But it is also, of course, what one can never seriously oppose to it, since affirmation is never simple (it must be further affirmed or affirm itself) and since, not being simple, it is paradoxically always too simple, clutching its own *will* [*vouloir*] and consequently incapable of dispersing itself without falling back well beyond its supposed point of detachment, in the infinite but closed exchange of philosophical theses.

All of this is well known, but it is perhaps worth repeating, first in order to note this: if the Heideggerian reading is to be called into question, it would be naïve, to say the least, to imagine that we can do it simply. Its power of encirclement practically eliminates the recourse to anything but "ruse," so that it is necessary to deploy a whole strategy of infinite complexity in which, as we know, repetition itself, in the Heideggerian sense, must be repeated, and this in such a way that, separating from itself, it folds back and comes to intersect itself, drawing within itself the outer limit of the closure. This strategy bears a name: *deconstruction*. And if, for simplicity's sake, we might say that deconstruction does not proceed by concepts, in the classical, philosophical sense of the term, we also know that it at least has a "site," a "field," or a "terrain" (but is it still a matter of "property"?) in which to function: the *text* of philosophy insofar as we can distinguish it from *discourse*, or, more exactly, insofar as we can follow its work in discourse — assuming the text is that on account of which discourse, in general, does not function, decomposes and resists itself, fails to reach completion.

To take into account, in Nietzsche's case, the text so defined is a task that could in some fashion be taken for granted (I say this very cautiously, conscious of the risk one always runs of *restricting* the concept of writing), since Nietzsche, of all the "philosophers" (Kierkegaard included), was the one who distinguished himself the most systematically (partly in spite of himself, but with his usual ostentatious rage) by his contradictory and multifarious, enigmatic and, let us say, disruptive practice of writing. Indeed, without him the "question" of the text would doubtless never have emerged so forcefully, at least not in the exact form it has taken today. This task naturally led, therefore, to a shift of emphasis, in a rereading of Nietzsche, onto the irreducibly "literary" part of his discourse (or discourses), in order to follow the contorted, tortuous path of the philosophical *disengagement* [*démarque*][2] and retrace at least the outline of this complex textual apparatus in which the philosophical as such becomes variously but unceasingly blurred.

This aim is, of course, not Heideggerian. In fact, up to a point, it corresponds to none of Heidegger's questions — ultimately incapable of allowing itself to be subsumed under the general form of a question. But this is only true up to a certain point, since, at least concerning Nietzsche, if Heidegger does not take into account "literature," "form," "style," etc. (still less the "text"), this is done deliberately. It is neither a gap nor a silence, but a refusal, and an explicit refusal at that. (As everybody knows, we cannot say as much about all refusals.)

Here is, quite simply, where I wanted to enter into the discussion: if, on the one hand, concerning Nietzsche, focusing on the text inevitably raises the question we can designate as "the question of literature" (with, as you might guess, all the requisite skepticism), and if, on the other hand, Heidegger (from whom we have the strategic project itself, whatever displacements it may have undergone) resolutely dismissed this problematic, is this not the sign that we should guard against a certain haste? Is this not, above all, an indication that we should begin by patiently reading Heidegger, by examining the reasons for this refusal or this dismissal? For by imagining that we could take advantage of this ambiguous silence [*non-dit*] (by hastily confusing it with the text's unthought and its correlative: the profoundly philosophical privilege unreservedly granted by Heidegger to the concern for presence, being, truth, etc.), do we not run the risk of remaining well within the limit to which Heidegger succeeded in carrying the interpretation of Nietzsche?

It is this simple question that I would like to raise here. But one immediately sees the immensity of the task it sets us: nothing less than the systematic deconstruction of the whole Heideggerian reading of Nietzsche. As it is clearly out of the question to undertake this today, I will limit myself to proposing a kind of programmatic outline. Still, we will also see, or at least I hope we will see, that in following even a short way the thread of this suspicion, one cannot avoid introducing, concerning Nietzsche's writing, a texture infinitely more complex than any we could have imagined.

Poïesis and *Dichtung*

There is, then, in the Heideggerian commentary, a refusal to consider the "literary" process in Nietzschean discourse. More precisely, since it is obviously *Thus Spoke Zarathustra* that is involved (but we will no doubt have to reexamine this obviousness), there is the clearly marked refusal to confirm the opposition of the "theoretical" and the "poetic" in which classic commentary on Nietzsche operates as it were spontaneously.

Let us begin by reading this refusal.

Everything turns upon what we might consider as the connection between the first two courses devoted to Nietzsche, where, in the mode of a complex exchange of their principal themes (the will to power and the eternal return), the question of the "poetic form" of *Zarathustra* and of the relation this "form" maintains with the teaching and doctrine of the eternal return surfaces, or, more exactly, resurfaces, at least twice. Here is what Heidegger says:

> We must free ourselves straightaway of a prejudicial view. The editors say (XII, 425) [here Heidegger is referring to the *apparatus criticus* of the large *octavo* edition]: "Right from the start two different intentions run parallel to each other; the one aims at a theoretical presentation [*eine theoretische Darstellung*] of the doctrine, the other at a poetical treatment [*eine poetische Behandlung*] of it." Now, to be sure, we too have spoken of a "poetic" presentation [*"dichterische" Darstellung*] of the doctrine of eternal return in *Zarathustra*. Yet we avoided distinguishing it from a "theoretical" presentation [*Darstellung*], not because the passages cited from *The Gay Science* and *Beyond Good and Evil* are not theoretical presentations, but because here the word and concept *theoretical* do not say anything, especially not when one follows the

lead of the editors and of those who portray Nietzsche's "doctrine" by equating *theoretical* with "treatment in prose" [*eine Prosabehandlung*]. The distinction "theoretical-poetical" results from muddled thinking. Even if we were to let it obtain in general, such a distinction would in any case be out of place here. In Nietzsche's thinking of his fundamental thought [*In Nietzsches Denken seines Grundgedankens*], the "poetical" is every bit as much "theoretical," and the "theoretical" is inherently "poetical." All philosophical thinking—and precisely the most rigorous and prosaic—is in itself poetic [*dichterisch*]. It nonetheless never springs from the art of poetry [*Dichtkunst*]. A work of poetry [*ein Dichterwerk*], a work like Hölderlin's hymns, can for its part be thoughtful [*denkerisch*] in the highest degree. It is nonetheless never philosophy. Nietzsche's *Thus Spoke Zarathustra* is poetic [*dichterisch*] in the highest degree, and yet it is not a work of art [*ein Kunstwerk*], but "philosophy." Because all actual, that is, all great philosophy is inherently thoughtful-poetic [*denkerisch-dichterisch*], the distinction between "theoretical" and "poetical" cannot be applied to philosophical texts.[3]

As we can see from just one reading, the operation attempted here is particularly contorted. So as neither to distort its logic nor miss its results (for it is, literally, an *operation*), we must quickly break it down.

What is in question is the *Darstellung* of *Zarathustra*, which is not its "form" but, if we must translate, its mode of *presentation* (and, for that matter, that of philosophy in general). As regards this *Darstellung*, the conventional opposition of the "poetical" and the "theoretical" (of the *poetisch* and the *theoretisch*) is strictly irrelevant, all the more so if it comes to correspond to the distinction between "poetic version" and "prosaic version" (*poetische Behandlung* and *Prosabehandlung*), which is to say the prose/poetry distinction itself. Moreover, regarding what is at stake in *Darstellung* (that of *Zarathustra* as well as of philosophy), and which is *Denken*—thinking—the terms "poetical" and "theoretical" are completely interchangeable.

On the other hand, the *Darstellung* of *Zarathustra*—philosophical *Darstellung* in general—can be characterized using a word that is radically untranslatable (except perhaps by clumsy, if handy, recourse to the resources of Greek and to the difference, which Heidegger never fails to stress, between Greek and Latin, though we will soon see that even this recourse is irrelevant): philosophical *Darstellung*, says Heidegger, is *dichterisch*—"poïetic," therefore (but above all not poetical). This does not mean that philosophy (including *Zarathustra*) is *Dichtkunst*—poïetic art or Poïesis. For the relation of philosophy to Poïesis (*Dichtkunst* or, better still, *Dichterwerk*—the work of Poïesis, in other words) is not symmetrical: just as philosophy, however little it may be thoughtful, is always poïetic, so Poïesis, precisely because it is thoughtful, is never philosophical. There is, therefore, an absolute privilege of Poïesis over philosophy, and one can clearly see that if Poïesis never fails to be thoughtful, the same cannot be said for philosophy.

The *result* is simple: as philosophy, as thinking philosophy, *Zarathustra* is poïetic. Were it written otherwise, moreover—less "poetically"—matters would remain the same. But it is a book of philosophy, and thus has nothing in common with a "work of art," that is, with a work of Poïesis. What this means, if we know how to calculate and deduct, is that it simply has nothing in common with a work. And this is what Heidegger implied some pages earlier, when he broached for the first time the question of the *Darstellung* of *Zarathustra*:

> What is difficult to grasp about this work is not only its "content," if it has such, but also its very character as a work. Of course, we are quick to propose a ready-made explanation: here philosophical thoughts are presented poetically [*dichterisch*]. Yet what we are now to call *thinking* [*denken*] and *poetizing* [*dichten*] dare not consist of the usual notions, inasmuch as the work defines both of these anew, or rather, simply announces them.[4]

This remark, noticeably prudent concerning the work-being of *Zarathustra*, and the operation it consequently assumes, are in fact comprehensible only if we refer at least to the three lectures on contemporary art included in the course and since collected in the first text of *Holzwege* under the title "The Origin of the Work of Art." It is here, indeed, in the painstaking study of the work-being of the work, that that which—following a connection unremarked by all of philosophy at least since Plato—essentially ties art to truth (to *aletheia*), or more precisely, *Dichtung* (which is the essence of art) to Being itself (to the meaning or the truth of Being), is determined. We will soon have to return to this determination of *Dichtung*, but if we also remember that "The Origin of the Work of Art" assumes the "destruction" of aesthetics carried out in the first course on Nietzsche (*The Will to Power as Art*) in reference to the Nietzschean stance on the question of art, we see by which endless detours we would have to travel in order to attempt this deconstruction of the Heideggerian interpretation which is our horizon here.

To simplify things and try in spite of everything to move as quickly as possible to the heart of the matter, we might content ourselves with the following remarks. They are, of course, only reminders:

1. In Heidegger's view, Nietzsche's thought is fundamentally determined as an anti-Platonism (a reversal or an inversion of Platonism), which is also to say that it is determined as the most extreme, the most radical, application of the post-Kantian onto-theology of the will against metaphysical nihilism (which amounts, as we know, to the devalorization of the sensible in general).

2. This reversal, which proceeds from Platonism and which consequently fulfills it, is carried out on the theme of art ("at present art wants its revenge,"

Nietzsche said in 1870), that is, within and at the limit of the (Platonic) field of aesthetics such as it has been reworked by the metaphysics of modern times from Baumgarten (or Kant) to Wagner. However much Nietzsche distances himself from this tradition, nothing is ever disturbed (from *The Birth of Tragedy* to the last texts) in the "physiological" ontology of modern aesthetics (of "aïsthetics" *stricto sensu*) or in the mimetology constitutive of Platonism.

3. Though philosophical in nature, this reversal is *thought* (*gedacht*), and, as such, it does affect the decisive question (decisive for the fate of metaphysics) of the relation between art and truth. But if it touches upon this relation, it does so according to the Platonic determination of the two concepts of art and truth, that is, first of all, according to the Platonic interpretation of *aletheia*, and this in such a way that even if the "discord" between art and truth, wherein is concealed (and revealed to interpretation) the whole question of the oblivion of Being, is displaced in this reversal—for example, in the saying: "Art has more value than truth"—it is nonetheless renewed and remains "unsurmounted." This, as one might suspect, does not mean that it remains *unsublated*.

4. It is to this that Heidegger "opposes," in a purportedly nondialectical (non-Hegelian) manner, another understanding of *aletheia*—following the unity of lighting and concealing, of presence and withdrawal—but which is such that "the *impulse toward the work* [this pull, *Zug*, once again untranslatable] lies in the nature of truth as one of truth's distinctive possibilities by which it can itself occur as being in the midst of beings."[5]

5. This truth at work, this position (*thesis*) or implementation of truth, is art itself—which in turn is essentially determined as *Dichtung*, or, let us say, still tentatively, Poïesis, in the sense least considered in Platonic thought. For *Dichtung* is basically nothing other than language itself (*die Sprache*), as we see if we free ourselves of all instrumental interpretations of language and are able, in language, to make ourselves attentive to its "inaugural," "enlightening" power—to its *speaking* or its *saying*, to that *Sage* which is both diction and fable (*muthos* in the most archaic sense) and which constitutes it in this historial relation to the access or the destination [*envoi*][6] of truth.

In the last analysis, everything in this refusal to consider the "poetic" character of *Zarathustra* depends upon this determination of the *work* wherein we find at stake the difficult destruction of the metaphysical "discord" between art and truth. To put it another way, everything depends upon this *position* of *Dichtung*, which we see (despite the "metaphysical" emphasis on the motif of speech and saying, despite the manipulation of an apparently conventional opposition between *phusis* and *thesis*, etc.) corresponds to none of the classical or modern positions of Art, and which, it would still be necessary to prove, is not, as regards the philosophical oppositions (of the "poetic" and the "prosaic," the "literary" and the "theoretical," etc.) that it comes to paralyze or perturb, in a position, let us say, of *supplementarity*. I am thinking in particular of this enigmatic *Zug*, of this *pull* which comes *in addition* and which complicates the simple structure of *aletheia*, that is, the unity apparently without remainder of presence and withdrawal. But, of course, this would require an analysis all its own.

Furthermore, it is doubtless the object of this other analysis, which is the most intractable part of the Heideggerian text, that renders the whole interpretation of Nietzsche unavoidable and compels us to envision its deconstruction. We will always be able to reduce Heideggerian discourse to some negative theology of the most contorted variety, but we can still not prevent (despite the interpretation that Heidegger, moreover, was the first one tempted to give) the text (the *Dichtung?*) in which all of this is laboriously woven—and provided we do not imagine that we have always already read it—from forbidding us to take lightly, and as the compulsive repetition of the old, this extreme forward thrust of philosophical discourse which forces it to reach, under this or that far from innocent name (*Dichtung*, *Sage*, etc.), its very limit.

Nevertheless, let this not prevent us from observing that, for the Heideggerian operation to be possible, at least three conditions must be met:

1. that on the one hand, support confirming the dissymmetry between *Dichtung* and the philosophical be provided. And this is the whole problem of the Hölderlinian *Dichterwerk* as an unexamined resource, which, in *Nietzsche* as in "The Origin of the Work of Art," fulfills the same strategic function. We will return to this;

2. on the other hand, that, in Nietzsche's work, a certain privilege be granted *Zarathustra*, even if we must immediately—though a little in the fashion of ritual precaution—adjust its scope. Here it would be appropriate to follow, without being overly hasty, the many descriptions given by Heidegger of Nietzsche's whole work, published or not. We would see that, ultimately—and with the exception of *Zarathustra*—nothing but *The Will to Power* is taken into consideration, in other words, only what remains of the great *philosophical* work intended to follow *Zarathustra*—to fulfill or reorient it. Hence, that *Zarathustra* be considered " 'eccentric' to [Nietzsche's philosophy as a whole]," [7] that, in spite of everything, it bears in secret and, as it were, silently the weight of the "highest thought," does not mean that it is, of the same Nietzsche, "the highest peak attained by [his] thinking." [8] If silence or secrecy are criteria—and they are—then *The Will to Power*, if only by virtue of its incompleteness, which is also to say its nondisclosure, outmatches *Zarathustra* in "depth." Yet for all that, Zarathustra is certainly the "vestibule" (a Nietzschean word Heidegger adopts; see 1: 12) of this great promised work; everything preceding it was "foreground" ["*hors- d'œuvre*"] (1: 9); and the last opuscules from the year 1888 are regarded as simply the products of an anxious urgency, having no other finality (on the eve of the presaged collapse and with a clear awareness of the inevitability of incompletion) than to "prevent anyone's confusing that basic position with any other." [9] Conse-

quently, everything is organized around this *work* which is missing, but which *Zarathustra* prefigures, and which, because it is missing, keeps all of Nietzsche's production within the realm of the philosophical and on the threshold of *Dichtung* as such;

3. finally (this is the last condition), that "the question of art" itself, its position and its function in the history of the modern completion of metaphysics, become the object of a certain skepticism. Art is here considered in its philosophical determination, as the art of aesthetics, which arises when "the magnificent art of Greece" (which had no need for aesthetics), as also "the great philosophy" corresponding to it, come to an end,[10] and when in Plato, and a fortiori in Platonism, what went before is no longer understood. This "event"—this accident, this fall or decline (*Verfall*)—is at bottom nothing other than the end of *muthos*. But this can only be understood if we conceive of *muthos* outside of its philosophical opposition to *logos*, in that exteriority which is precisely that of *Sage* (*muthos* in German) and of *Dichtung*. Only Hölderlin had access to this exteriority, this (nearly) pure outside; and it is because he did not sufficiently reflect upon pre-Platonism, or, which amounts to the same, because he thought Platonically about pre-Platonism, that Nietzsche—whose intuition of the Greeks and of the fundamental antagonism governing their thought is nevertheless so close to that of Hölderlin,[11] and even though he suspected what was at stake behind the question of art—could not go beyond the "liquidation" of aesthetics in which post-Kantian metaphysics culminates. For the question of art, far from being a fissure portending the crumbling of the philosophical edifice, is precisely the means by which metaphysics pulls itself together. As long as art is thought within the horizon of Platonism, and even more so as long as it is thought, against Plato, in the categories of the physiological, of creativity or productivity (whatever name we use to dress it up and whatever "subject" one imputes to it), of lived experience, of sensibility, of energy, of desire, of *aïsthesis*, etc.—and all this despite its extraordinary complexity and its internal contradiction, the deep sense of the Dionysian—the question of art, which is not "fortuitous," still does not bear on what is "essential."[12] The opposite is the case, as we have just seen. What is essential takes place when what is called into question and interrogated is, through *Dichtung* and *Sage*, the relation between Being and humanity, between *aletheia* and language.[13] And it is only at this price that we can consider the "poetic" and, in general, poetics, as negligible—beginning with that of Plato (*Republic*, III, for example)—meaning that we can subordinate *poïesis* (as an already distant echo of *muthos*) to *techne*, which corresponds, as we know, to the form/matter opposition and refers to the understanding of being as *eidos*. This is the reason why Poïesis does not translate *Dichtung*. But it is above all the reason why, in the text of the *Republic*, no distinction is established between the two formulations of the question of *mimesis*, the "poetics" of Book III, and the general "mimetology" of Book X, and why the first is summarily assimilated to the second.[14]

What Is Nietzsche's *Zarathustra?*

I would like to pause here for a moment. The last remark makes clear that we have already begun to use the language of deconstruction, that is, to consider how, textually, Heidegger's commentary sidesteps or cuts across the question of the philosophical text in general — in the case at hand, Plato's, though at the same time, and for a reason, Nietzsche's as well. The example of Plato is remarkable, however, in that it suggests the place, the location at which the general configuration of the whole conceptual apparatus of poetics (of forms and genres) is decided. Whatever our skepticism, we cannot avoid mobilizing this apparatus when we ourselves broach the question of the text. This is hardly the moment, of course, to explore the full dimensions of this question. But it is at least possible to take advantage of its occurrence here to try to measure what is at stake in it. It is, after all, very clear.

When we attempt to apply a textual reading to Nietzsche, in order to follow, in the text, the very *trace* [*remarque*], as Jacques Derrida says, of the question of the text; when we search, in other words, for the "birth of textuality" in Nietzsche's text, are we sure to avoid *art* (the poetic) and, at the same time, since one does not go without the other, *Dichtung*? In order for us to gain such assurance, the text would have to be reducible neither to art nor to *Dichtung*; it would have to exceed each of them; and consequently, we would have to be able simultaneously to hold that *Dichtung* is still a metaphysical concept and show that, in the concept of art, something has always been at work to disintegrate its very conceptuality and weaken somewhat its philosophical impact.

Doubtless, the question never arises in such simple fashion and we know that, unlike "destruction," deconstruction does not work exclusively on words or concepts but on a combination and a system, on a syntax.

When it comes to Nietzsche, and from the very point of view of syntax, it is still surprising that, despite an entirely different approach to the texts, despite the privilege granted (in opposition to Heidegger) to *The Birth of Tragedy* and the early fragments, despite the emphasis given to the problematic of language, we are necessarily led, in a textual as in the Heideggerian reading, to treat *Zarathustra* as a kind of "center" (however "eccentric" it may be), no doubt held (although for different reasons) to be equivocal, but such indeed that around it gravitates the unbalanced remainder of the work, whose whole weight is supported sometimes by the beginning (*The Birth of Tragedy*) and sometimes by the end (*The Will to Power*). To schematize in the extreme, one could almost say that the difference between *Dichtung* and text is established or played out in *Zarathustra* alone, considered in the one instance as the pivot of an aborted system, and in the other as the culmination, or at least the major component, of a system [*dispositif*] of writing. How can a single text serve both to keep Nietzsche within the realm of philosophy and to remove him from it?

Provided we resign ourselves to not being fearful of emphasizing yet again the excessive aridity of this question, one could if necessary formulate all of this in the following manner. The three possibilities are:

1. Heidegger is right, as they say. *Zarathustra* is a philosophical book and, by not entirely wishing to consider it as such, we risk paradoxically letting ourselves be governed by those philosophical presuppositions already denounced by Heidegger;

2. or else, Heidegger does not see (or even does not wish to see) how *Zarathustra* departs from the philosophical, and how it does so (this is an indispensable condition) more radically, that is, more deliberately, than any other philosophical text. Here would perhaps be a sign that, for Heidegger himself, something remains unthought in his use of the word or concept of *Dichtung* (fiction, for example, or as Derrida says more rigorously, fictioning [*fictionnement*]; or even writing, if we may here strategically use against Heidegger an etymology he would contest);[15]

3. or else, lastly, *Zarathustra* is not, at least by itself, the privileged site of Nietzschean writing. One could therefore say: the Nietzschean text in general, as such, is no more privileged than any other philosophical text.

This is a bit of a caricature but perhaps allows us to see that the bundle of questions is tightened and that everything converges clearly enough on this final (and pretentious) question: not, Who is Nietzsche's Zarathustra? but, What is Nietzsche's *Zarathustra*?

Nietzsche in "Jena"

In order to provide a new departure here, we will begin by following a path of apparently minor interest, but that may nevertheless lead us rather quickly to where we would like to go. In so doing, we will continue to follow Heidegger's reading a little further. And this quite simply in order to raise two points:

1. When he broaches the question of the "discovery" of the struggle between the Apollinian and the Dionysian,[16] Heidegger, even while noting that Nietzsche can effectively lay claim to it as far as its public elaboration is concerned, traces it immediately back to Burckhardt, on the one hand, and on the other, more distantly, to Hölderlin, who, of course, "had seen and conceived of the opposition in an even more profound and lofty manner." Were it not for this reference to Burckhardt (one of the very few, in this whole commentary, to recall the scholarly history of the sources), we might think Heidegger had dealt adequately with this stunning connection established, in the mode of a "thinking dialogue," between Hölderlin and Nietzsche. But even if it reiterates Nietzsche's final declarations (in *Twilight of the Idols*), the reference to Burckhardt, ostensibly consented to in order to take "various clues" into account, creates the impression of a symptom because it sounds out of place. And, in fact, no one is unaware (because there

is no lack of "clues") that between Hölderlin and Burckhardt—from Schelling to Ritschl, or, if you like, from F. Schlegel to Bachofen—an entire tradition of academic philology (which, on his own initiative, Nietzsche had joined) revolved around precisely this opposition. And even Andler knew that. Why, then, this silence, if not to occult romanticism (the romanticism of Jena), which is, in fact, the "source" of this tradition and, whether Nietzsche knew it or not (this is of absolutely no importance), one of the principal "places of origin" of his thought?

This, moreover, is confirmed by the second point I would like to make.

2. In the genealogy of Nietzsche's *philosophy* that he repeatedly retraces, Heidegger always emphasizes the relation of direct filiation that, over Schopenhauer, unites the doctrine of the Will to power with the determination of Being as will common to all post-Kantianism and in particular to Hegel and Schelling.[17] For this reason, disregarding the profound difference that separates Hegel from Schelling, Heidegger always speaks, using the established expression, of "German idealism." From the point of view of the fulfillment of onto-theology, there is doubtless no "essential" difference between these variants of speculative philosophy. But to say this is only possible on the condition—if we may be allowed this expression—that we "Hegelianize" Schelling, that is, understand Schelling in the perspective of philosophy's systematic-*dialectical* completion. This is in turn an operation that can only be carried out if, first, we underestimate Schelling's hostility toward Hegelian onto-*logic*; second, we simply accept the Hegelian critique of Schelling and of romanticism in general; and third, we do not take into consideration their respective texts—to wit, in the case of Hegel, what Bernard Pautrat calls the "hidden Dionysianism" informing the system (and which, moreover, does not fail to recall the *patent* Dionysianism with which the manuscript of *The Ages of the World* concludes); and, in the case of Schelling, the incompletion, the rupture, the breakup of the systematic project itself.

As these remarks may appear a bit simplistic or historicizing, it will be objected that the occultation of romanticism is minor relative to the historial. This is doubtless true. But it does not mean that what is at stake is a matter of indifference, for it is nothing other than the question (itself philosophical) of the *form* of philosophy's completion. True though it be that the debate pitting Hegel against Schelling cannot be reduced to this one question, it is no less true that the determination of the system is decided on this question and that the romantic goal of a "literary" (poetic, mythical, novelistic, etc.) completion of philosophy—even assuming that this goal too is encompassed by a logic of *Aufhebung* and that, as such, it arises [*relève*], if we dare say, within Hegelian jurisdiction (though this would still have to be proven)—inevitably re-poses the question of the relation between "literature" and philosophy, art and philosophy, etc. This is the question to which Hegel replies by saying that "art is a thing of the past." And it is the question that Heidegger *repeats*[18] in displacing the concepts of art and truth at play in it, or, more exactly, in trying to go beyond Hegelian "*parousia*" by taking into account *aletheia* and *Differenz als Differenz*.[19] And, as we have seen, for this to happen, nothing ultimately need be done except to endorse the Platonic/Hegelian determination of art as an *intra-philosophical* determination (condemnation or subordination), so that the art that has always survived philosophical sublation is precisely not art pure and simple but, essentially, *Dichtung*.

Through their project for a "literary" completion of philosophy, the romantics also mobilize the concept of *Dichtung*. Furthermore, there is, there has perhaps always been, haunting (or confirming) the assurance of philosophical discourse, this nearly immediate proximity of poetry, this risk (or this opportunity) of a possible intermixing of the poetic and the philosophical. This is also true for Hegel, who, we might remember, must draw upon all the resources of dialecticity to sever the "affinity" of speculative thought with "the poetic imagination."[20] Thus, to the extent that Heidegger does not consider romantic *Dichtung* for a single moment and says not a word about the debate it triggers between Hegel and romanticism—in other words, because of this impressive silence—we must ask what should keep us from thinking that his use of *Dichtung* is informed, as though by the very precise effect of a return of the repressed, by the entirety of romantic conceptuality itself?

The question, here again, is naïve—but not without interest, if only because it indicates the lack of an effective reading of Hegel's relation to the romantics. This is not the place to begin such a reading, nor even to turn to the relevant romantic texts. But as it is still necessary to give at least an idea of this project for a *dichterisch* completion of philosophy, I will ask to be given credit for analyses I cannot produce, and I will simply emphasize these points:

1. The fulfillment of philosophy in *Dichtung* takes the general form of a "return to myth" (whatever its complexity and problematic character). I will limit myself to recalling here the famous text known as "The Oldest Systematic Program of German Idealism" (of which we do not know whether its author was Hegel, Hölderlin, or Schelling; it dates from 1794), where the "philosophy of the spirit," defined as an "aesthetic philosophy," must yield to *Dichtkunst* in order to engender a "new mythology," itself conceived, according to the principle of an absolute exchange between the mythological and the philosophical, as a "mythology of reason." We would also find, with only slight shades of difference, an analogous program in, among other texts, the final pages of the *System of Transcendental Idealism* or the "Talk on Mythology" published by F. Schlegel in the *Athenaeum*.

2. This demand for a "new mythology" forces us to consider *Dichtung* as a kind of narrative or story. This is why, for example, in the introduction to the never-finished first draft of the great philosophical myth that he dreamed of writing (*The Ages of the World*, in other words), Schelling could make a statement of this sort:

After science has achieved objectivity with respect to the object, it seems a natural consequence that science seek objectivity also with respect to form.

Why has this remained impossible until now? Why cannot that which is known, even in the highest science, be related with the same directness and simplicity as every other *known* thing? What holds back the anticipated golden age when truth again becomes fable and fable truth?[21]

We know that for Schelling—*The Philosophy of Art* is explicit on this subject—this grand philosophical story was conceived of as a "speculative epos" and was to be modeled on Dante's *Divine Comedy*, privileged for, among other reasons, its "speculative tripartition." But we must also note that this epic model competes with a novelistic model (the idea of a "philosophical novel") whose outlines are provided by a dialogue (itself unfinished) entitled *Clara*, of which Schlegel attempted to produce the theory and the text under the name "absolute novel" (I am thinking in particular of the first part—here again the only one to be written—of *Lucinde*).

3. All of this is of a piece, moreover, and without there being, properly speaking, any incompatibility, with the idea of a fragmentary, aphoristic exposition of philosophy—based, for Schlegel at least, on a theory of *Witz*—as with the project of a "carnivalesque" muddling of genres as they are defined by the Platonic poetics of the *Republic*.

Such a description is obviously very schematic (we will take up these questions again elsewhere)[22] and, above all, does not take into account the textual network in which this program is at once inscribed and engulfed. As such, however, that is, as a *program*, we must still insist that it is indeed an absolutely philosophical program and based wholly on the idea of a reversal and an overcoming, of a completion of science (and hence of Platonism). The reference to Plato, whether implicit or explicit, is constant, not only because all of this rests on the distinction between form and content (the text of Schelling's to which I just referred amply demonstrates this), and not only because the theory of genres is implicated, but also, and especially, because Plato's "literary" practice is itself at stake. So we might understand, at least from this strictly programmatic point of view, why Heidegger never feels the need to speak of it.

All of this should still not prevent us from feeling some surprise that Heidegger does not seize the occasion to confirm his own disdain for Nietzsche's "literary" pretensions, and his refusal to consider the "poetic" character of *Zarathustra*. As one might have guessed, if we stress here the philosophico-literary program of German romanticism, it is of course because it is not difficult to read in it, particularly in the motif of a new mythology and in the dream of a philosophical epic, the indication, almost point for point, of what will be carried out (perhaps—although this is not certain—minus the speculative rigor, but including still the rivalry with Dante) by *Zarathustra*. We must not forget that Nietzsche also thought it one of the components of the myth (to be written) of the future;[23] and this is, furthermore, what Bataille suspected during the period of *Acéphale*, when the task was to free Nietzsche from the fascist, Nazi interpretation of romanticism. That Nietzsche did not know (but, then, he did not want to know everything) that this project implied the absolute completion of science, that he was inspired, as they say, by more marginal texts (Masonic ones, for example), changes nothing. This can be demonstrated.

Aristotle's *Zarathustra*

An insurmountable difficulty remains: namely, that nothing allows us to assume that the Platonic dialogue model haunted, as it did the romantics, Nietzsche's literary work. We know how *The Birth of Tragedy* describes the role played by Socrates (a role already informed by the oratorical, dialogic decline of Sophoclean tragedy, it is true) both in the dissolution of the tragic brought about by Euripides and in the perversion of Plato, or, at least, in Plato's renunciation of poetry (*The Birth of Tragedy*, §14). We might recall that this is the reason why Plato "invented," through a suspect method of mixing genres (which, by the way, Schlegel had already noted), a hybrid genre, closer to the new comedy than to tragedy, and which Nietzsche pejoratively characterized as a "novel." I won't belabor the point. Jean-Michel Rey recalled it here just two days ago.[24] Of course, Nietzsche leveled this whole accusation, at the time of *The Birth of Tragedy*, from the point of view of what Pautrat calls "melocentrism," that is, as far as *Dichtung* is concerned, from the point of view of *Sprachliteratur* as opposed to *Leseliteratur* (to literature properly speaking, written and intended to be read). Hence, in this well-known note of 1870, we find: "The philosophical drama of Plato belongs neither to tragedy nor to comedy: it lacks the chorus, the musical element, and the religious theme. It derives from the epic genre and the Homeric school. It is the *novel* of Antiquity. Most especially, it is not meant to be played, but to be read: it is a rhapsody."[25]

But if I here call attention to what is conventionally (naïvely) called Nietzsche's "Wagnerian" period, it is not in order to suggest that things would subsequently change. From a certain point of view—that is, in a certain stratum of the Nietzschean text—things in fact never changed. In *Twilight of the Idols*, Nietzsche will still say (pretty much) the same thing, Plato will still be portrayed as "the first *decadent* of style," Platonic dialogue will be compared to the *Saturae Menippeae*, etc. But this does not mean that Nietzsche never wrote the opposite—in another layer of the text and yet in the *same* text. And these (unsublatable) "contradictions" we will have to take into account here. In the text, Plato or

"Plato" (the system of propositions, figures, strategic usages, etc., which appear under the name "Plato") is never simple, nor even simply double. And even if we spoke here of ambivalence (all the more so if we imagined it to be "psychological"), it goes without saying that we would still have said nothing.

For example (and this will be but one example), in the course Nietzsche gave at Basel between 1874 and 1876 on the history of Greek literature (must we excuse ourselves for speaking here of *Professor* Nietzsche?), regarding Plato—the artist and the writer and, as we will read, the *text* passed down to us under this name— nothing is advanced that might be construed as a condemnation. Quite the contrary. In conformity with the "deep" logic, I mean with the textual logic of *The Birth of Tragedy*, the opposition between oral and written literature, between prose and poetry, etc., on which, officially, the first texts still lived, gradually but systematically begins to blur. The clearest sign of this is provided by a certain reevaluation of writing, to which a saying of Heracleides Ponticus concerning the existence of Hymns to Dionysus consigned and conserved on Mount Haemos in Thrace allows us to assign, through the intermediary figure of Orpheus—"the terrestrial image of Dionysus of Hades, of Zagreus"—a Dionysian origin.[26] Moreover, the same Dionysian-Orphic tradition (and the same saying of Heracleides) is used in the first part of the same course (1874–75) to account for the origin of philosophy itself.[27]

This, of course, does not mean that the opposition of writing and speech purely and simply ceases to function (that will never happen), nor that writing, *literature* as such, is brutally, with one simple gesture (which itself would not be above suspicion), raised up *against* speech. On the contrary, the appearance of *Leseliteratur* very much remains a sign of "degeneration." But what happens is that, between written and oral literature, a third term arises, that of *Kunstprosa* (artistic prose), which partakes of "writing" but whose role is also paradoxically to have contributed to the enlargement of the oral tradition, of the *sprachliches Kunstwerk*.[28] This is so because *Kunstprosa* is fundamentally rhythmic, not according to the metrical demands of poetry (which are arrived at by convention, like currency), but according to the measure of a *meter in itself*, of a *metron in sich*, of which oracular discourse, for example, provides a rather good model. It is precisely for this hybrid but fundamental type of *Kunstprosa* that philosophy disposes of neither term nor concept. Proof of this is provided by the famous passage from the beginning of the *Poetics* (1447b) where, in effect, the Aristotelian classification of genres becomes confused regarding this "anonymous" non-genre in which *mimesis* is carried out "by language alone" (whether in prose or in verse) and by which is perhaps already engraved, precisely where the system of the poetics no longer functions, the place in which the modern concept of literature will come to rest and immediately founder. This is the text that Nietzsche paraphrases approximately in these terms:

According to popular opinion, it is meter that distinguishes poetry from prose. Against this criterion Aristotle, who only confers the name of poet on the basis of imitation, set himself: he denounces the granting of this name to one who merely states [*vorträgt*] a medical or musical doctrine in meter. He depores the lack of a common name allowing one to convey the concept under which fall Sophron's nonversified mimes . . . Socratic dialogues, as well as poetic presentations [*Darstellungen*] in hexameter, distichs, etc.[29]

Thus, *Kunstprosa* as such eludes the categories of philosophical poetics, and we can see clearly here how the return (barely predating this text) of the question of rhetoric and of rhythmics comes to inform and displace Nietzsche's whole "former" conception of writing. This is all the more striking given that it is very precisely in this *Kunstprosa* that not only great history (Herodotus, Thucydides) and great eloquence (Isocrates), but also philosophy itself "at its acme," between Plato and Aristotle, finds, so to speak, a home. In order to establish this, it is further necessary radically to detach Plato from Socrates, hypothesize that Plato did not write before the end of his second trip to Sicily, reclassify all the dialogues, and prove that Platonic dialogue is in no way modeled on Socratic dialogue (of which we get an idea from the "little dialogues" falsely attributed to Plato). The proof is that in the *Phaedrus*, the first of the properly Platonic texts, Plato "discusses the cardinal question of why one must write."[30] On the other hand, it has yet to be shown that in the philosophy that follows, in Stoicism and Epicureanism, the decline of this *grand style* in philosophy begins.

From this the principal characteristics of Platonic writing derive: the intermixing of genres, the tendency toward comedy, the indifference toward philosophical demonstration, and the liberty taken with regard to historical truth (the life of Socrates, for example), which is comparable to the liberty taken by poets with regard to myth, etc.[31] And from this also comes—as paradoxical as this may appear—the chaotic elaboration of the work (through the arbitrary and belated assembly of old drafts), which represents the height of artistic refinement and of which only Goethe (the great initiator, as we know, in matters of writing) could provide an equivalent. It is even uncertain whether Plato "himself" carried out this assembly, so true is it that, very often for Nietzsche, the great writer was not the same as the author.[32] But what is most remarkable is that, in the final analysis, Plato wrote *against himself*, meaning he practiced the style that Aristotle, as reported by Diogenes Laertius, says is intermediary between prose and poetry— and that he thus "violated the severe anathema" that he himself had proclaimed on the genres.[33]

Far from having precipitated the decline of *Dichtung*, Plato therefore carried it to its highest point (at least in the already inevitable register of writing), and this—if we take into account the equivocal status of *Kunstprosa*—at once against and *between* the foundational distinctions of poetics he himself had developed. Nor is this all. A short but decisive tradition of philosophical writing also evolves from him, a tradition that involves Aristotle but barely survives him (assuming, however, that we keep in mind, as far as Aristotle is concerned, the lost dialogues and not simply the course notes, which are all that remain). This tradition comprises six consecrated models, or types, of dialogue: the banquet, the *magikos*, the dialogue on the last moments of life, the protreptric, the *peri poieton*, and finally, the *erotikos*. Here is what Nietzsche says about the second of these:

> 2. *magikos*—this is a dialogue of Aristotle's in which a magus, Zoroaster, comes to Athens and talks with Socrates, for whom he predicts a violent end. According to Suidas, this was perhaps a work by Antisthenes. There is a dialogue of Heracleides: *Zoroaster*, in which Zoroaster comes to Gelon; Clearcus (fragment 69 M) represents Aristotle in conversation with a Jew during a trip to Asia. Aristoxenus recounted that Socrates had met an Indian in Athens.[34]

The (to us) Borgesian style of this note is not likely to diminish the vertiginous quality of this "revelation." Modeled on a Platonic dialogue, there was, therefore, an Aristotelian *Zarathustra*. If we add Kant's, of which Jean-Luc Nancy has spoken,[35] and even, for good measure, Heracleides', which Nietzsche mentions here, that would make for no fewer than four *Zarathustras* in the philosophical tradition opened by Platonism. And to think that people considered *Zarathustra*, our own, to be one of a kind . . .

It is no doubt appropriate to be wary of this kind of "miraculous" coincidence. And, in fact, *Zarathustra* is not a "dialogue." In *Ecce Homo*, Nietzsche will sooner portray it as a dithyramb and will in any case trace its derivation to music and great poetry. We could multiply the counterexamples. In the case at hand, however, wariness may be entirely out of place. All of this would in fact remain on the level of a nominal analogy if the distinctive criterion or relevant feature of the Platonic model did not consist, in accordance with Plato's unfaithfulness to his own doctrine, in the *dissimulation* of the author (of the subject of writing) as a character. In Platonic dialogue, Plato himself does not speak or intervene in his own name. I use the word *dissimulation* on purpose here, if only to appeal to that condemnation of the "apocryphal" author Plato brings up in Book III of the *Republic* (393a-e), where it is a question of defining, between simple narrative and pure imitation, between dithyramb and tragedy, the epic as a narrative mixed with imitation—and where it is in fact in the name of the conformity, of the *homoïosis* between the speaking subject [*sujet de l'énonciation*] and the subject of speech [*sujet de l'énoncé*] (and hence in the name of truth already thought, beginning with the question of language and the rectitude of discourse, as adequation) that, for the first time in the *Republic*, Plato "belittles" art and *mimesis*. Inversely (though out of faithfulness to the specific mode of Platonic writing), Nietzsche himself uses no other criterion to measure the decline of the grand philosophical style: in Plato, pedagogical necessity already weakens stylistic intent; but when a certain loosening of writing works with the success and adoption of the Aristotelian model of the course, when philosophers write (as they speak) in their own name, that will be the end of great art, of style, and of formal beauty – and the birth of the pure philosophical genre, the "scientific genre."[36] If this criterion is decisive, it is understandable why Nietzschean *dissimulation* in the figure, character, and discourse of *Zarathustra* does not coincide simply by chance with the "literary" will of Platonism.

Dissimulation – Dissimilation

That *Zarathustra* is "Platonic" (and it is clearly much more so than if it were *simply* romantic or Masonic, etc.) is what Heidegger both says and does not say. More precisely, this is basically what he thinks, but for reasons other than those we have attempted to foreground. But should we wish to pursue this reading to its conclusion, one suspects we would have to stress the question of truth. If what constitutes Platonic *Darstellung* is first of all the dissimulation of the author (a certain "hypocrisy"), and if, consequently, the problematic of *Darstellung* in general assumes the horizon of truth already determined as *homoïosis*, adequation – then as long as Heidegger thinks (or tries to think) something like a break accompanying the "Platonic interpretation of *aletheia*," he will, in the final analysis, have to reduce any question asked about *Darstellung* to an "aesthetic" question. That Heidegger himself, or rather the Heideggerian text, worked to mend this break (this is evident everywhere, at least since *Holzwege*), of course does nothing but complicate matters.

We cannot, therefore, envision settling, against Heidegger and in a simple way, the question of Nietzschean writing. Moreover, in the case at hand (limiting ourselves at least, as does Heidegger, only to the case of *Zarathustra*), it is less Nietzschean writing than Platonic writing that requires examination. And even if, in order to measure the magnitude of the shake-up Plato causes in the edifice of philosophy (that is, of *his* philosophy), we could be satisfied with the lone Nietzschean criterion of the contradiction so introduced, in the Platonic text, between content and form – a contradiction it would be easy to show is established precisely in this content – would we go so far as to ratify the Nietzschean reversal (but it is only, as Heidegger says, a reversal) of the relation between content and form?[37]

It is clear that, in fact, these questions must remain answerless, for we cannot answer for writing.

Still, since it is never true either that we can resign ourselves to leaving a question suspended, I would like to conclude by taking one last shot at this *dissimula-*

tion, where, at least in part, the infinitely ambiguous relation between Nietzsche and Plato is played out. I do this to correct (the time has come) the effect this embryonic analysis risks provoking; in other words, to reverse, or rather deteriorate, its most obvious result.

If both withdrawal and dissembling (*dissimilation*) are at play in *dissimulation* (in textual dissimulation, and not in the concept of which Nietzsche, moreover, makes extensive use); if truth and truth (*aletheia* and *homoïosis*) are interlaced; if "truth itself" begins to come undone, what happened when, in the "last" year, as though brutally reversing the whole "Platonic" strategy of *Zarathustra* (or the "Aristotelian" strategy of *The Will to Power*), Nietzsche suddenly spoke (wrote) in his own name? Was it in order to speak the truth? *Ecce Homo*, me, Nietzsche—the truth, I speak . . .

But we read: "I have a terrible fear that one day I will be pronounced *holy*: you will guess why I publish this book *before*; it shall prevent people from doing mischief with me. I do not want to be a holy man; sooner even a buffoon."[38]

A buffoon, that is, a "real" buffoon. Not Socrates, that buffoon who "wanted to have himself taken seriously"—and who did not write. Rather, a buffoon like the one in the *Saturae Menippeae*, or the buffoon of the Cynics (who are also, in the post-Platonic debacle of the grand philosophical style, the only ones who, *through dissimulation*, put up some resistance).

Yet why? In order to write some "buffooning" letters, rehash one last time some old ideas, lose oneself in all names, sign all names, write in all styles, rewrite one's own books—never finish exhausting the inexhaustible content, the inexhaustible lack of content of what we still call, so naïvely, the "subject of writing."

Once engaged (though who can say when that is?), *dissimulation* never ends. This is what we call madness, even when we suspect (like Gast or Overbeck) that it is simulated.

But perhaps it is urgent to say here that no writer (no "philosopher," for example) has ever been unaware of it.[39]

Translated by Timothy D. Bent

Chapter 4
Obliteration

To free Diction [Dichtung] *from literature* [Schriftstellertum] *is one thing.*
And the other thing we need:
To save the earth for the world.[1]

To think is surely a peculiar affair [Um das Denken freilich ist es eine eigene Sache]. *The word of thinkers has no authority. The word of thinkers knows no authors, in the sense of writers* [Schriftsteller]. *The word of thinking is not picturesque* [bildarm]; *it is without charm* [ohne Reiz]. *The word of thinking rests in the sobering quality* [Ernüchterung] *of what it says. Just the same, thinking changes* [verändert] *the world. It changes it in the ever darker depths of a riddle, depths which as they grow darker offer promise of a greater brightness.*[2]

Access (1): Reading Heidegger

The publication of *Nietzsche*[3] in the fall of 1971 was doubtless "untimely." Its repercussions were, moreover, practically nonexistent. But its publication in Germany ten years before was perhaps also untimely. Already. And, at least in part, probably for similar reasons. For such a "monument" (and with such a signature), there is still something rather strange or unexpected about this. Let us dwell on it for a moment.

In France, the situation has never been very clear. As everyone knows, *Nietzsche*, before actually being translated, had already practically been "read." Let us be clear: we knew it existed, we were concerned about it, and we had come to know at least the broad outlines of its "content" (its theses, the dominant themes of the interpretation of Nietzsche it proposed). With a few exceptions, there was nothing, therefore, that resembled a genuine reading. From this (double) book, from this "synthesis," if you will, people most often contented themselves with remembering, in order to subscribe to it or feel irritated by it, the way in which Heidegger demonstrated Nietzsche's adherence to metaphysics. But this is at least a sufficient reason to be able to say that *Nietzsche* did not need to be accessible in our language in order to act and to have an effect (or even to be exploited) and to leave its mark, if only superficially, on a certain philosophical "field." Doubtless, one must recognize as well that the whole "renewal of Nietzschean studies" in France, all the more or less clear instances of a certain "return to Nietzsche,"

even the whole "rereading" of Nietzsche—in short, in whatever form, the new in-
vasive irruption of Nietzsche (the "fashion," if we must say so) does not really
or only derive from Heidegger. The major role played—in different ways, needless to say—by Jaspers, for example, or Bataille, is well known. Heidegger has
nevertheless occupied a position such that one could just as well show that, when
all is said and done, this return *of* Nietzsche will have taken place, and not without
discomfort, as though *around* this book which is "missing" from our catalogues
and our library, but diffracted—openly (correctly, favorably) or not—in everything that, regarding Nietzsche, has been taught, written, published (or even
translated)[4] in France for the last ten years. One of numerous books ended, moreover, in a symptomatic manner with a "critical exposé" of "Martin Heidegger's
interpretation," on the assumption that it must be possible to summarize in a few
pages (as Heidegger forced himself to do, albeit in an entirely different style) the
theoretical or thematic armature of these two volumes.[5]

There would be a great deal to say about this new "Nietzscheanism" (which
it would be a mistake to consider as being homogeneous and, especially, as simply a Nietzscheanism) and on the exact role played by Heidegger in this whole
story—whether one has rejected or avoided him, opposed him or attempted to "go
beyond" him, etc. But this is not what interests us here. So let us simply (and tentatively) say that this book, despite this rather "lateral" divulgence and "reading,"
will have counted for something in recent times and that its French translation
may very well coincide, as a result, with the foreseeable end of the stir it has
created.

It remains to be seen, however, whether it is indeed this book *itself* that should
thus be called into question. For it is also fair to note, however incongruous this
proposition may appear, that *Nietzsche* was in fact already read before even being
published. In a certain number of short texts, on this or that theme of Nietzsche's
thought, Heidegger had actually revealed in advance, at least in its principle and
in certain of its trajectories, the essence of his interpretation: "The Word of
Nietzsche: 'God is Dead' " figured in *Holzwege* (1950); "The Overcoming of
Metaphysics" and "Who is Nietzsche's Zarathustra?" (with the "Note on the Eternal Return") in *Vorträge und Aufsätze* (1954); the entire first part, devoted to
Nietzsche, of the course of 1951–52, had been published in *Was heißt Denken?*
(1954); the *Einführung in die Metaphysik* itself, where the debate with Nietzsche
had been "inaugurated" in 1935, appeared in 1953. And the persistence with
which, since 1947, since the *Letter on Humanism*—despite (that is, because of)
the dispersion of texts—Heidegger had tirelessly recalled the major theses (reversal of Platonism, "completion" or culmination of metaphysics, etc.) could very
well have led one to think—on the condition, as always, of not looking too
closely—that there was in fact nothing more to be expected or learned. So that
in 1961, when it appeared, *Nietzsche* seemed to offer no more than a systematic

(and "pedagogical") synthesis of the interpretation and to have no greater bearing or function than that, suggested by Heidegger himself in the foreword, of a kind of retrospective.[6] If we add to this that almost all the texts that had thus "anticipated" it had already been translated in France at the time,[7] it becomes clear that there was not, and will therefore never really have been, any urgent need to undertake the actual *reading* of this book, of which the least one can say is that it did not arrive, in either case, on time.

This "double" (restricted, empirical) *untimeliness* probably implies another, much more fundamental one. It nevertheless suffices to explain a certain silence. Regardless of Germany, where it is said that Heidegger has for a long time been a "thing of the past," the French translation doubtless comes too late (the Nietzschean "wave" is receding) to have any chance of reorienting, or even of seriously affecting, the reading of Nietzsche – and too early (or again too late: it's been some time since Heidegger was arrogantly consigned to his idealism, his Nazism, or his Black Forest) to interest a possible reading of Heidegger. That this translation bears the signature of Klossowski – and that one is indeed entitled to consider it of debatable quality[8] – is a fact that, despite all of the statements on the relation between writing and translation generalized today, will probably be considered negligible as far as Klossowski's own work (or as far as the question of translation) is concerned.[9] There is thus nothing left to do but await the historians.

Unless this translation arrives in fact "in time," assuming it is urgent, for many reasons, to resist the kind of precipitous "liquidation" of Heidegger that is currently in season and that seems to have taken over, quite smoothly, from the devout and voluble pathos of the recent past. Unless, therefore, this translation affords the opportunity to persist a bit more, despite the "unfashionableness" of such an activity, in *reading* Heidegger, assuming it is not entirely futile to try to break the "systematic" opposition of Heideggerianism and anti-Heideggerianism, whose only result will have been, in the final analysis, to have prematurely exhausted Heidegger's text, as well as all those questions which, on its own or not, this text raised. It is true that, in this case, "to resist" (or "to persist") is doubtless a way of reinforcing *untimeliness*. But aside from the fact that this is certainly not a bad thing, there are also moments when necessity knows no law. And besides, in general, urgency never dates from today.

But to look at things in this way is obviously, as they say, to relegate *Nietzsche himself* to the background, that is, to place between him and us the hardly transparent screen of Heidegger's interpretation. It is, therefore, also to risk, at the same time, unwittingly sanctioning the opinion that prevails virtually everywhere, and first of all in academic philosophy, as to the "real" interest – as to the (philological) seriousness and the (historical) accuracy, indeed quite simply the honesty—of Heidegger's interpretations. Such a risk is more serious than one thinks. We must, therefore, begin by dispelling this misunderstanding.

It is well known that most of the time, and contrary to custom, this distrust provoked by Heidegger is expressed rather clearly. This is also because the threat is strong: no one is unaware of all that Heidegger has rendered definitively obsolete. Thus, we do not have to look very far. For example, in the "critical exposé" to which we have already alluded, we find the following passage, which summarizes rather felicitously the essence of the debate: "These theses of Martin Heidegger—theses of which we have just given a brief survey—are philosophically very stimulating. But they seem to me more apt to inform us about Heidegger's than about Nietzsche's thought. From a strictly Nietzschean point of view, Heidegger's interpretation is, in my opinion, inadmissible."[10]

It will be said that we here reach a kind of limit. But nothing is less certain. For if we allow for, let us say, the rigidity of tone, this grievance, with its strange but significant logic (what is *philosophically* stimulating may eventually be instructive, but remains inadmissible), is indeed the same one that has always been brought against Heidegger, and not only concerning his interpretation of Nietzsche. It would be tedious to show that Granier's book is the first essentially to refute what it itself asserts, or that it amounts, in other words, to no more than a gigantic (or at the very least voluminous) "anti-Heidegger."[11] But what is remarkable in an accusation of this kind is that it assumes, as is now well known, against some of the most decisive, that is, the most "vertiginous," affirmations of Nietzsche's text,[12] that there is a truth of Nietzschean *doctrine*, safe within his text, initially pure, prior and external to any reading (beginning with Nietzsche's own), on the basis of which the "correct" interpretation must be built, that is, on the basis of which the coherence of a system must be (re)built.[13] Up to a point— but only up to a point, and, of course, without this ever being confused with a compulsive obsession with *accuracy*, be it assimilated to Nietzsche's "philological integrity"—an analogous *obliteration*, a certain erasure of the letter, animates the very style of interpretation practiced by Heidegger (with its most spectacular effects, its moments of coercion, the violence to which the texts are deliberately subjected, etc.) and contributes to the maintenance of his method, to a large extent, within the strict limits of a *hermeneutics*, in the ultimately classical sense of the term.[14] Heidegger also concerns himself, if not with a system, at least with the coherence of a basic Nietzschean doctrine, which, in spite of everything (particularly in spite of a certain *worklessness* [*absence d'œuvre*]), is organized according to the style and structure of philosophizing in general, that is, according to the conformity of "form" to what is in *question* [*en cause*] in thought (to the matter, *Sache*, of thought).[15] Moreover, from a certain angle, all of the *courses*, properly speaking, in *Nietzsche*, would perhaps turn out to have no other object than the rigorous reconstitution of this doctrinal economy. Why, then, this opposition? For what exactly is Heidegger being criticized? And what precisely is the focus of the debate?

As one may suspect, the focus is none other than that from which Heidegger's entire interpretation proceeds and to which, in that interpretation, all philosophy, whichever it may be, must be referred in order to be constituted as such—but which people persist in thinking is the major theme of the "philosophy of Heidegger": the question of being (or of truth) and that which it governs, the problematic of the delimitation of metaphysics. This is something of which Granier, incidentally, is not unaware, even if he does not acknowledge it and imagines himself able to identify it with a "personal" conception of metaphysics, to which one could oppose another (Nietzsche's, for example),[16] or better yet, for which one could substitute a "metaphilosophy" based on an ontology of "Being-interpreted" (and which doubtless has no other fault than that it reveals itself to be completely rooted in the misinterpretation, foreseen by Heidegger, of the very nature of the attempt to delimit metaphysics).[17]

What is troubling, what must be fought, is therefore the question of being. And first of all that which, in this question, makes impossible, forbids, a whole nostalgia for the philosophical in its most banal or best-documented variations (positivistic, anthropological or vaguely theological, historicizing, messianic, etc.). This is why the claims of academic philosophy are so easily transmissible to the great liquidation (in the sense, it is to be feared, in which we speak of a "liquidation of inventory before reopening") that is taking place, in principle, "outside" of the academy. To say that "Heidegger is inadmissible," or, as in the discourse that is all the rage today, that "we've had quite enough of metaphysics, of the question of being," amounts to the same thing, the difference between them being stylistic (assuming, however, that this difference will not some day appear slighter than now). As though one could quite simply *decide* to "dispense" with the question of being and to move on to "something else." It is quite obvious that all of this must be seen in its proper perspective. This "encounter" nevertheless has the paradoxical merit of indicating where the real questions lie. For either we seriously question what is at stake in the question of being, or else we remain and condemn ourselves to remain on this side of the question, subjected to its (secondarily but radically) critical power, and in this case it is more or less as though we had done nothing. All the more so if one lays "primitive" claim to Nietzsche himself, without asking for a second what is at stake in what must indeed be called, whether this pleases anyone or not, Nietzsche's *thought*. At least tentatively.

We must therefore go through Heidegger. Not in order to repeat or *settle* a bit more some kind of ritual of sacralization, but for the single reason that without Heidegger—saying this has become banal, but nothing is more quickly forgotten than this kind of banality—Nietzsche's *philosophy* as such would never have been rigorously taken into account. Before Heidegger, neither Jaspers nor Löwith, and Andler and all the others even less, managed to do this. Whether one likes it or not, one should recognize that there is today no access to Nietzsche that does not oblige one to follow the itinerary of Heidegger's interpretation. This does not mean that we must purely and simply "ratify" this interpretation. It means that it is necessary, assuming it is still of matter of *reading* Nietzsche, to subject Heidegger's interpretation to this preliminary question (which "anti-Heideggerian" commentary, whatever its degree of opposition, never asks itself, so deeply is it unwittingly influenced by what is most fundamental in Heideggerian thought): On what basis can one make of Nietzsche a philosopher? On what basis, by what right, can we *treat* him like a philosopher and include him within metaphysics? And at what price?

The Stratagem of *É-loignement*[18]

"Nietzsche"—the name of the thinker stands as the title for the matter *of his thinking.*

. . . der Name des Denkers steht als Titel für *die Sache* seines Denkens.[19]

In its very formulation and despite the apparent simplicity of its principle, this question is, as is after all well known today, infinitely problematic. At least, first of all, insofar as it is immediately followed by another. Whence, indeed, can we ask it of Heidegger? And how? In what concepts and in what kind of discourse, according to what logic, that are not themselves inevitably compromised by what Heidegger himself recognized or experienced as the closed and omnipotent systematicity of metaphysics? The question is, therefore—and it is hard to see what sort of assured, definitive answer one could give to it—before all others, that of the *access* to Heidegger himself. A question that is strictly necessary. For want of having raised it, the entire "critique" of Heidegger has most often risked becoming mere babble.

But this *metonymic* (convenient?) use of the "author's name" threatens to obscure its particular difficulty. What then, indeed, is "Heidegger himself"? To what (to whom?), in "Heidegger," is it a question of gaining access? Is it enough to question oneself about the mode of access? Or does the question of access also depend on that to which we must secure access?

This suggestion may appear a bit flimsy. It is, nevertheless, not impossible that this displacement of the question determines, by itself, all that is at stake today in the *reading* of Heidegger (and therefore, at the same time, in that of Nietzsche). We will take our example (but, to tell the truth, the examples in this area are not that numerous) from one of the texts Granel has brought together in *Traditionis traditio*[20] and whose title—"Remarques sur l'accès à la pensée de Martin Heidegger: *Sein und Zeit"* — inscribes within itself, and deliberately besides, the difficulty we must confront here. For to speak of Heidegger's *thought* — to make of *Heidegger's thought* that to which, from the outset, it is a question of gaining access — is not only to use a word that Heidegger himself uses (and in the sense — the major one — in which he uses it); it is also, in fact, by means of this word, to grant him *everything* and hence to *decide* what "Heidegger himself" is — or rather, and even though such a formulation is not self-evident, simply and purely to subscribe to what "Heidegger himself" is for Heidegger himself.

In speaking of Heidegger's thought, one grants no less, indeed, than the difference between *thinking* and *philosophizing*. This difference is never simple.[21] It is nevertheless upon it, as we know, that Heidegger's entire "strategy" concerning metaphysics is organized. I refer to the *double* gesture that, beginning from this *untenable* (and yet constantly *held*) position, namely, that *"there is no philosophy of Heidegger,"* is ceaselessly reiterated against metaphysics with a view toward its overcoming *and* its appropriation (*Überwindung/Verwindung*),[22] and consists (need we recall?) in turning back upon metaphysics, in unheard-of fashion, its own questioning (in questioning metaphysics about its own foundation, that is, about that which, in it, has remained for it *unthought*), in attempting, as through an almost stationary movement of twisting upon itself (*Windung*), at once to *tear itself away from* and to *penetrate into* metaphysics *itself.*[23] This is what defines, at "the end of philosophy," "the task of thinking," *die Aufgabe des Denkens*.

If we speak of Heidegger's thought, if we accredit the difference between *thinking* and *philosophizing,* we sanction the very possibility of this movement, with all its consequences. And we are obviously obliged, among other things, to ratify, along with the entire Heideggerian interpretation of metaphysics, his interpretation of Nietzsche, of Nietzsche's metaphysics. But to what other difference than that between *thinking* and *philosophizing* could one really appeal? From what other "place," which is neither that of thought nor that of philosophy, would one have some chance of gaining a panoramic view of Heidegger? If need be, what other Nietzsche could possibly be opposed to "his"? And if *by some miracle* one of these operations could be seriously contemplated, what would be its meaning and implications? It is clear enough that in subordinating the access to "Heidegger" to no other condition save that dictated by Heidegger himself, one leaves intact the problem of whether *Heidegger himself* is, in each instance, *the same.* But what else could he be than what he himself must be, that is, *already,* not *himself* — if not the pure and simple spokesperson of thought?

In order to answer all of these questions, it would *at least* be necessary that what "Heidegger" calls thought be in one way or another something *assignable.* The difference between thought and philosophy would itself have to be clearly determined. But this is certainly not the case: the distinctive feature of thought seems to be its evasiveness; nothing appears more elusive than thought itself. This withdrawal or retreat of thought, this fleeting quality, is precisely what Granel has in mind as the unavoidable difficulty of Heidegger; it is this and nothing else[24] that constitutes the whole difficulty of the *access* itself:

> The more [Heidegger's thought] offers itself to us, the more it becomes obvious that it is not open to us. It is true that this would "already" obtain for any great philosophy. Yet it does not simply "also" obtain for Heidegger, even with a greater degree of complexity. The reason for this is that Heidegger's thought does not constitute one more "great philosophy": it no longer belongs at all to metaphysics. However, it does not belong either to one of those dimensions which are familiar to us and which, in Western history, have repeatedly been found to be "related" to metaphysics: religion, or art, or history. Heidegger's thought no longer belongs at all to metaphysics and yet it does not belong to anything else. It is completely turned toward metaphysics, like those Egyptian figures which generally walk with their necks turned, looking behind them.[25]

It is hard to see, under these conditions, what "beyond," what "beside," quite simply what "other," in relation to thought, one could bring into play, assuming at least that the possibility of retrieving a philosophical position prior to the extreme limit touched here is excluded. There is, nevertheless, in this necessarily paradoxical and vertiginous "uncoupling" of thought, in the very movement by which it is produced, something troubling and discomforting enough to cause a certain suspicion. Not that all of this is lacking in "positivity." On the contrary, no doubt: it would sooner be the very possibility, and the effectiveness, the indisputable power of this "uncoupling," that would be problematic. Of course, it is not a question of claiming that there is no difficulty here. Nor, having acknowledged the difficulty, of wanting at any cost to reduce it. It is merely a matter of asking whether this difficulty of thought is not also, and at the same time, the whole *resource* of thought. Is it really thought, as such, that constitutes the *whole* difficulty of "Heidegger"? Why — if formulating these questions as suspicions is unavoidable — why does Heidegger himself constantly foreground it? Why is thought, in its difference from philosophy, the only matter or cause (*Sache*) for thought? And do all of the questions Heidegger has asked amount at bottom to the single question of "what is called thinking"? Is there not something here that, in spite of everything, is less difficult than it appears?

As will be suspected, nothing is less easy to certify. If the difficulty of thought can be construed as the resource of thought, it is, if we may insist on this point, because difference, on the basis of which thought draws away or aside, determines by itself the possibility of a nonphilosophical relation to (the history of) philosophy, to (the history of) metaphysics. In one of the most explicit texts on the subject, *Identity and Difference*,[26] it is this difference that allows of separating the "step back" (the *Schritt zurück*, which leads back "from metaphysics to its essence" and in so doing opens the way to the unthought of metaphysics) from the Hegelian *Aufhebung*, on which in fact relies, in the last (as perhaps also the "first") instance, any *philosophical* "conversation" "with the earlier history of philosophy."

Now it just so happens—and the resource is here very close to the difficulty—that for Hegel himself, "the matter of thinking is: Thinking as such"; "für Hegel ist die Sache des Denkens: Das Denken als solches." This is the reason why, as Heidegger says in another text,[27] Hegel is "the only Western thinker who has thoughtfully experienced the history of thought," the only one who, "in thought, has been affected by the history of thought" ("der einzige Denker des Abendlandes, der die Geschichte des Denkens denkend erfahren hat"). Where, then, is the difference? What can distinguish ("Hegelian") thought from thought? What more (or less) is there in thought than what Hegel thinks as thought?

Thus, the difficulty is not "nothing." It consists entirely, as one might have expected, in the question of the "relation to Hegel": in both cases, in Hegel as in Heidegger, the *cause of thought* is the same, namely, thought. In other words, what constitutes the difficulty of thought—and hence the difficulty of the access to Heidegger—is nothing other than the difficulty of the *excess* (outside) of Hegel (and so also, according to the law of return and appropriation, of *retrocession* in Hegel). And this, moreover, since the "beginning," since the first paragraph of *Sein und Zeit*, where the question of the meaning of being is oriented *against* the indetermination of the concept of being (being as "the most universal and the emptiest of concepts") that has governed philosophy since Aristotle and is realized in the *Science of Logic* (that is, as *Identity and Difference* will recall, in the thinking in which being, thought "in its most empty emptiness," is also and indissociably—inasmuch as it is the cause of thought—thought itself).[28] "Thought" is thus the word with the greatest proximity to Hegel. It is, therefore, also the word with the greatest danger.[29] But just as the closest is the farthest (this too was expressed in *Sein und Zeit*: the question of being has never even been raised elsewhere than in this paradoxical gap [*béance*], this *é-loignement/Ent-fernung*, that is proximity),[30] so: "But where danger threatens / That which saves from it also grows," to cite a verse of Hölderlin's hymn *Patmos* that Heidegger often invokes: "Wo aber Gefahr ist, wächst / Das Rettende auch." This is indeed why "thought" is at bottom the word of resource, that is, of "salvation," in the debate or the struggle with Hegel—this disagreement, this dispute (*Streit*) always provoked by the calling into question of what is in question in thought. The same comprises difference; the separation from Hegel, from the whole of the philosophical—excess itself—has thus always been and is still able to occur. Heidegger states, in *Identity and Difference*:

Thinking can stay with its matter [*bei seiner Sache*] only if it becomes ever more rigorous in its constancy, only if the same matter becomes for it ever more sharply contested [*strittiger*]. In this way the matter requires thinking to stay with it in its own manner of being [*in ihrem Sachverhalt*], to remain steadfast toward that manner of being, answering to it by sustaining the matter to its completion [*Austrag*]. If its matter is Being, the thinking which stays with its matter must involve itself in the perdurance of Being [*Austrag des Seins*]. Accordingly, in a conversation with Hegel we are expected to clarify in advance the sameness of the same matter [*die Selbigkeit derselben Sache*] for the sake of that conversation. According to what has been said, we are required in our conversation with the history of philosophy to elucidate the otherness of the historical [*die Verschiedenheit des Geschichtliches*] at the same time as we elucidate the otherness [*Verschiedenheit*] of the matter of thinking.[31]

Difference, separation (*Verschiedenheit*) must be *clarified*: separation can, therefore, *manifestly* occur; it can *appear*. And not only can it appear, but it appears with the clarity of a break or an incision. For the matter of thought, as we know, is nothing other than difference (*Differenz*) itself, the difference between Being and beings (that *on the basis* of which, the one differing from itself, *Hen diapheron heauto*, Being differentiates itself from beings, and *vice versa*), which, *as such*, has remained unthought throughout the history of thought. Separation thus assures itself of the step back. The step back "frees" difference, *die Differenz als Differenz*, that is, difference insofar as it resists identity, sublation (*Aufhebung*) in and as identity. So it is that to the three questions asked in order to clarify the separation from Hegel—"1. What is the matter of thinking for Hegel, and what is it for us? 2. What is the criterion for the conversation with the history of thinking for Hegel, and what is it for us? 3. What is the character of this conversation for Hegel, and what is it for us?"—Heidegger can successively reply (it is necessary here to follow the text itself, at least in part):

To the first question: For Hegel, the matter of thinking is: Being with respect to beings having been thought in absolute thinking, and as absolute thinking. For us, the matter of thinking is the Same, and thus is Being—but Being with respect to its difference from beings. Put more precisely: for Hegel, the matter of thinking is the idea [*der Gedanke*] as the absolute concept. For us, formulated in a preliminary fashion, the matter of thinking is difference *as* difference.
    To the second question: For Hegel, the criterion for the conversation with the history of philosophy is: to enter into the force [*Kraft*] and sphere [*Umkreis*] of what has been thought by earlier thinkers. . . .
For Hegel, the force of each thinker lies in what each has thought, in that their thought can be incorporated [*aufgehoben*] into absolute thinking as one of its stages. . . . For us, the criterion for the conversation

with historical tradition is the same, insofar as it is a question of entering into the force of earlier thinking. We, however, do not seek that
force in what has already been thought: we seek it in something that
has not been thought, and from which what has been thought receives
its essential space. But only what has already been thought prepares
what has not yet been thought. . . .

To the third question: For Hegel, the conversation with the earlier
history of philosophy has the character of sublation [*Aufhebung*], that
is, of the mediating concept in the sense of an absolute foundation. For
us, the character of the conversation with the history of thinking is no
longer sublation, but the step back. Sublation leads to the heightening
and gathering area [*in der überhöhend-versammelnden Bezirk*] of truth
posited as absolute, truth in the sense of the completely developed certainty [*Gewißheit*] of self-knowing knowledge [*Wissen*]. The step back
points to the realm which until now has been skipped over [jumped
over and omitted, forgotten, neglected / *in den bisher übersprungenen
Bereich*], and from which the essence of truth becomes first of all worthy of thought.[32]

But it is immediately clear—whatever may be the force of opposition, the
change in "point of view" and terminology, the distance taken with respect to
Hegelian systematicity—that things are not in fact as simple, that is, as clear-cut,
as one might have believed. Although these three answers, as well as the very
questions that give rise to them, are explicitly presented as a "short and sketchy"
way of drawing the line of separation, nothing very clear manages to inscribe itself here, and the separation, which is supposedly so brutal, *also* does not stop,
at the same time, blurring and coming undone. At least in part. This has nothing
to do with the unavoidable paleonymic compromise (that is, here, with the very
name difference). Heidegger is the first to emphasize this compromise.[33] Nor
does it have anything to do, at least at this point in the text, with the "sameness"
of the subject or matter (thinking, being), since the possibility of gaining access
to difference as such is not for a moment placed in doubt, and since the thinking
of difference cannot be confused with absolute thinking or the Idea. Rather, it
would have to do with the nature of that toward which, in the step back, one must
retrocede, assuming that the step back is to be distinguished from the *Aufhebung*
—and which is therefore the *unthought*. How can one *distinguish* the unthought?
How can one make sure that the unthought will not be the same thing as what absolute thinking—despite the presence "next to us" *already* of the Absolute, despite
the *will* to *parousia* of the Absolute—must gather "in the end," after having
waited? The fragility, the precariousness of the gesture are such here that it is
necessary, in order to reinsure the possibility of the step back, to insist a second
time that, for Hegel, the thinking of thought is the thinking of the *already thought*
and that, therefore, the memory of thought—whatever the whole "historical" lack,

the whole *delay* of the Absolute in manifesting itself as thought, analyzed with such precision in another text[34] – is never more than the recollection of questions already asked:

> Since the step back determines the character of our conversation with the history of Western thinking, our thinking in a way leads us away from what has been thought so far in philosophy. Thinking recedes before its matter, Being, and thus brings what is thought into a confrontation in which we behold the whole of this history – behold it with respect to what constitutes the source of this entire thinking, because it alone establishes and prepares for this thinking the area [*Bezirk*][35] of its abode [*Aufenthalt* – halt, delay, sojourn]. In contrast to Hegel, this is not a traditional problem, already posed, but what has always remained unasked throughout this history of thinking. We speak of it, tentatively and unavoidably, in the language of tradition. We speak of the *difference* between Being and beings. The step back goes from what is unthought, from the difference as such, into what is to be thought. That is the *oblivion* of the difference.[36]

We will return to this unprecedented affirmation of the necessity of thinking the forgetting of that which has never been thought. It is obviously the extreme to which thinking is reduced by the gesture of separation. But it is also clear, already, at the price of what difficulties such an operation is "possible." Not only must we, like "Hegel himself" (that is, absolute thinking), speak in the first person plural (*Wir/für uns*),[37] but we must also, as it was already possible to read in the answers to the second and third questions, constantly find support, with a view to marking the difference between the philosophical and thinking, in a separation *already* produced (and yet never made explicit) between the Hegelian relation to the "history of philosophy" and the relation of thinking to the "history of *thought*" or to the "historical *tradition*." The risk of this operation – whatever may be, at the same time, its assurance – is therefore sufficiently inscribed to hinder its simple and smooth progress [*le déroulement simple et "sans histoire"*], or even to prevent the subsistence of any *certainty* as to its *result*. Heidegger knows this: the step back precedes itself: "the 'whither' to which the step back directs us, develops and shows itself only in the execution of the step."[38] Moreover, this whole movement, if indeed one can describe it as a sort of strategic movement, must also be recognized, in a larger way, as, after all, rather insufficiently military or political (that is, philosophical) to be able, when all is said and done, to rely on "nothing" (or almost "nothing" – an "imperceptible" gap, says Granel), assuming it actually turns out to rely, since *Sein und Zeit*, only on an ultimately *impossible* "determination" of the meaning or the truth of being:

> The difficulty resides in the fact that the question concerning the meaning of being, itself asked on the basis of the meaning it seeks, and

which is entirely other than the one in which being is understood in metaphysics, does not lead us *positively* anywhere else; that is, it does not lead us into an "other" of metaphysics that would itself be situated, posited, subsisting or consisting in any way whatsoever. The discrepancy with respect to the metaphysical meaning of being is rather an "imperceptible" gap, which never loses its inappearance in all the paragraphs of the introduction to *Sein und Zeit* and even in all the movements that lead the work as a whole to the break where all of a sudden it stops.[39]

What Granel says here about *Sein und Zeit* could be said about the entire remainder of the "work." It is certainly not by chance that the break of *Sein und Zeit* was never reduced as such—not even in the lecture *Zeit und Sein*, whose title is that of the broken, missing hinge between the two initially planned parts of *Sein und Zeit*. Nor is it an accident that, as we may say looking ahead, Heidegger's "work," in its dispersion, its rupture (caused by the repercussion, within it, of this first break), does not constitute an *œuvre*, at least in the classical sense of the term.

In short, thinking itself risks being "nothing." If Heidegger constantly stresses the difficulty of thinking, if, correlatively, his thinking knows no other matter than thinking, it is indeed, as was already known, because the difference of thinking is not assignable. The question "What is called thinking?" receives, in fact, no answer. None of Heidegger's questions, as such, can receive one. This is why the answer awaited since *Sein und Zeit*, the answer to the question of being, will always have been, in all the texts and in all the books without any exception, necessarily *deferred*. Necessarily and rigorously, assuming that, as the *Postscript* to *What Is Metaphysics?* says, there is no *authentic* question other than the one that does not allow itself to be *sublated* by and in the answer.[40] But this also means, consequently, that the step back is practically nil (either always to be taken or always already taken), that the distance with respect to philosophy is without space (or in the "only space" of a *pure sustained* question). The separation could, therefore, very well not *appear*.

It must nevertheless appear, however little, if thinking cannot avoid having nothing else to think but the unthought of thought, and if, for that reason, it must not be purely and simply the same thing as philosophy. As for Hegel, paradoxically (as, doubtless, for the whole tradition since Parmenides and Plato), the most serious threat is that of mixture, mingling, confusion (*Mischung, Verwirrung*, etc.). There is thus always *also*, in spite of everything, a decisive "moment"—and this does not fail to occur in *Identity and Difference*—where it becomes necessary, in order to mark the separation, to envision and to *posit* difference as such, to place difference *itself* in a confrontation from which it can *present* itself:

Unexpectedly it may happen that thinking finds itself called upon to ask: what does it say, this Being that is mentioned so often? If Being here shows itself concurrently as the Being of . . . , thus in the genitive of the difference, then the preceding question is more properly [*sachlicher*]: what do you make of the difference if Being as well as beings appear *by virtue of the difference*, each in its own way? To do justice to this question, we must first assume a proper position face to face with the difference [*zur Differenz in ein sachgemäßes Gegenüber*]. Such a confrontation becomes manifest to us once we accomplish the step back. Only as this step gains for us greater distance [*Ent-fernung*] does what is near give itself as such, does nearness achieve its first radiance [*kommt Nähe zum ersten Scheinen*].[41]

But what is the difference here with the confrontation in which, as we have seen, it was a question of first positing the *already thought*—and through which one passed closest to the Hegelian relation with the history of philosophy or the "totality" of the history of thought? No doubt this confrontation is now the one that opens to the unthought. No doubt it also, for this reason, remains "objectless" (*gegenstandlos*), and difference as such is no more objectifiable or representable than was, for example, the "nothing" or nothingness disclosing itself in the *unheimlich* drift of being-in-totality and in accordance with which, in the aftermath of *Sein und Zeit*, the question of being began once again to repeat itself.[42] But inasmuch as it is indeed a matter of *position*, the problem remains intact as to how precisely this position differs from a philosophical position, that is, from a *thesis*. Is it not the unthought (difference as such) that "gives account" ["rend raison"] of what has been thought and that "founds" the foundation on which metaphysics in its onto-theological constitution has been elaborated? Is it not in this confrontation that one can "follow difference in its essential provenance" and that the very origin of the unthought, the *oblivion* (the veiling) constitutive of difference itself, gives itself to be thought? "The oblivion here to be thought is the veiling [*Verhüllung*] of the difference as such, thought in terms of *Lethe* (concealment) [*Verbergung*]; this veiling has in turn withdrawn itself from the beginning. The oblivion belongs to the difference because the difference belongs to the oblivion."[43]

Here we run into a kind of "circularity," which of course is not just a hermeneutical circularity (even less a logical circularity),[44] but rather, if we may again anticipate what follows, something like the course of the impossible. Whatever may be the rigor with which this "test" of the impossible is sustained (but is the impossible absolutely unsublatable? and does this question even make sense?), the circularity cannot fail to come unhinged; there is always a "forced passage," or, which amounts to the same, a "brake." This is why the recourse to *Lethe*, however "abyssal" it may be, also functions, in a certain way, *positively*. This is why difference, in order to be (the oblivion of) difference, must necessarily differ from itself and be given as nondifference, the settling or conciliation (*Austrag/Versöhnung*) of the Same. Here again we must read:

> Being shows itself as the unconcealing overwhelming [*als die entbergende Überkommnis*]. Beings as such appear in the manner of the arrival that keeps itself concealed in unconcealedness [*die in die Unverborgenheit sich bergenden Ankunft*].
>
> Being in the sense of unconcealing overwhelming, and beings as such in the sense of arrival that keeps itself concealed, are present [*wesen*], and thus differentiated [*als die so Unterschiedenen*], by virtue of the same, the differentiation [*Unter-Schied*]. That differentiation alone grants and holds apart the "between" [*das Zwischen*], in which the overwhelming and the arrival are held toward one another, are born away from and toward each other [*auseinander-zueinander getragen sind*]. The difference [*Differenz*] of Being and beings, as the differentiation [*Unter-Schied*] of overwhelming and arrival, is the *conciliation* of the two in *unconcealing keeping in concealment* [*der entbergendbergende Austrag beider*]. Within this conciliation there prevails a clearing [*Lichtung*] of what veils and closes itself off [*das sich verhüllend Verschließende*] — and this its prevalence bestows the being apart, and the being toward each other [*das Aus-und-Zueinander*], of overwhelming and arrival.[45]

In this practically "mad" laboring of the language, in this almost unreadable "forcing" of syntax, and this dislocation of the semantic,[46] what this text says, as it tries to name this difference more ancient than metaphysical being, is nothing other than *truth itself, aletheia*, such, no doubt, as it has never been thought, but such also as it governs all thinking, in its history and its fate, as the thinking of presence. To the extent, therefore, that there is no thinking save that of the same, of the dif-ferent, the step back, if it is not to lead to the *unthinkable*, must necessarily seek support from a *determination* of being or of truth *preferably* [*plutôt*] *as presence* — whatever the difficulty of (re)presenting it and however indissociable from its (own) withdrawal, however weakened ("absent" as presence) it may be.[47]

We could go on like this for a long time: this back-and-forth is doubtless interminable. It may be said that thought is in fact nothing but this sort of "perpetual movement," which neither can nor should ever be settled, between the philosophical (the already thought) and its other; that thinking "consists" entirely in this between, in this *Zwischen* without consistency. But can we really say this? And above all, can we think it?

In other words: does this not allow itself to be thought, that is, conceived, too well? Is not this between, this intermediate "place," this pure distance which thinking must "occupy," precisely what allows it to "grasp" itself, to come back to itself, to retrieve itself, and, so doing, to retrieve everything? How does the distance, the between, assume a position and fulfill a function other than that of *mediation* in general? And at the same time—however rigorously one may distinguish between the *same* and the *identical*—what separates the necessary differentiation of difference, the return of difference in conciliation, of the distant in the near, of the other in the proper, etc., from the *movement* of sublation? Did Hegel ever *think* anything but the impossibility for difference to *be* difference without deferring and differing from itself? What distinguishes the "return" of difference from identification, or rather from *determination*? That it is "provisional"? But this "provisional" also repeats itself. And in re-petition (that is, first of all, in the suspension of answers), what proves that the *authenticity* of questioning does not sublate questions as well as, if not better than, the answer or answers themselves? Or again: what prevents all that which has successively been called "repetition of the question of being," "introduction to (into) metaphysics," "appropriation [*Verwindung*] of metaphysics," "remembrance [*Erinnerung*] in metaphysics," "return to the foundation of metaphysics," etc.—this whole long process, in the mode of the future anterior (or of anteriority to come), which governs the movement of all the texts—what prevents this from merging (let us say, for the time being, though not without reservation: formally) with the movement of philosophical *anamnesis* in general? How call all of this avoid becoming a kind of uncompletable "Phenomenology of the Unthought"?

Nothing in this is intended to resemble a "critique." This would be derisory, all the more so as these questions are clearly not *right* [*justes*]. It is rather a question of recognizing a kind of fatality (of destiny?), even if it takes the form of a refusal to resign oneself to it and *nothing more*. But this is intended also (or rather first of all) as a way of doubting (if not of disputing) that if something really distinguishes "Heidegger," this something must be primarily what Heidegger himself calls thinking. Emphasizing thinking would sooner involve running the risk of consolidating or aggravating the proximity of the philosophical. The paradox is obviously that the more thinking distances itself from the philosophical, the more it resembles it. What saves thinking is its ruin. And it is perhaps not out of the question that where the chances of salvation increase, danger also appears. At bottom, the "privilege" of thinking is entirely contained in what one could call, on the model of the Platonic *mechane* or of the Hegelian *ruse* of reason (and because it is decidedly hard to forego all reference to war), the stratagem of *Entfernung*, of *é-loignement*. But this stratagem works in two directions. It can at least be turned around; it may be quite simply reversible. That it is not completely so, that it *sooner* functions in one direction—that "Heidegger" is not a philosopher—this the recourse to thinking could not decide. If it wished to (and it doubtless wishes to; we must indeed learn to recognize here the *whole* difficulty), the stratagem would *already* have come into play, as Hegel says, "behind its back." Unbeknownst to it, then, and of course, in the "other" direction. In favor of the philosophical.

The (De)constitution of the Subject

Still, in all this what remains decisive is to hear Nietzsche himself; to inquire with him and through him and therefore at the same time against him, but for [für] the one single innermost matter [Sache] that is common to Western philosophy.

Like all Western thought since Plato, Nietzsche's thinking is metaphysics.[48]

We should now be able to ask the question once again: if it is not to thinking, if it is not *exclusively* to thinking, then to what, in "Heidegger himself," is it a matter of gaining access?

We will, however, suspend this question a while longer. Not that we wish to escape it or abandon it, even though one may already suspect not only that it cannot be answered in a simple way (that is, it cannot be simply answered), but also that we will probably have to modify its formulation and give up, in any case, speaking of "Heidegger *himself*."

But first, there is something more urgent.

Whatever its infinitely problematic character, the "strategy" of thought *functions*. Also. It is efficient. It is even fearsome. Perhaps nothing escapes its "enveloping" power, not even, in spite of everything, Hegel. It is therefore also necessary to take stock of this power and first of all to reveal, if only schematically, the *mechanism* [*dispositif*] on which it relies. As we shall see, Nietzsche is implicated in this. But the position he occupies is especially ambiguous.

As expected, this mechanism is double. There is what we might call, while we're at it, "alliances." And it is known that "against" metaphysics – and more so than in the Greeks themselves, who probably never thought what, in their own language, was given them to think – Heidegger finds these alliances on the side of those who began to *repeat* the unthought of Greek thought and whose real *force* Hegel was unable to recognize (perhaps because they were *too close* to him): that is, Kant[49] and Hölderlin. Of course, nothing is automatic in the conjunction of these two alliances. On the one hand, because they were not entered into at the same time (and what separates the "repetition" of Kant from the "clarification" of Hölderlin is nothing less than the break of *Sein und Zeit*, the abandonment of the "terrain" of phenomenology, the declared renunciation of ontology); on the other hand – but this is in fact the *same* story – because in its duplicity, the alliance implies nothing less than the extreme difficulty of the relation that unites and separates, according to the "logic" of *é-loignement*, poetry and thought, *Dichtung* and *Denken*. We will therefore content ourselves here with a simple reminder. It would in fact be necessary, in order to sketch a less summary description of this, to relate this (double) alliance to its origin (the break of *Sein und Zeit*) and to analyze its *dissymmetrical* functioning. It would thus be necessary to show at the same time what, in *Sein und Zeit*, inevitably causes the break, how this break affects, at least in part, the reading of Kant (initially planned for the "second part"), and how, finally, this same break (this obstruction)[50] governs, through the eruption of the problematic of the work of art, the return to the question of being (that is, the question of the relation of being to the being of humanity) as a question of language or of idiom (*Sprache*), of speech or of "myth" (*Sage*), and of diction or "poetry" (*Dichtung*).[51] It is thus understandable that the surest and most incontestable alliance is the one with Hölderlin, that is, more generally, with (authentic) *Dichtung*. It is also understandable why there is, at bottom, no properly philosophical alliance and how thought itself, in a certain way, remains subordinated to the sovereign "word" of *Dichten*, which, alone, manages to make the "voiceless voice" of being itself "resonate" as such. But this is not exactly our subject.[52]

So there are the alliances. After all, these things are well known. It is no less obvious, however, that these alliances could never have been concluded, that the "allies" could perhaps never have discovered one another, if the "enemy" had itself not previously been *recognized*. This is a truism, but it conceals a problem. The whole question of the determination of metaphysics—the whole question of the necessity (that is, at the same time, of the unavoidability) of the *Überwindung*, of the "overcoming" of metaphysics, depends on it.

And this is precisely where Nietzsche comes in.

But Nietzsche's intervention is complex. We should therefore follow rather closely its ramifications.

The whole "strategy" of thought, as we have seen, can be interpreted—if we agree to harden its contours a bit—as an "anti-Hegelian" strategy. And this (which must be recalled yet again) as of *Sein und Zeit*, as of the protest against the oblivion of the question of being and the revolt (or insurrection) against the "ontological dogma" of the emptiness (of the "pure indetermination" and the "pure void," as Hegel says) of the concept of being. But from where is this protest raised? Where does the decision to revolt come from? Nothing, in *Sein und Zeit*, points to it, neither in the first paragraph, nor in the "subtitle," nor in any of the introductory paragraphs, where the program for the re(in)stitution of the meaning of the question of being and for the elaboration of the question of the meaning of being is set up as a whole. It is only quite a few years later, in 1935—when, once again, after the break (the constraints of teaching increasing the effect of repetition), it is a question of taking up again, on a new basis, the question of being—that a first indication appears. This happens in the first part of the *Introduction to Metaphysics*. Despite the changes that have taken place since *Sein und Zeit*, the question is the same. Must we resign ourselves to the idea that being is only an "empty word"? But this time, the source of the protest is clearly indicated. It is Nietzsche himself, although not unambiguously:

But being remains unfindable, almost like nothing, or ultimately *quite* so. Then, in the end, the word "being" is no more than an empty word. It means nothing real, tangible, material. Its meaning [*Bedeutung*] is an unreal vapor. Thus in the last analysis Nietzsche was perfectly right in calling such "highest concepts" as being "the last cloudy streak of evaporating reality." Who would want to chase after such a vapor, when the very term is merely a name for a great fallacy? "Nothing indeed has exercised a more simple power of persuasion hitherto than the error of Being."

[T]hat preliminary question which sprang necessarily from our main question "How does it stand with being?" ["Wie steht es um das Sein?"] [is] a sober question perhaps, but assuredly a very useless one. And yet a *question, the* question: is "being" a mere word [*ein bloßes Wort*] and its meaning a vapor or is it the spiritual destiny of the Western world?[53]

No doubt Nietzsche himself is inscribed, albeit in a contradictory way, in the unfolding of this decline or this loss of the meaning of the question of being. It remains, nonetheless, that the extreme (ultimate) violence, the share of rage and spite it comprises, *also* make of his accusation concerning the "error of being" something like the announcement of the necessity and urgency of a "new" formulation [*position*] of the question of being: "Does Nietzsche speak the truth? Or was he himself only the last victim of a long process of error and neglect, but *as such* the unrecognized witness to a new necessity?"[54]

Therein lies the whole ambiguity of Nietzsche's situation. Nietzsche indeed committed the error, but he did so as a victim, the last victim. As such, he bears witness. He is a *sign*—indeed, an oracular or prophetic sign. He recognized—more precisely, he designated—the evil, the enemy to be fought. It was essentially Nietzsche who was able to bring out, in Hegel, in the culmination of idealism, obscurely but also by virtue of an exceptional lucidity (the intrication of blindness and insight, the ambiguity of prophetic knowledge is such that it will require no less than the two volumes of *Nietzsche*, and doubtless much more, to untangle its skein), the accomplishment of philosophy in and as *nihilism*. No doubt, in the struggle he waged against nihilism, and first of all because he used the very "arms" of his opponent (the Will), Nietzsche allowed himself to be enclosed within what he was fighting. But he continued to fight nonetheless. He even, and with rigor, fought against himself. This is why, having recognized "the reign of nihilism" in the whole history of Western philosophy,[55] he sensed that nihilism is founded precisely on that (multiple) oblivion of being, on that "indetermination" of being according to which what Heidegger will call the "onto-theological constitution of metaphysics" is organized—and which Nietzsche himself will, therefore, have been the first to denounce. In this, his role is *decisive*. For if this is Nietzsche's *ambiguity*, it is not impossible to interpret the whole enterprise of what was initially called the "destruction of the history of ontology"[56] as the corrective repetition, the rectification, or, better yet, the *removal* [*levée*] of that ambiguity. When it comes to the commentary on Nietzsche himself, the thrust will, in any case, be *unambiguous*: "Nietzsche transformed himself into an ambiguous figure [*zweideutige Gestalt*], and, within his world and that of the present time, he had to do this. What we must do is to grasp the forward thrust and the uniqueness [*das Vorausweisende und Einzige*], what is decisive and ultimate [*das Entscheidende und Endgültige*], behind this ambiguity."[57]

The fact remains, however, that at the moment when the project for a destruction of the history of ontology was being elaborated, Nietzsche himself did not appear (the references to Nietzsche in *Sein und Zeit* are few in number and limited in length). So it is as though, at the time of *Sein und Zeit*, Nietzsche had not been read, or, more precisely, as though this reading had to be concealed, as though Heidegger had to keep, regarding Nietzsche, a certain reserve, a certain silence. After the fact, but only after the fact—and as if it were the effect of constraint, of the break—Nietzsche was revealed to be the one whose (ambiguous) protest already governed, surreptitiously, the strategy of *Sein und Zeit*. But then why this silence of *Sein und Zeit*? Why this kind of belated admission? If Nietzsche was already *active* in *Sein und Zeit*, why not let any of it show?

The problem raised here is not the empirical, anecdotal problem concerning whether Heidegger had actually read Nietzsche at the time of *Sein und Zeit*. Nietzsche's belated intrusion says a lot more than any proof. The problem is of an entirely different nature. What we must try to understand is what *delayed* Nietzsche's entry. Why did so many years elapse before this entry took place? Why, as well, does Nietzsche appear accompanied (or even preceded) by Hölderlin?[58] Why is this double entry contemporaneous with the moment when the question of art is first asked? And why does this asking of the question of art (as the *Überwindung* of aesthetics) already take place against Nietzsche?[59]

These questions are doubtless too sweeping for us to even hope to answer them here. It is nevertheless perhaps not impossible to sketch in a very rough way a kind of hypothesis. A hypothesis that would, moreover, necessarily have, here again, the form of a suspicion. It would amount to asking whether, in this silence of *Sein und Zeit*, in the delay imposed on Nietzsche's entry onto the scene, in the "refuge" sought, at the same time, on the side of Hölderlin (and especially in the persistence with which, for more than ten years, Heidegger will doggedly comment on Nietzsche *against himself* in order to subordinate him to metaphysics), we could not find the symptoms of a certain worry or a certain fear (more than a distrust, in any case) experienced before Nietzsche, before a *threat* represented by Nietzsche. The threat would, of course, be that of a proximity. But as opposed to the "Hegelian" proximity, this proximity would be such (so slightly or poorly perceived, so difficult to pinpoint as such) that the "strategem of *Ent-fernung*" might reveal itself to be powerless, that is, unable to contain or remove it, and that there would perhaps be no way — except in force or denial — to disengage oneself from it.

Such a suspicion is not self-evident. Formulated in these terms, it is doubtless even incongruous or shocking. What could *fear* possibly have to do with it? A little further and we would lapse into psychology. It is true that, since we are talking about Nietzsche, one could still nurture the hope of not proving to be too unable to maintain a certain "inspiration" and of being able to avoid falling from "grand psychology" back into psychologism. But what exactly would be in a position to guarantee such a hope? We must therefore observe a certain prudence. This is why we will seek justification for this suspicion in the obligation, to which Heidegger himself submitted, of bringing into relation or of comparing, with respect to the question of the *Sache des Denkens*, Hegel and Nietzsche. There are plenty of examples. Let us cite just one of them, the passage from "The Anaximander Fragment" to which we have already referred and in which Hegel appears as "the only Western thinker who has thoughtfully experienced the history of thought." Nietzsche is also mentioned here: "In his own way the young Nietzsche does establish a vibrant rapport [*lebendiges Verhältnis*] with the personalities [*Persönlichkeit*] of the pre-Platonic philosophers; but his interpretations of the texts are commonplace, if not entirely superficial, throughout. Hegel is the only Western thinker who has thoughtfully experienced the history of thought."[60] It is clear where the differences are, or rather where the difference is: Nietzsche did not undergo, like Hegel, the thoughtful experience of the history of thought. This does not mean that he did not *think*. It means that his relation to the history of thought is not itself a thoughtful — *denkend* — relation. It is a living — *lebendig* — relation, not with thought itself, but with the *personalities* of thinkers. By emphasizing this, moreover, Heidegger remains absolutely faithful to Nietzsche's own statements.[61] But how can this "inadequacy" of Nietzsche's clarify the threat or the danger supposedly in question? How would the indication of this inadequacy by Heidegger be symptomatic?

There would doubtless be nothing all that significant in it if we did not recall that the whole "strategy" of thought vis-à-vis metaphysics is played out precisely in the thoughtful relation to the history of thought, in the dangerous but salutary (or at least what Heidegger hoped would be salutary) proximity to Hegel. As we have seen, it is "against" Hegel (*right against* Hegel) that the very possibility of the *Überwindung* of metaphysics — Hegel obviously included — is "decided." And even though one can begin to see that the Nietzschean insurrection against nihilism played an innovative or provocative role in that "decision," the Heideggerian gesture with regard to the whole history of thought models itself, in order to disrupt it and dissociate itself from it, on the Hegelian gesture with regard to the whole history of philosophy. The symptom here is the scorn or aversion for, the indefatigably repeated refusal of, anything that might resemble an empirical, historical (historicizing), psychological relation with the past of philosophy. The history (*Geschichte*) of philosophy is the history of thought, that is, the destiny of being, of which each philosophy is a dispensation, a mark or imprint, a trace. As such, thought is *anonymous*. A little, mutatis mutandis, like literature for Valéry or Borges (or for Blanchot—except that Blanchot has read Heidegger),[62] philosophy (thought) has no author. It [*Ça*] thinks, being (or truth) gives us to think—*almost* in the way in which the Absolute, in Hegel, gives (itself as) food for thought. The difference is just a certain positivity, that is, reflexivity. But there is also not a single philosophy's name that can be written without quotation marks. A philosopher's *proper* name is thought itself.

Of course, this refusal to take the *author* into account (and with the author, the character, the personality, the subject, etc.) is rigorously justified. Nietzsche's gesture with regard to the "living figures of philosophy" is actually bound up, as we know, with the simple reversal of (the values of) metaphysics, that is, in this case, with the substitution of art for the "truth instinct" ("We have art in order not to perish from truth") on the basis of which is organized the whole reading of Greek philosophy outlined in 1873.[63] Similarly, this gesture is of a piece with the effort to turn rhetoric against philosophy (being is a metaphor, etc.),[64] as also with the plans, more tenacious perhaps, for a "physiography" or a typology of philosophers—plans which, as is known, all remain forever imprisoned within the very conceptual economy they claim to denounce. This no longer needs to be proven today.

But this is perhaps not what is essential. Or at least we may ask if, in this refusal, however justified it may be, to consider the *author*, there is not something else hidden, another refusal, or the refusal of something besides the author (the "philosophical subject") and which the concept of author would nevertheless cover up. This is why it is not a matter of indifference to point out that, twelve years before *Sein und Zeit* (before the "beginning," then), in the habilitation thesis on Duns Scotus, Nietzsche's name, sure enough, appears, and the question of the "philosophical subject" is debated. This takes place in the introduction, in a preliminary development devoted to the notion of the history of philosophy. The whole text must be read:

> The history of philosophy has a relation to philosophy other than that, for example, of the history of mathematics to mathematics. This difference has to do, not with the *history* of philosophy, but with the history of *philosophy*.
>
> Those who judge this from the outside, and sometimes also those who are supposedly inside, imagine that one must see in the history of philosophy a succession of more or less oft-repeated, alternating "errors." Add to this that philosophers remain divided on what philosophy

itself is, and the quite uncertain nature of philosophy as science seems to be an established fact.

Yet, another reality is revealed to the eye truly capable of understanding.

Philosophy certainly has, like any other science, a cultural value. But at the same time, what is most its own is its claim to be valuable and effective as a *life-value*. The basis of philosophical thought is more than a scientific subject to which one devotes oneself by personal preference and by a desire to promote or to participate in the configuration of culture. Philosophy lives also in a tension [*Spannung*] with the living personality [*lebendige Persönlichkeit*], from whose depths and fullness of life it draws content and the claim to value. Mostly, then, there is, underlying any philosophical conception, a personal stand taken [*eine persönliche Stellungnahme*] by the philosopher concerned. This fact for philosophy of being determined by the subject [*Dieses Bestimmtsein aller Philosophie vom Subjekt*] was expressed by Nietzsche in his inexorably harsh style of thought and in his aptitude for plastic representation [*plastische Darstellungsfähigkeit*], with the phrase: "*The drive that does philosophy*" ["*Trieb, der philosophiert*"].

Given the constancy of human nature, it thus becomes understandable that philosophical problems are repeated in history. What it allows us to establish is not so much a *development* [*Entwicklung*] in the sense in which one would proceed constantly toward new questions from a foundation provided by previously acquired solutions, as chiefly an *unfolding and exhaustion* [*Auswicklung und Ausschöpfung*] of a limited philosophical sector. This effort forever ready to begin again with a more or less identical group of problems, this enduring identity of the philosophical mind not only allows, it *demands* a corresponding conception of the "history" of philosophy.[65]

It is indeed a question here of the *philosophical subject*, that is, of the subject of philosophy. And not only is it a question of the subject, it is also a question of "life-value," of "living personality," of "a personal stand taken," etc. It is obvious that Nietzsche—and even if it is here rather a kind of Nietzschean vulgate—is "working" this text. But it is also clear how, in terms already close to those which will be used later, the real problem stirring here is the Kantian one of whether human nature is predisposed toward metaphysics—and how the reference to Nietzsche, to the *philosophical drive*, so "diverted," serves in fact to *dismiss, already*, the question of the subject of philosophy (and, at the same time, that of the "Hegelian" *Entwicklung*) to the benefit of the law of repetition, of the *Auswicklung* and *Ausschöpfung* of the same.

The subject is thus indeed already, between the lines (and thanks to a retrospective reading), what *threatens*. And what threatens, in reality, under the name of the "enduring identity of the philosophical mind," no less than thought itself, or at least what will later be called thought, once the double crossing of phenomenology or the crossing of the two phenomenologies has been completed.

But why is the subject threatening? And what is it, in the subject, that threatens?

The explicit reasons for which Heidegger always "distrusted" the subject, that is, always "condemned" the modern oblivion of being in and as the ontology of subjectivity or "subjectity" in all its variants (Cartesian, Leibnizian, Hegelian, Schellingian, etc.) and in all its consequences (anthropology in general, historicism and psychologism, the theory of images or of worldviews, etc.), are well known. But when Nietzsche is at issue, is that all there is to it? Are these reasons sufficient? Does not something else come into play? More precisely: when the question of the subject is the question of the *subject of philosophy*, and when this question and the question of the *author* are one and the same, what happens? What is entailed by the refusal to take the author into account and the desire to refer thought only to itself?

Let us look, for example, at the beginning of the third course on Nietzsche: *The Will to Power as Knowledge* (1939). The answer to our questions is given here:

"Nietzsche as the Thinker of the Consummation of Metaphysics."

Who Nietzsche *is* and above all who he *will be* we shall know as soon as we are able to think the thought that he gave shape to in the phrase "the will to power." Nietzsche is that thinker who trod the path of thought to "the will to power." We shall never experience who Nietzsche is through a historical report about his life history, nor through a presentation [*Darstellung*] of the content of his writings. Neither do we, nor should we, want to know who Nietzsche is, if we have in mind only the personality [*Persönlichkeit*], the historical figure, and the psychological object and its products. But was not the last thing that Nietzsche himself completed for publication the piece that is entitled *Ecce Homo: How One Becomes What One Is*? Does not *Ecce Homo* speak as his last will — that one occupy oneself with him, with this man, and let oneself be told by him those things that occupy the sections of his book? — "Why I am so wise. Why I am so clever. Why I write such good books. Why I am a destiny [*Schicksal*]." Is this not the apotheosis of uninhibited self-presentation and boundless self-mirroring?

It is a gratuitous and thus often practiced procedure to take this self-publication of his own nature and will [*diese Selbstveröffentlichung seines eigenen Wesens und Wollens*] as the harbinger of erupting madness. However, in *Ecce Homo* it is a matter neither of the biography of Nietzsche nor of the person of "Herr Nietzsche." In truth, it is a matter of a "destiny," the destiny [*Geschick*] not of an individual but of the history [*Geschichte*] of the era of modern times, of the end of the West. . . .

Nietzsche transformed himself into an ambiguous figure, and, within his world and that of the present time, he had to do this. What we must do is to grasp the forward thrust and the uniqueness, what is decisive and ultimate, behind this ambiguity. The precondition for this is that we look away from the "man" and also from the "work" insofar as it is viewed as the expression of his humanity, that is, in the light of the man. For even the work as work closes itself off to us as long as we squint somehow after the "life" of the man who created the work instead of asking about Being and the world, which first ground the work. Neither the person of Nietzsche nor even his work concern us when we make both in their connection the object of a historiological and psychological report.

What solely concerns us is the *trace* [*Spur*] that that thought-path toward the will to power made into the history of Being—which means into the still untraveled regions of future decisions.

Nietzsche belongs among the essential thinkers. With the term *thinker* we name those exceptional human beings who are destined to think one single thought, a thought that is always "about" *beings as a whole* [*das Seiende im Ganzen*]. Each thinker thinks only one *single* thought.[66]

There is nothing in this text to which one cannot or even should not subscribe. As it is said in *The Gay Science*, which is no more absent from these lines than *Ecce Homo*: "But let us leave Herr Nietzsche."[67] We do not, therefore, have to *go back on* this condemnation or this exclusion (from the point of view of thought) of the subject and the author, biography, psychology, etc. Or, if you prefer, it is not a question of opposing in turn Herr Nietzsche to "Heidegger," nor the "rights" of the subject to the "imperialism" of thought. Even less of seeking in Nietzsche—in the books and the rest—the wherewithal to debunk Heidegger's "treatment" of him: we know perfectly well that we would run up against contradictory texts, and this would be, at least in terms of these purposes, insignificant. No one is any longer unaware, at any rate, of what psychology and all the "returns to the subject" are worth in this area. Or rather of what they mask, namely, the absence of *thought*.

As one might already have surmised, what interests us here is neither the subject nor the author. Nor is it the "other"—whatever this may come to mean—of the subject or the author. Rather (and to limit ourselves for the time being to the question of the subject alone), what interests us is what is *also* at stake in the subject, while remaining absolutely irreducible to any subjectivity (that is, to any objectivity); that which, in the subject, deserts (has always already deserted) the subject *itself* and which, prior to any "self-possession" (and in a mode other than that of dispossession), is the dissolution, the defeat of the subject in the subject or *as* the subject: the (de)constitution of the subject or the "loss" of the subject—if indeed one can think the loss of what one has never had, a kind of "originary" and "constitutive" loss (of "self").[68]

Now it is precisely this that Heidegger's text touches upon. But it does so only in order immediately (or even in advance) to take it back, to sublate it (meaning also to sublimate it) in and as thought. *This* is "madness," and "madness" as it declares itself, or rather does not declare itself, in *Ecce Homo*, in that exhibition of the subject, of its "essential being" ["être propre"], which one could take for "the apotheosis of uninhibited self-presentation," if "Nietzsche," fortunately, had not spoken of "himself" as a *fatality* or a *destiny*. It is as though – and this is perfectly legible in the text – the "strategy" of thought had no other *reason* (and first of all to destroy the subject) than in this exorcising gesture with regard to madness. In the subject, in the concept of the subject, the most fearsome danger, the greatest threat would be precisely what threatens the subject *in a certain way*. And under the name of the subject, what would be dismissed, refused, is in fact the "loss," the bad "loss," of the subject.

But this operation does not happen all by itself. Nor all at once. It may even implicate the whole reading, or rather the whole interpretation, of Nietzsche. This is what we must try to understand now.

Exorcising Madness: The Appropriation of the Unthought

"Man" means "thinker": this is where madness lies.
                    Nietzsche, note for Tragedy and Free Spirits

The parallelism between Heidegger's descriptions and this position is incontestable. It is established:
—despite my reservations regarding Heidegger;
—despite the different roads taken. Even more than the text of the first volume of Sein und Zeit, *however, his inability (at least according to appearances) to write the second volume brings me closer to Heidegger. I would like, on the other hand, to indicate some important differences:*
—my point of departure was laughter and not, as in Heidegger's Was ist Metaphysik?, *anguish: this may give rise to certain consequences on the very level of sovereignty (anguish is a sovereign moment, but a self-fugitive, negative one);*
—Heidegger's published work, as it seems to me, is more a factory than a liqueur (it is even just a treatise of manufacture); it is a professorial piece of work, whose subordinate method remains stuck *to the results: what matters in my eyes, on the contrary, is the moment of* unsticking, *what I teach (if it*

is true that . . .) is an intoxication, not a philosophy: I am
not a philosopher but a saint, *maybe a madman.*
Bataille, Méthode de méditation

What forces me to write, I suppose, is the fear of going mad.

I adopt these lines as my own: "I do not want to be a holy
man; sooner even a buffoon. . . . Yet in spite of that—or
rather not *in spite of it, because so far nobody has been more*
mendacious than holy men—the truth speaks out of me."[69]
Bataille (Sur Nietzsche, Preface/Part I, "M. Nietzsche," III)

If it could only concern "madness" (if one could isolate, in one way or another, "madness" itself), the operation would doubtless be relatively simple. Besides, it always is to some extent, or at least it is always animated, initially, by the hope of a certain simplicity. The schema is familiar. It would suffice to show that Nietzsche's "madness" cannot easily be considered within the categories of "medicoscientific representation" and that, in its originality, its singularity, its specificity, it resists clinical description, nosography, diagnosis, etc. Psychiatric discourse would prove unable to master it, just as, for example, it has no real grasp of Hölderlin's "madness." This discourse would not be false (it is, on the contrary, *correct*), but insufficient. This insufficiency would obviously be due to the strict subordination of the categories of medical representation to those of the (modern) philosophical representation of subjectivity. Medical representation, in other words, would already presuppose representation itself, the certainty (or the consciousness) of thought as subjective thought. As a result, it would rely on a predetermined concept of the subject as *being-oneself* [*être-propre*] (self-proprietary, self-identical, adequately represented or representable in its name, its acts, its discourse, etc.)—or inversely, but this amounts to the same thing, as *being-other* (alienated, dispossessed, divided, unrepresentable, etc.). It would then be no trouble to show that this representation of the subject, in its very contradiction, is never more than a secondary effect of the powerlessness of representation to explain thought as such. The sublation of "madness" would thus be assured from the very outset of the operation. And in such a way, finally, that the operation could even not take place, or be reduced, practically, to nothing. One could do this with unparalleled ease; a word would suffice.

But this is quite obviously what cannot be done. And for at least two reasons.

Because, on the one hand, it would involve, in fact, a pure and simple exclusion of madness, founded on the presupposition of the very thing that should have been "taken out" of (or saved from) the operation—that is, thought. In other words, it would amount to denying in advance the very possibility of madness, as if by the sole authority of this definitive "argument" (which Heidegger never entirely gives up): a *thinker* could not possibly be *mad*.

Because, on the other hand—but it is the same problem—by bringing into play thought in the strong sense of the term, that is, the essence of thought as such (so as to oppose it as well to what "Nietzsche himself" could think as thought), one would never completely avoid the risk of effacing at a stroke the singularity or originality of "Nietzsche's case" (in the nonclinical sense of the term), even if one subsequently tried to emphasize the *single thought* that inhabits and constitutes each thinker and to transform the *case* into an *example*. Exemplarity would be nothing more than that of thought in its very generality, that by which there is thought only of *being in totality*.[70]

This is why the operation, caught, as is only natural, between its desire for simplicity and what makes the operation itself impossible, is never easy, but long, tortuous, fragile, and threatened in its fragility. It must, in particular, always be resumed; it is never completed. It must ceaselessly forge a path through its own impossibility. If this impossibility consists entirely in the *position* of thought, this means that the path must always be forged in the question: What must we understand by thought? What is called thinking? What must we understand in Nietzsche's thought and in thought generally? This is the hermeneutical question par excellence. It amounts therefore to saying that the (desired) sublation of madness assumes interpretation (which, however, at the same time, it must authorize). Madness cannot be isolated; madness cannot be excluded. The whole interpretation treads within this enclosure. But how?

In the opening section of the course on *The Will to Power as Knowledge*, it is a matter of pulling what one could call the *say-I* of *Ecce Homo* away from narcissism, egocentrism, subjectivism. It is a question of showing the loss of the subject. Everything depends, therefore, on the interpretation of "I Am a Destiny [*fatalité*]," thought immediately not as the destiny of the *say-I* but as the very destiny of thought. It is always this kind of *fatal* loss that holds Heidegger's attention. But it goes without saying that if destiny is here the very destiny of the thought of the thinker, nothing can guarantee that the loss of the subject will be an actual loss. One must, then, in the destiny of thought, in the *I am a fatal thought*, aim at something besides the thought of the thinker; or, more precisely, aim in the thought of the thinker at what escapes the thinker, escapes the strictly "conscious" thought of the thinker. A delicate task, if indeed it is impossible to refrain completely from referring to what the thinker himself thought as thought. It is thus necessary—this is the only "possible" solution—to understand in fate, in destiny (*das Schicksal*), beyond the meaning Nietzsche wished to give to this word, and yet with a certain faithfulness to what he sensed, that which transcends, in thought, thought itself. It is probably this necessity that governs, from beginning to end, the general movement of *Nietzsche* and obliges the interpretation to complete itself through a return to the question of the "history of Being," in which we read, in fact, the following:

> Every thinker exceeds [*überschreitet*] the internal limit of each thinker. But such an exceeding does not constitute a knowing better since it itself consists only in maintaining the thinker within the immediate claim [*Anspruch*] of Being and thus in remaining within his own limits. But these limits in their turn consist in the fact that the thinker can never say of himself what is most his own [*sein Eigenstes*]. The latter must remain unsaid [*ungesagt*] because the sayable word [*das sagbare Wort*] receives its determination from the Unsayable [*das Unsagbare*]. However, what the thinker has that is most his own is not his possession [*sein Besitztum*], but the property of Being [*das Eigentum des Seins*]. . . .
>
> The historiality of a thinker (the manner in which he has been claimed by Being for history and in which he corresponds to this claim) is never measured according to the historically calculable role that his opinions, always necessarily misinterpreted during his lifetime, might play when they are publicly circulated. The historiality of the thinker, which does not mean the thinker himself, but Being, finds its measure in the thinker's original fidelity to his own internal limit. *Not* to know this limit and not to know it especially by virtue of the proximity of the unsaid unsayable—this is the hidden gift [*das verborgene Geschenk*] that Being presents to its elect, called to make their way along the path of thought. . . .
>
> It is not a question here of the psychology of philosophers, but exclusively of the history of Being.[71]

It is clear that recourse is still being taken here to the "strategem of *é-loignement*." But this is not at all surprising, whatever the conclusions to be drawn regarding the relation thus established between proximity and the unsayable, between the word (*das Wort*) and what is *most proper* to the thinker and which the internal limit of his thought prevents him from reaching. What matters to us for the moment is that, in this movement, the loss of the subject—if it is not yet madness—requires that thought, in its most intimate essence, in its own destiny, be thought as the *unthought* itself. The only possibility of warding off the threat of madness, that is, the (de)constitution of the subject, would be to think the (de)constitution of thought *as* the unthought—which is precisely how Heidegger sought to effect the separation from Hegel (from this, too, conclusions will have to be drawn).

Thus, when, several years later, Heidegger will come back to Nietzsche—in the 1951 course (necessarily) entitled *What Is Called Thinking?*—the same movement will be recapitulated in one page, but this time in an even more explicit way. *Loss* will therein be portrayed indeed as the *unthought*. And the question of thought (that is, the question of madness) will be gathered in the interminable ex-orcising litany of the "what gives the most food for thought is that we are not yet thinking," in which it is perhaps not forbidden to hear the barely muted (but in-verted) echo of another litany, more openly linked to the hope for salvation, and which goes something like this: "you would not seek me had you not already found me":

> But to encounter Nietzsche's thinking at all, we must first find it. Only when we have succeeded in finding it may we try to lose again what that thinking has thought. And this, to lose, is harder than to find; be-cause "to lose" in such a case does not just mean to drop something, leave it behind, abandon it [*etwas bloß fallen lassen, es hinter sich las-sen und preisgeben*]. "To lose" here means to make ourselves truly free of that which Nietzsche's thinking has thought. And that can be done only in this way, that we, on our own accord and in our memory [*zum Andenken*], set Nietzsche's thought free into the freedom of its own es-sential substance—and so leave it at that place where it by its nature be-longs. Nietzsche knew of these relations of discovery, finding, and los-ing. All along his way, he must have known of them with ever greater clarity. For only thus can it be understood that at the end of his way he could tell it with an unearthly clarity. What he still had to say in this respect is written on one of those scraps of paper which Nietzsche sent out to his friends about the time when he collapsed in the street (Janu-ary 4, 1889) and succumbed to madness. These scraps are sometimes called "epistles of delusion." Understood medically, scientifically, that classification is correct. For the purposes of thinking, it remains in-adequate.
>
> One of these scraps is addressed to the Dane Georg Brandes, who had delivered the first public lectures on Nietzsche at Copenhagen, in 1888.
>
> "Postmark Torino, 4 Jan 89
>
> "To my friend Georg!
> After you had discovered me, it was no trick to find me: the difficulty now is to lose me. . . .
>
> The Crucified."
>
> Did Nietzsche know that through him something was put into words than can never be lost again? Something that cannot be lost again to thinking, something to which thinking must forever come back again the more thoughtful it becomes? He knew it. For the decisive sentence, introduced by a colon, is no longer addressed only to the recipient of the paper. This sentence expresses a universal fateful state of affairs [*ein geschickhaftes Verhältnis*]. "The difficulty now is to lose me. . . . " Now, and for all men, and henceforth. . . . How are we to give thought to Nietzsche's thinking if we are still not thinking? . . . Part

of what is thought-provoking is that Nietzsche's thought has still not been found. Part of what is most thought-provoking is that we are not in the least prepared truly to lose what is found, rather than merely pass it over and by-pass it. Bypassing of this sort is often done in an innocent form—by offering an overall exposition of Nietzsche's philosophy. As though there could be an exposition [*Darstellung*] that is not necessarily, down in its remotest nook and cranny, an interpretation [*Auslegung*]. As though any interpretation could escape the necessity of taking a stand or even, simply by its choice of starting point, of being an unspoken rejection and refutation. But no thinker can ever be overcome by our refuting him and stacking up around him a literature of refutation [*eine Widerlegungsliteratur*]. What a thinker has thought can be mastered [*verwinden*] only if we refer everything in his thought that is still unthought back to its originary truth. Of course, the thoughtful dialogue with the thinker does not become any more comfortable that way; on the contrary, it turns into a disputation [*Streitgespräch*] of rising acrimony.[72]

Thus *to lose* does not mean *to just drop*. To lose, which is more difficult than to find, is not to lose. What one does not just drop, what one takes up again in order not to lose it, is not just what one picks up (what one finds), but properly what one raises and takes over [*relève*].[73] "Loss" is here the *Aufhebung* itself.

This is why "loss" means—and this is the economic gesture par excellence—"to make ourselves free of that which Nietzsche's thinking has thought." One must therefore "obey" Nietzsche only when (and insofar as) his thought demands that one lose it. This exigency is that of "madness." It is not by chance that this exigency is to be found in the quotation from *Thus Spoke Zarathustra* with which the preface to *Ecce Homo* concludes. But neither is it an accident that Heidegger chooses to refer to a text written by Nietzsche himself rather than to one issuing from the mouth of Zarathustra (it is a *letter*), and that he refrains from pointing out the strange signature (the crucified) at the very moment when he erases the singularity of the addressee ("the decisive sentence . . . is no longer addressed only to the recipient of the paper").[74] One must obey the exigency of loss, but only to the extent that this loss may not be the mad, demented, in-sane [*in-sensée*] loss of "Nietzsche" in all the names of history and all the characters of universal fabulation. The exigency of "loss" is thus the exigency of the *sublation* of thought in the unthought, that is, in that which, not yet being thought, results in our not yet thinking, but which for that very reason we are called upon to think. And, as it is clearly stated in the end, "loss" is nothing other than *appropriation* itself, the *Verwindung* of the unthought. In the same way as in the debate (*Streit*) with Hegel, and perhaps for the same reasons, the movement of *Verwindung* and that of *Aufhebung* are so alike that it is difficult to tell them apart.

The Operation on the Work (Disorganization)

Verwindung—"loss" so understood—insofar as it could be realized, would be a protection against madness, like the *Aufhebung*, which, as Bataille doubtless suspected, fulfills an analogous function[75]—and whatever the difference separating their respective *results*, that is, whatever, in either case, the ("positive" or "negative") *quality* of the refuge sought.

It remains to be seen, however, what is *more precisely* threatening in madness. Why should one want to ward off madness at any price? What is madness, that it can instill fear to this point and push thought to such *extremes*? And what exactly must be exorcised in madness? The very nature of the Heideggerian gesture with regard to madness—its allure, so to speak—allows one to glimpse, as we have tried to indicate, that the "subject" (there is no other word) is still what remains in question. But what must we understand here by "subject" if, in any case, we have ruled out any consideration of the *subject* itself, of the psychological and philosophical subject (of consciousness, will, desire, affect, etc.)?

The exclusion of madness assumes, as we have seen, not only the appropriation of the thought of the thinker, but, according to the *logic* of "loss," the appropriation of the unthought of that thought. This is, of course, where hermeneutics reaches its extreme limit. But both appropriations, as the text of *What Is Called Thinking?* shows, are in close solidarity with each other. In *Identity and Difference*, it is claimed that the already thought prepares the way for the unthought. The interpretation ventured in *What Is Called Thinking?* could never have been established without the immense *preparation* represented, in its larger part, by *Nietzsche*. The preparation, the appropriation of the already thought (or, more rigorously, the "finding," *das Finden*)—interpretation, in the most classic sense of the term, at the very moment when it proceeds, as we have also seen, from a first effort to ward off madness, involves itself in a specific work of *preparation* (but this time, in the pharmacological acceptation of the word) of Nietzsche's "work." Because a certain distrust informs Heidegger's attitude toward the earliest texts, as also toward *Zarathustra*, it is a matter of examining the status of what Nietzsche himself called his "major work," his *Hauptwerk*, that is, the status of the so-called *Will to Power*. This is not the place to examine in detail his long analyses, which, besides, necessarily continue to punctuate, as does the question of madness, the whole interpretation of Nietzsche. A strict relation of mutual dependence unites, in what is perhaps a wholly classical manner, the three questions of interpretation, madness, and the work—or rather seems to consign the question of madness and that of the work to a hermeneutical treatment. It is enough to recall briefly that neither the first texts (for example, *The Birth of Tragedy*), nor the aphoristic books, nor *Zarathustra* can be considered as works—works in the traditional sense, or (since the problem is raised for the "poetic" text that is *Zarathustra*) as a *work* in the sense in which Heidegger understands it in "The Origin of the Work of Art," that is, as a work of *Dichtung*.[76] "Nietzsche" is literally *worklessness* [*absence d'œuvre*]:

> We call Nietzsche's thought of will to power his *sole* thought. . . .
> Ever since the time when Nietzsche's thought of will to power first scintillated and became decisive for him (from about 1884 until the last weeks of his thinking, at the end of 1888), Nietzsche struggled for the *thoughtful configuration* [*um die* denkerische Gestaltung] of his sole thought. As far as the writing goes, in Nietzsche's plans and sketches this configuration looked like what he himself in accordance with tradition called the "major work." But this "major work" was never finished. Not only was it never finished, it never became a "work" at all in the sense of modern philosophical works [*Werke*] such as Descartes' *Meditationes de prima philosophia*, Kant's *Critique of Pure Reason*, Hegel's *Phenomenology of Spirit*, and Schelling's *Philosophical Investigations into the Essence of Human Freedom and the Objects Pertaining Thereto*.[77]

But for this *worklessness*, as previously for what concerned so-called "madness," all empirical explanations are immediately impugned, without the slightest hesitation, and in terms in which one can easily detect what unites the problem of madness with that of the work: "Why did Nietzsche's thought-paths to the will to power fail to converge in this kind of 'work'? Historiographers, psychologists, biographers, and other propagators of human curiosity are not caught short of explanations in such cases. In Nietzsche's 'case' especially there are ample reasons that explain the lack of the major work adequately enough for the common view."[78] The reasons one might invoke, and that have generally not failed to be invoked, are of little importance here. Even if they were *right*—and they are as right as medical discourse—they would not touch upon what is essential, that is, on the *necessity* of the work's impossibility, given what is at *issue* in the thought of "Nietzsche":

> These and other explanations for the fact that the "work" never got written are correct. They can even be documented by Nietzsche's own remarks. However, what about the assumption with regard to which these explanations are so zealously offered? The assumption that we are talking about a "work," written in the style of already familiar philosophical "major works," is unfounded. Nor can it be founded. The assumption is untrue, because it goes against the essence and kind of thought that will to power is.[79]

The *operation* undertaken here on the "work" corresponds so well to the one previously undertaken on "madness" that it is no longer really possible to be surprised that the renunciation of the "work" is ascribed to Nietzsche's *lucidity* and that, correlatively, the *reorganization* of the *Will to Power* according to "the hidden thought-path to the will to power" is done on texts from the years when "Nietzsche reached the point of greatest luminosity and tranquility in his thinking":

> The fact that Nietzsche himself speaks of a "major work" in letters to his sister and to the few, and ever fewer, sympathetic friends and helpers does not alone prove the justifiability of that assumption. Nietzsche clearly knew that even these few "closest" friends to whom he still expressed himself could not judge what was facing him. The constantly new forms in which he tried to expound his thinking in various publications [*Die immer wieder anderen Gestalten, in denen er sein Denken durch die verschiedenen Veröffentlichungen zum Wort zu bringen versuchte . . .*] clearly show how decidedly Nietzsche knew that the configuration of his fundamental thought had to be something other than a work in the traditional sense. The lack of completion, if one may dare to assert such a thing, in no way consists in the fact that a work "about" will to power was not completed. Lack of completion could only mean that the inner form of his unique thought was denied the thinker. . . .
>
> However, we still have to follow some kind of order when we try to penetrate to the thought-path of the will to power. . . . [W]e shall initially keep to those passages from the years 1887–88, the time in which Nietzsche reached the point of greatest luminosity and tranquility in his thinking [*in der Nietzsche die größte Helle und Ruhe seines Denkens erreichte*]. From these passages we shall again choose those in which the whole of the thought of will to power comes across and is expressed in its own coherence [*Geschlossenheit*]. For this reason we cannot call these passages fragments or pieces at all. If we nevertheless retain this designation, we then note that these individual passages converge or diverge not only in content but above all according to their inner shape and scope, according to the gathering power and luminosity of thought, and according to the depth of focus and the acuity of their utterance [*das Sagen*].[80]

To the extent that it assumes this "essentialist" justification of worklessness, the *preparatory* interpretation, the interpretation of the already thought, returns us, however, paradoxically—despite what had to be excluded of the subject so that the equally "essentialist" reduction of madness could succeed—to a kind of subject, defined by its lucidity, its knowledge, and the lucidity of its knowledge. This is the classical subject of intentions, of meaning, without which no interpretation is possible. But this return, this reference, are conditional, that is, made with the proviso that the form, the figure (*Gestalt*) of the "work," internal to his unique thought, could well have escaped the thinker himself, the lucidity and knowledge of the thinker. We know what is designated by this limit internal to thought: it is the limit that thought transgresses unbeknownst to itself, *without knowing it*, in the movement that necessarily leads it back to the unthought as to its essence and its truth. The form of the "work"—that is, the form of worklessness, the essential incompletion of the "work"—could thus very well be the specific form required by the unthought itself, by the "presence" or the labor of the unthought in thought. This is why "Nietzsche" is disquietingly ambiguous. And this is why it is necessary, in a way, to save him from this ambiguity—or, more precisely, to emphasize, in this ambiguity, what carries Nietzsche off course and draws him away from his own knowledge. Up to a point, the form *willed* by Nietzsche, the form imposed on his thought by his knowledge and his lucidity, hides or conceals the unthought of his thought. The knowledge of form masks the absence of thought. The knowledge of form, because it is a knowledge (and therefore also because it assumes a "subject," however fleeting it may be), *threatens* the essence of thought—with a threat as serious, as pressing, as irredeemable as that of madness.

What is, in its turn, this knowledge of form? In a way, *Nietzsche* offers no direct answer to this question, even though the whole analysis of the question of form and style in the first course and the whole debate conducted on *Dichtung* and on the *undichterisch* character of *Zarathustra* in the first volume as a whole, actually contain the answer. On the other hand, in its very brevity—and because it is concerned only with the commentary on *Zarathustra—What Is Called Thinking?* immediately indicates what is at stake. Several times, in fact, it is a question, not of form itself, but of *writing*—of the constraint or obligation of writing (*das Schreiben*) and of literature (*Literatur/Schriftstellertum*). It is not that the knowledge of form consists in the acceptance of writing or in the choice of this or that type of writing, of this or that style, even though this is a consideration and even though *Zarathustra*, in its way, is *too written*. Rather, and more rigorously, it is because the knowledge of form as such, as a knowledge, runs the risk of colliding with the obstacle of writing (with the bad danger of writing) and of *not knowing* how to surmount or remove it. There is a powerlessness to knowledge, which lets itself be taken in by writing: so it is that *Zarathustra*, because it is a *book*—and despite Nietzsche's great distrust of writing—conceals from thought what is most essential in thought itself:

> Learning, then, cannot be brought about by scolding. Even so, a man
> who teaches must at times grow noisy. In fact, he may have to scream
> and scream, although the aim is to make his students learn so quiet a
> thing as thinking. Nietzsche, most quiet and shiest of men, knew of this
> necessity. He endured the agony of having to scream. . . . But riddle
> upon riddle! What was once the scream "The wasteland grows . . . ,"
> now threatens to turn into chatter. The threat [*das Drohende*] of this
> perversion is part of what gives us food for thought. The threat is that
> perhaps this most thoughtful thought will today, and still more tomor-

row, become suddenly no more than a platitude, and as platitude spread
and circulate. This fashion of talking platitudes is at work in that endless profusion of books describing [*Beschreibungen*] the state of the
world today. They describe what by its nature is indescribable, because
it lends itself to being thought about only in a thinking that is a kind of
appeal, a call—and therefore must at times become a scream. Script
easily smothers the scream, especially if the script exhausts itself in
description. . . . The burden of thought is swallowed up [*verschwin-
det*] in the written script, unless the writing is capable of remaining,
even in the script itself, a progress of thinking, a way. About the time
when the words "The wasteland grows . . . " were born, Nietzsche
wrote in his notebook (GW XIV, p. 229, Aphorism 464 of 1885): "A
man for whom nearly all books have become superficial, who has kept
faith in only a few people of the past that they have had depth enough—
not to write what they knew." But Nietzsche had to scream. For him,
there was no other way to do it than by writing. That written scream of
Nietzsche's thought is the book which he entitled *Thus Spoke Zarathustra*.[81]

The powerlessness of knowledge here is not exactly a nonknowledge. It still
belongs to knowledge. It still assumes a consciousness and a subject. This is why
the threat of writing is all the more dangerous. But it is indeed a *bad* danger, that
is, a danger that, once again in an exorcising gesture, is to be denied as such and
opposed to the real danger, to the danger of thought itself. This theme is well
known:

Once we are so related and drawn to what withdraws, we are drawing
into what withdraws, into the enigmatic and therefore mutable nearness
of its appeal. Whenever a man is properly [*eigens*] drawing that way,
he is thinking—even though he may still be far away from what withdraws, even though the withdrawal may remain as veiled as ever. All
through his life and right into his death, Socrates did nothing else than
place himself into this draft, this current, and maintain himself in it.
This is why he is the purest thinker of the West. This is why he wrote
nothing. For anyone who begins to write out of thoughtfulness must inevitably be like those people who run to seek refuge from any draft too
strong for them. An as yet hidden history still keeps the secret why all
great Western thinkers after Socrates, with all their greatness, had to be
such fugitives. Thinking entered into literature.[82]

The gesture is clear enough here—including in what it saves from writing: the
progress of thinking, the way[83]—for us to understand now the meaning and the
function of the operation to be performed on Nietzsche's "work." What holds,
in fact, for *Zarathustra* (the obligation to write what one knows should be
screamed) does not hold for the major "work" in which Nietzsche's thought culminates, and which is precisely not "written," does not constitute a book. Whence

the possibility of following therein, "in its movement," the "progression of thought toward the will to power." Whence the necessity of beginning the interpretation of *Zarathustra* only belatedly, when the thinker's unique thought has been interpreted in the realm of what has, as far as possible, escaped writing. Whence, above all, the possibility of understanding the incompletion of *The Will to Power* as the form most appropriate for the essential movement of thought. In *The Will to Power*, the subject that chooses the form, that knows, that "writes," that, in writing, makes its spokesperson (the spokesperson of its thought)[84] speak, disappears or tends to disappear — the *"subject" of writing*, if you will, as fearsome (because it is in fact inseparable from it, because it is the same "subject") as the encumbering but enigmatic, abyssal "subject" of *Ecce Homo*, the "subject" of madness. This is why, in the end, thinking does not take place in writing. The thought of the will to power consists, on the contrary, in a pure joining of words (*Wortgefüge*) or in the pure joining of the words *will* and *power*. And when, beyond the recognition of the unique thought, it is a matter of "losing" what that thought thinks, it becomes necessary to listen to "what has no language," the unexpressed or the unsaid (*das Ungesprochene*) in the very language of the thinker[85] — that is, in the writing and language (at least a certain language) where thought, what is beyond writing and language, always risks losing itself [*s'abîmer*]. The movement that leads from "madness" to the unthought is therefore the same as that which leads from writing to the unexpressed. Writing and madness must be sublated together. This is why the hermeneutics of the unthought finds in *obliteration* — in a certain erasure of the letter — its surest defense against madness. It is in *obliteration* that all of Heidegger's operations ultimately take place. And if, as we have seen, what is most *proper* to each thought, what is *closest* to each thinker, is nothing other than the unexpressed or the unsayable — the most distant, the most concealed gift ("present") of being itself — *obliteration* is the other name of the "stratagem of *é-loignement*" and the primitive operation or maneuver on which the whole strategy of thought is built. If danger lies in madness, the enemy is the letter — thought in the letter or the becoming-letter of thought, in which there is the threat of something much worse than death. This becoming-letter of thought is philosophy *itself* insofar as, in it, the unsayable itself, or perhaps the unthinkable, is or might always be irreversibly, irredeemably lost.

As is known, all of this is not unrelated to *nihilism*, "whose essential interpretation [Nietzsche] concentrates in the terse sentence: 'God is dead,' " even though his metaphysics is "the ultimate entanglement [*die letzte Verstrickung*] in nihilism" and does not at all manage to overcome (*überwinden*) nihilism.[86] It is hardly possible here to reconsider the question of the interpretation of Nietzsche's word: "God is dead." But perhaps it is necessary now to read these three texts together, as the unique testimony to what the Heideggerian obliteration inevitably brings into play. For it is indeed this that we intended to confront:

The thinkers' thought is laid down in books. Books are books. The only allowance we make for books in philosophy is that they may be difficult to read. But one book is not like another, especially not when we are concerned with reading a "Book for Everyone and No One." And that is here our concern. For we cannot get around the necessity of finding Nietzsche first, in order that we may then lose him in the sense defined earlier. Why? Because Nietzsche's thinking gives voice and language to what now *is*—but in a language in which the two-thousand-year-old tradition of Western metaphysics speaks, a language which we all speak, which Europe speaks—though in a form transposed more than once, timeworn, shallowed, threadbare, and rootless. . . .

We do not hear it rightly, because we take [the language of the thinkers] to be mere expression, setting forth philosophers' views. But the thinkers' language tells what is. To hear it is in no case easy. Hearing it presupposes that we meet a certain requirement, and we do so only on rare occasions. We must acknowledge and respect it. To acknowledge and respect consists in letting every thinker's thought come to us as something in each case unique, never to be repeated, inexhaustible—and being shaken to the depths by what is unthought in his thought.[87]

The theological character of ontology does not come from the fact that Greek metaphysics was later assumed by the church theology of Christianity and transformed by it. It comes rather from the manner in which being, from the beginning, un-concealed itself as being. It is this unconcealing of being that first made possible Christian theology's seizing upon Greek philosophy—for better or for worse, the theologians will decide, beginning with the experience of the fact of Christianity, if they meditate on what is written in the first letter to the Corinthians by the apostle Paul: *Ouchi emoranen ho theos ten sophian tou kosmou*: "Has not God made foolish[ness] [*Torheit*] the wisdom of the world?" (I Cor., I, 20). *Sophia tou kosmou* is what, according to I, 22, the *Hellenes zetousin*, what the Greeks seek. *Prote philosophia* (philosophy proper) is explicitly called by Aristotle *zetoumene*—the one that is sought. Will Christian theology finally resolve to take seriously the word of the Apostle and accordingly consider philosophy to be folly?[88]

What is given to thinking to think is not some deeply hidden underlying meaning, but rather something lying near, that which lies nearest, which, because it is only this, we have therefore constantly already passed over [*übergehen*]. Through this passing over we are, without noticing it, constantly accomplishing the killing [*Töten*] in relation to the Being of whatever is in being.

In order to pay heed to it and to learn to pay heed, it can be enough for us simply to ponder for once what the madman [*der tolle Mensch*] says about the death of God and how he says it. Perhaps we will no longer pass by so quickly without hearing what is said at the beginning of the passage that has been elucidated: that the madman "cried incessantly: 'I seek God! I seek God!' ". . . .

The madman . . . is . . . the one who seeks God, since he cries out after God. Has a thinking man perhaps here really cried out *de profundis*? And the ear of our thinking [*Und das Ohr unseres Denkens*], does it still not hear the cry? It will refuse to hear it so long as it does not begin to think. Thinking begins only when we have come to know that reason, glorified for centuries, is the most stiff-necked adversary of thought.[89]

Access (2): Throwing Off the Safeguard

The "strategy" of thought is *obliteration*. We now begin to understand how and why this is the case. But the meaning of *obliterate* is ambiguous at the very least: it means at once to efface and to surcharge (superimpose). In each case, it is obviously a question of making an inscription disappear. But in each case, the erasure and the sense of the operation are no less completely different. Here is what our dictionaries, which it would be naïve in this case not to consult (however tedious this may be), say (or think) about the matter:

Obliterate. (*Littré*)
   1. To efface letters, marks. Time has obliterated this inscription.
   2. By extension, to make forget. Time has obliterated this opinion.
   "The further they move into the future, the easier it is for them to obliterate the past, or to give it the aspect they wish." J.-J. Rousseau, *Third Dialogue*.
   3. To close the hollow of a conduit.
   4. By extension, to obliterate an organ, make it disappear.
   5. To be obliterated, *ref. v.* — To be effaced; to be obstructed.

—Syn[onym]. To cross out, obliterate. To cross out a stamp is to annul it completely, remove all value from it by marking it with the canceling stamp.
—Hist[orical]. Sixteenth c. "It is so obliterated that it cannot at all be read," *Paslgr.* p. 740.[90]
—Etym[ology]. Lat. *obliterare*, from *ob*, on, and *littera*, in the sense of a stroke of writing.

Obliterate. (*Robert*)
   1. *Obsolete and archaic*. To make progressively disappear, but in such a way as to leave some traces. (See efface.) *The circulation of money imperceptibly obliterates the figures and letters imprinted on it.* (See wear off.)
   Esp. Render illegible, incomprehensible. *Obliterate a text*, cover it with erasures.
   Fig. Suppress, efface. *Images, memories, obliterated by time.*

It is clear from this brief sample that there is more than a simple ambiguity. And it would doubtless be easy (but "facile") to turn almost all of the senses of the word to account. But we will limit ourselves to the ambiguity, which will be, for our precise purposes here, largely sufficient. But why, exactly?

Because we have been led back, in the end, to the question that had to be asked at the beginning, but that we had to leave suspended, and that still awaits, at least in principle, an answer. This question was formulated more or less in the following way: To what, if not simply to *thought*, must we gain access in "Heidegger himself"? This was, we recall, a preliminary question. It was itself to open the way to "Nietzsche." It was supposed, at the very least, to allow us to ask that other question, namely, to what extent, how, and by what right it is possible to reconsider Heidegger's interpretation of "Nietzsche," that is, of Nietzsche's *thought*. This has obviously required going through—or else outlining, in the broadest strokes, the movement of going through—that interpretation itself. It has been unavoidably necessary to undertake the *reading* of this interpretation, and therein to let ourselves be guided by the necessity of calling into question the "strategy" of thought itself. An obligatory ruse, but a crude one. The answer was already known: it was merely a question of the text, of writing . . .

Now this is not at all the case. Or at least this appearance is misleading. And it is here that the ambiguity of obliteration comes into play. Appearances are misleading because it has never been a question in all of this of playing the "writing trick" on "Heidegger." Even less that of the subject or of madness. Nothing could have been more irrelevant. Or, if you will, this ruse would have been so crude that it could not have failed to turn back against itself—immediately. Precisely as we were able to say of the "stratagem of *é-loignement*" (whose relation to *obliteration*, to the erasure of the letter, is now known) that it is, after all, reversible. The ruse would have been turned back against itself (if we had yielded to it) for the simple reason that it would have ended up merely *opposing* writing (or the subject, or madness) to thought. We know full well what an opposition is, or rather how it functions: opposition as such is never maintained; on the contrary, one of the terms constituting it—because they constitute it—has always *already* sublated the other. And sublation always occurs in the direction [*sens*] of ideality, that is, in meaning [*Sens*] period. All the more so if it is a question of opposing thought to "something else": the sublating term can never be anything but thought itself, be it "negatively" or under *another name* (for example, as we see every day, under the name of writing, of the text, of the signifier, of madness, of desire, etc.). In other words, the ruse would have been turned back against itself because it would have entailed *deciding*, "against" Heidegger, what "Heidegger himself" is (in the same way that Heidegger decides, "against" Nietzsche, what "Nietzsche himself" is). But the power (and the desire) of *decision* belongs to thought, is even its distinguishing feature, as Heidegger never tires of repeating. We could, therefore, have very well insisted on speaking of writing, and nothing other than thought would in fact have been at stake.

What, then, has all this been about? An operation, certainly. And even, if you will, a "counter-operation." But provided we agree on the value of this *counter*. For it is precisely on this value that the entire operation itself will have been brought to bear. We have simply attempted—and nothing, indeed, is less clear, less definite, nothing resembles less a critique, a refutation, a "countering"—to render suspect the practice of *contra-diction*, that is, the utopia of *decision* (which is the utopia, and yet the only *topos*, of hermeneutics, of commentary). For example: the *questioning of Nietzsche against himself*, which governs (*animates*) all of Heidegger's interpretation, and which is like its motto. Doubtless, the question of what could be the *other* of thought that thought would not in advance have sublated, or would have been powerless to reappropriate, has never ceased to be raised, at the risk—and this is a fact—of nonsense (of insanity [*l'insensé*]). Doubtless, it has been necessary to bring into play, while wandering along this question, that which, in "Nietzsche," has some *chance*, as Bataille would have said, of resisting thought as such, that is, the incoherence or extreme violence (or the weakness, the fall, the shipwreck) of thought, all that which communicates, at bottom, with "empiricist," "naïve" virulence, with a certain type or style of writing, of which Derrida has spoken in *Of Grammatology* (and precisely in order to "oppose" it to Heidegger's interpretation).[91]

We have, therefore, never been able to avoid playing Nietzsche *against* Heidegger. But we have at least tried to contest or undo, as far as possible, this gesture of opposition.

But how does all of this concern the *ambiguity of obliteration*?

In that, contrary to all expectations, *effectively* nothing else is happening in Heidegger's interpretation of Nietzsche. It is true that *Heidegger himself* (let's accept one last time this fiction) does not know this. It is true that for *him* it is indeed a question of avoiding, in "Nietzsche," a threat, of preventing the irruption of that *other* of thought which would not be thought itself or would not be—like the un-thought that must be written un-*thought*[92]—of the order of thought. A threat much worse, probably, than that of nihilism, which can be thought and therefore mastered. The incoherence, the excess, the lack of control (the irreversible escape or loss of thought itself in all thoughts, in the frenetic multiplicity of words, of languages, and of names—philo*sophy* and philo*logy* unleashed), this whole movement of a racing motor, a mad machine, which is that of the "last Nietzsche," this, indeed, escapes mastery. Or else one must *oppose* it, blindly, so to speak, with all the deepest, the most deeply buried resources of thought. *Arrest* thought, or remove it, by a *step back*, from this danger: draw back. And so measure, maintain, economize. Save and safeguard: the earth for the world, *Dichtung* against literature, truth against everything that could shake it. Nothing is accidental if *safeguard* is the proper name of truth, the very truth of *aletheia*—the master word: "One day we shall learn to think our exhausted word for truth [*Wahrheit*] in terms of the guard [*Wahr*]; to experience truth as the safeguard [*Wahrnis*] of Being; and to understand that, as presencing, Being belongs to this safeguard."[93]

And yet, once all of this has been acknowledged—once all of this has been understood as that which governs and imposes, within the interpretation of Nietzsche, the *obliteration* of the Nietzschean text—we must observe that this *obliteration obliterates itself*, that is, takes the "form" of an interminable surcharge or of an interminable superimposition. The erasure of the text engenders its proliferation, forces it. Interpretation is written, and not only is it written but it is as though writing, from the moment it starts, carried interpretation outside its own limits, obliged it to take itself up again, to begin again, to repeat itself in every possible way, without, precisely, being able to stop. The thinking that does not want to hear anything about the text, or that wants to hear the least possible about it, never stops producing text, and a text about which one will have said very little if one is content merely to deride its incantatory, archaicizing, or laboriously "poeticizing" allure. It would be better to try to understand:

1. What necessity of writing—perceived, moreover, from the beginning[94]—played a part in the break of *Sein und Zeit*;

2. Why this break—at the moment when thought seemed to become fixed on the theme of truth—triggered the passage through the question of language and of *Dichtung* and through the reading of Hölderlin and Nietzsche;

3. Why this passage definitively confirmed or consecrated a radical *worklessness* (the proliferation of multiple texts that constantly overlap one another, summarize one another, call to one another, etc.), as though the crossing of the Nietzschean text had *contaminated* Heidegger's own;

4. Why, despite all the denials, this sort of textual "adventure" is to such an extent attentive and concerted, as evidenced by the uninterrupted maze of prefaces, postfaces, forewords, notes, clarifications, datings, localizations, etc.;

5. Why the impulse was so strong to attempt such a working through of language (of vocabulary and syntax) and of "form" or "style"—"forms" and "styles" (the course, the essay, the poem, the dialogue, etc.).

One can always ascribe writing, especially when it is precautionary, to an exorcising mania or to the repetition compulsion. But perhaps it is strictly impossible to write anything but this: "What forces me to write, I suppose, is the fear of going mad."

This applies as much to "Nietzsche" as to "Heidegger."

Translated by Thomas Trezise

Chapter 5
The Scene Is Primal

The joy aroused by the tragic myth has the same origin as the joyous sensation of dissonance in music.

Nietzsche, *The Birth of Tragedy*

Eros: *You ask too much, Thanatos.*

Pavese, *Dialogues with Leuco*

The remarks that follow are based on Freud's text published by Max Graf in 1942: "Psychopathic Characters on the Stage." There are at least two major reasons for taking an interest in this text. First, of all the posthumous texts, this one is the most puzzling, not only because Freud did not publish it (or did not wish to publish it, or did not write it with publication in mind), but also because he quite probably "forgot" that it even existed, and, at any rate, *relinquished* it.[1] The case, if not unique, is nonetheless rare enough to attract attention, even to pique curiosity — and merit examination: which of course means looking first of all at the history of Freudian thought and the position that this semiclandestine text might have occupied (and may still occupy) in that history. The other, more far-reaching reason is that by virtue of its object — the theater — this text (which nearly everyone would now agree to consider one of Freud's most important on the subject) openly poses, and in terms that may not be found anywhere else, the decisive question (on which is focused a whole contemporary critique of Freud) of the relationship of psychoanalysis to theatricality, or, more generally, to *representation*.

"Somewhere," it is likely that these two reasons are one and the same, and this is what I would like to try briefly to indicate here.

The Scene of the Anti-scene

In order to accomplish this, we need to refer to the French situation (or "scene") — the philosophical and political debate surrounding Freud that has been going on for several years, particularly since the publication of *Anti-Oedipus*, and, in a less dramatic way, the disclosure of the results of Girard's research.[2]

Indeed, we must bear in mind what happened once the value of theatricality as a *model* or even a *matrix* in the constitution of analysis had been theoretically buttressed (Lacan, of course) and then confirmed through commentary (for instance, Starobinski or Green)[3] – once, consequently, so-called "applied psychoanalysis" had been refuted, and not only one of Freud's most enduring metaphorical networks but also the very construction of the "analytic scene" had been rigorously situated and defined. Because, at the same time, but elsewhere, the consequences of the Heideggerian disruption [*sollicitation*][4] of representation were beginning to be felt and (accentuated and displaced) actually to *work*,[5] the reaction was not long in coming: whatever the problematic nature of the analytic "sceno-morphy" thus revealed, whatever the strict precautions surrounding the account of the "closure of representation" (and first of all the determination of the very concept of "closure"), a certain critical haste, which could not be called beneficial simply because it shakes up academic habits a bit and opposes to capital what capital itself is quite likely to encourage, was only too happy to have the opportunity to get rid of one more burdensome "cultural cadaver" that – so it was said – had had its day.

It appeared then that Freud had quite simply remained a prisoner of the Western system or mechanism of representation – Greco-Italian scenography, classical dramaturgy, etc. – and that he had even reinforced its constraining power by identifying it with a structural necessity of the human subject in general. This explained at once the timorous, relatively sterile, and conservative quality of his aesthetics, the regressive (not to say reactionary) ambiguity of his "politics," and above all the (institutionally, but also theoretically) repressive nature of analysis itself. This description is obviously schematic and needs to be "nuanced" (and we need above all to explain our quarrel with the obscure presuppositions of anti-Freudianism as well as our reservations vis-à-vis all summarily "anti" movements); but this corresponds more or less to what has happened in France – and probably elsewhere – during these past few years.

Let us cite as evidence (not only because it is essential to do so, but also because this is one way to pursue a discussion begun in different circumstances) a relatively recent piece by Lyotard that, in reference to the text of Freud's that concerns us here, recalls the main points of this critical motif. Lyotard writes:

> It has already been recognized that, compared with the other arts, the theatre enjoys a privileged status in Freudian thought and practice. Freud himself not only admits this; on at least one occasion he appears to offer justification for it. In a short paper of 1905–6 entitled "Psychopathic Characters on the Stage" he sketches the genesis of psychoanalysis in terms of the problem of guilt and expiation: the sacrifice designed to mollify the Gods is the parent form; Greek tragedy, itself

derived, as Freud believed, from the sacrifice of the goat, gives birth to socio-political drama and then to individual (psychological) drama, of which psychoanalysis is the offspring. This genealogy not only reveals the extent to which, by Freud's own admission, the psychoanalytic relationship is organized like a ritual sacrifice; it also suggests the identity of the various spaces in which sacrifice takes place: temple, theatre, the chambers of politics and doctors' surgeries—all *disreal* spaces, as Laplanche and Pontalis might call them: autonomous spaces no longer subject to the laws of so-called reality, regions where desire can play in all its ambivalence, spaces where for the "proper objects" of desire are substituted accepted *images*, which are assumed to be not fictions but authentic libidinal products that have simply been exempted from the censorship imposed by the reality principle.[6]

We are, of course, in no way suggesting that this is false. On the contrary, we should even stress that this is a necessary reading and thus acknowledge once and for all that it does truly turn up something in Freud that cannot be avoided—something, moreover, that Ehrenzweig has in fact been one of the few to point out. Nor do we intend to present "philological" reservations, as is often done in such cases, and, for example, to reproach Lyotard not only for forcing the text in order to make it yield a genealogy of analysis that is not really there (Freud, for his part, does not go beyond comparing),[7] but also for rather boldly and unceremoniously "mixing up" the text with the well-known paragraph seven of the fourth chapter of *Totem and Taboo* (where Freud places considerable emphasis on that which, concerning the origin of the theater, is here simply embryonic, and where he in fact speaks of the "tragic misdeed," of guilt, of the payment of debt, etc.). This would be of only secondary interest.

Let us say, therefore, that Lyotard is basically right.

But he is only right on one condition—or rather two, but these are merely two sides of the same coin.

He is right, first of all, on the condition that one posit (or imagine) that there is a *reality* "outside of representation"—that the real, far from being the impossible as it was for Lacan and Bataille, is what can actually present itself as such, and that consequently there is, in general, such a thing as *presentation*, a full, whole, virginal, inviolate, and inviolable presence. A wild state where we could be, where we would be, *ourselves*, unalienated and undissociated subjects (in whatever form), before any transgression or prohibition, before any war or rivalry—obviously also prior to any institution. Lyotard is right, then, on the condition that, once and for all and without further ado, we relegate the "reality principle" to the arsenal of outmoded metaphysical-civilizing ideas [*vieilleries métaphysico-policières*].

But his being right also depends, on the other hand, on our relating the analytic *necessity* of the representational mechanism (a necessity affirmed by Freud and that, practically speaking, determines analysis) exclusively to *desire* (and to a pleasure without hiatus, itself full, whole, etc.), or more precisely (if we are to remain faithful to the slippage that Lyotard's operation constantly implies), exclusively to "instinctual effects" ["productions pulsionnelles"], which in turn come down exclusively to *libido*. If analysis is only concerned with drives *as* libidinal, if, in general, there is only the libidinal—itself invulnerable, never jagged, or bruised, or paralyzed (that is, never run through by what darkens it or furrowed by what dooms it to die)—then one certainly can, and even must, call into question the derealizing function of what Luce Irigaray calls the "analytic practicable." The whole problem is to know whether analysis only concerns the libidinal, or whether the only drive that there is (we do not say: *that manifests itself*), is one reduced to libido—and a libido quite plainly "positive."

If we raise this question, it is obviously not out of respect for "Freudian orthodoxy": orthodoxy as such is of little interest to us, and we know only too well to what extent *orthopedics* (that is, ontological, virile, controlling, and properly political rectification) enters into any orthodoxy, any subservience to a master discourse. It is also clear that it is not in order to "save" Freud (who quite capably saves "himself") from a *univocal* reading: it is hard to see what interest would be served in the reestablishment of ambiguity. But it is in order to shield Freud, that is, "his" text, from an operation that concerns us at least insofar as it is in fact organized only in terms of uni- or equi-vocity. This is a question concerning the use of texts and the function of criticism. It is also a "political" question, if that is what one cares about. In Freud, if you prefer, things are always *a lot more complicated*; there is even nothing, ultimately—whatever might be Freud's desire and the incontestable (but *reversible*) critical power of analysis—that would allow one to *decide* with certainty on any meaning (first, last, hidden, etc.) in order to appropriate or exclude it. In order, in general, to appropriate *and* exclude. It is not a question here of preserving a benevolent "neutrality." Rather, we would take issue with the system of doctrinal *identification*, in the name of an idea of criticism that is, let us say, less simple, less assured, less triumphant—and consequently less "confiscatable." A little subtlety, given the enormity of the stakes, is doubtless not too much to ask.

Freud and Nietzsche: Aristotle

In point of fact, the charge brought against Freud by Lyotard is double.

On the one hand, it is concerned with the representational mechanism as a mechanism of derealization, that is, with the (en)closure (the *temple*) of the tragic site—the stage as a *substitute* for the site of the actual ritual sacrifice commemorating the murder of the *Urvater* (the *Totem and Taboo* version, but that hardly matters here). It even concerns already, if one reads between the lines, that thing which is not yet theatricality but ritual, in other words, the religious—

regardless of whether this implies any real violence, a sacrifice, an exclusion, etc. As such, it is closely akin to what Girard says (though Lyotard might object to this comparison) when, having conceived of Christianity as the only known explicit acceptance of violence, he critiques all of those substitute institutions (religious, political, aesthetic) which are intended to curb that violence, but which, by masking it or causing it to be forgotten, only aggravate it.

But, on the other hand, Lyotard's indictment of Freud has to do with the "psychic" *instrument* or *apparatus* of this derealization, with what makes this evocation of sacrifice and murder, this reminder of suffering, not only tolerable but desirable (even to the point of producing therapeutic effects). In other words, it also has to do with what Lyotard—calling into question the libidinal formalism of Freudian aesthetics, the whole intrication (nonetheless complex and extending far beyond mere "aesthetics") of *Lustgewinn, Nebengewinn, Vorlust, Verlockungsprämie*, etc.—calls the hypnotic, anesthetizing power of form.[8] As a result of this power, Freud was supposedly unable to take into consideration, or even simply to notice, what Ehrenzweig calls the *disruptive* (as opposed to the merely substitutive) function of art—modern art, in particular. This, moreover, implies, as one might suspect, that art takes on more than a simply "secondary" function, that it has the power to confront us with the real itself (with *presence*), that it can somehow or other constitute an *event*: that it does, if we may venture the expression, *effectively affect* us.

It is not hard to see that this double accusation is aimed less at Freud himself than at a whole philosophical tradition (if not practically *the* whole philosophical tradition), and in particular Aristotle—under whose authority Freud explicitly places himself at the beginning of "Psychopathic Characters," but under whose authority he perhaps in general always placed himself, either out of prudence, or, let us admit it, out of "academicism" (but also for other less anecdotal reasons that will be revealed in their proper time). It could be said that from the moment he takes cover in this way behind philosophical, Aristotelian guarantees, he is, if we may be allowed to use the metaphor, holding out the stick with which to be beaten. It remains to be seen, however, what exactly are the function and precise protocol of this apparently unqualified allegiance. And therein lies the whole problem.

How, in fact, does "Psychopathic Characters" function? How does this text present itself? Modestly, as is nearly always the case with Freud, as a simple development of Aristotle's theatrical poetics intended to "clarify" it: "If, as has been assumed since the time of Aristotle, the purpose of drama [*Schauspiel*] is to arouse 'terror and pity' and so 'to purge the emotions,' we can describe that purpose in rather more detail by saying that it is a question of opening up sources of pleasure or enjoyment in our emotional life."[9] But it is obvious that the gesture really masks—as is *also* always the case—the ill-concealed desire to produce the *truth* of that poetics, to size it up and sum it up. In other words, "Psychopathic Characters" presents itself as nothing but an analytic reading—an interpretation and, therefore, a *translation* (inevitably active, *transforming*, as we shall see) of the *Poetics*. Upon this reading, it is true (but this does not really change anything), is superimposed an analogous or homologous translation of the average response of "German romanticism" to the question of the difference between Ancient and Modern (Greek and Occidental, Oriental and Hesperian, etc.) as this question had been posed in Germany roughly from the time of Lessing and as, from Hölderlin, Hegel, or the Schlegels right up until Nietzsche, it had continued to occupy the whole field of historico-aesthetic investigation (that is, everything that was in fact eventually to produce a general theory of culture or civilization).

In order to evaluate precisely the meaning and significance of Freud's gesture, it is perhaps enough simply to compare it with what Nietzsche attempted in *The Birth of Tragedy*: the operations are basically similar even if the intentions at the outset are completely different. Let me stress that this is not an entirely random comparison: whatever may have been Freud's practically constant "denial" of this connection, we are nevertheless today very well aware of just how closely psychoanalysis is tied to certain of Nietzsche's major intuitions. In fact, the question raised by Nietzsche concerning tragedy—that is, concerning art in general, of which tragedy, in an utterly classical (or, we might say, utterly Hegelian) way, is the paragon—is exactly the same as the one Freud, by way of Aristotle, poses in the very first two paragraphs of "Psychopathic Characters." Even the terminology used by both (I am thinking in particular of chapter 22 of *The Birth of Tragedy*) is the same. One can formulate the question as follows: how is it that the spectacle of suffering, of annihilation and death, can lead to pleasure [*jouissance*]—and a pleasure superior to that aroused by any other spectacle? It is true that Nietzsche (who is not, for all that, unaware of the Aristotelian origin of the question) takes issue with any answer that does not ultimately refer to "aesthetic principles"—first and foremost with that of Aristotle. Nietzsche, in other words, challenges the *cathartic* interpretation of tragedy. And not without vehemence. But in favor of what? Let us reread the indictment:

> Never since Aristotle has an explanation of the tragic effect been
> offered from which aesthetic states or an aesthetic activity of the lis-
> tener could be inferred. Now the serious events are supposed to prompt
> pity and fear to discharge themselves in a way that relieves us; now we
> are supposed to feel elevated and inspired by the triumph of good and
> noble principles, at the sacrifice of the hero in the interest of a moral
> vision of the universe. I am sure that for countless men precisely this,
> and only this, is the effect of tragedy, but it plainly follows that all
> these men, together with their interpreting aestheticians, have had no
> experience of tragedy as a supreme *art*.

The pathological discharge, the catharsis of Aristotle, of which philologists are not sure whether it should be included among medical or moral phenomena, recalls a remarkable notion of Goethe's. "Without a lively pathological interest," he says, "I, too, have never yet succeeded in elaborating a tragic situation of any kind, and hence I have rather avoided than sought it. Can it perhaps have been yet another merit of the ancients that the deepest pathos was with them merely aesthetic play, while with us the truth of nature must co-operate in order to produce such a work?"

We can now answer this profound final question in the affirmative after our glorious experiences, having found to our astonishment that the deepest pathos can indeed be merely aesthetic play in the case of musical tragedy. Therefore we are justified in believing that now for the first time the primal phenomenon of the tragic can be described with some degree of success. Anyone who still persists in talking only of those vicarious effects proceeding from extra-aesthetic spheres, and who does not feel that he is above the pathological-moral process, should despair of his aesthetic nature.[10]

I have insisted on quoting this text at some length in order to show clearly just to what extent we seem to find ourselves here in diametrical opposition to Freudian discourse. One might even be tempted to say that there could be no better target of such accusations than Freud—although in order to do so one would have to credit Nietzsche with a strange gift of prophecy. In fact, this is not the case at all. Indeed, considering the specifically Nietzschean mechanism (that is, the opposition of the Dionysian and the Apollinian, of music and the plastic arts, of the "immediate reproduction" and the mediate, reduplicated reproduction of the originary One—of originary pain and contradiction), the response here is perfectly clear: tragedy, from whatever point of view one looks at it—including, therefore, its "properly" musical or Dionysian aspect—never *presents*, as such, the suffering that it (re)presents (*darstellt*), but on the contrary presupposes a space of derealization, if you will, circumscribed in advance and thanks to which the "deepest pathos" is in fact never anything but *aesthetic play*. I would emphasize that even music, even the worst music (that of *Tristan*, for example)—even *dissonance*—still (or already) arouses pleasure. And we know why: because somewhere, including on the ontological level (that is, still on the aesthetic level, assuming that the world itself is to be grasped as an "aesthetic phenomenon" or that art, in a narrow sense, is to be understood as an "imitation" of the process of production of what is)—somewhere, then, *suffering itself is pleasure*, if only the pleasure of being forced into *discharge* (*Entladung*), that is, into the catharsis of the contradiction that constitutes it.

This is precisely, mutatis mutandis (and minus the ontological "speculation"), the type of response that Freud puts forward—prudently—in "Psychopathic Characters." The apparent submission to the Aristotelian schema should not deceive us. It is true that Freud at no point goes beyond the limits of what Nietzsche designates as the "pathological-moral" interpretation of tragedy. One can at least superficially imagine this. And it is true that he seems to be merely translating Aristotle. The first few lines are even a quasi-literal translation of the text of the *Poetics*: for if Freud, at the outset, appears to commit or repeat the famous mistranslation concerning the catharsis of the passions in general,[11] it is clear, later in the text, when it is more specifically a question of drama (*Drama*), that is, strictly speaking, of tragedy, that he means catharsis in the narrower sense of a "purging" of suffering alone (that is, of terror and compassion). And we could show here precisely, with texts to back us up, how "libidinal derealization," that is, the law of economy (of savings) governing aesthetic pleasure, very faithfully transcribes the *charan ablabe*, the "joy without harm" that Aristotle, in the *Politics* (VIII, 1341b), attributes to catharsis in its specifically medical, homeopathic, "pharmaceutical" function (catharsis used *pharmakeias charin*).[12]

The fact remains, however, that on one fundamental point this "faithful" translation actually upsets the Aristotelian theory. This is when—doubtless going back, whether knowingly or not, from the medical to the religious, which is probably at the root of catharsis—Freud posits mimesis (that is, "mimetism," or, to use his term, identification) as what basically makes the "cathartic machine" itself possible. Even though, like Aristotle, he maintains the analogy between art and children's play[13] (and continues to do so until—*but not including*—*Jenseits des Lustprinzips*), Freud, as Starobinski has stressed, also does exactly what Nietzsche does in the last chapters of *The Birth of Tragedy*, that is, he transfers Aristotelian *recognition* (*anagnorisis*) to the relation between stage and audience in such a way as to "interest" the spectator in it.[14] In so doing, Freud actually introduces something that does not belong to the Aristotelian "program" but explains the connection between catharsis and mimesis that had remained *unthought* throughout the entire tradition (except for Nietzsche):[15] namely, that tragic pleasure is essentially a *masochistic* pleasure, and thus maintains some relationship with *narcissism* itself (this is not actually expressed in 1906, but we shall soon see why):

> Being present as an interested spectator at a spectacle or play [here
> written literally *Schau-Spiel*: the "play-of-view"] does for adults what
> play [*Spiel*] does for children, whose hesitant hopes of being able to do
> what grown-up people do are in that way gratified. The spectator is a
> person who experiences too little, who feels that he is a "poor wretch to
> whom nothing of importance can happen," who has long been obliged
> to damp down, or rather displace, his ambition to stand in his own person at the hub of world affairs; he longs to feel and to act and to ar-
> range things according to his desires—in short, to be a hero. And the

playwright and actor enable him to do this by allowing him *to identify himself* with a hero. They spare him something, too. For the spectator knows quite well that actual heroic conduct such as this would be impossible for him without pains and sufferings and acute fears, which would almost cancel out the enjoyment. He knows, moreover, that he has only *one* life and that he might perhaps perish even in a *single* such struggle against adversity. Accordingly, his enjoyment is based on an illusion; that is to say, his suffering is mitigated by the certainty that, firstly, it is someone other than himself who is acting and suffering on the stage, and, secondly, that after all it is only a game, which can threaten no damage to his personal security. . . .

Several other forms of creative writing [*Dichtung*], however, are equally subject to these same preconditions for enjoyment. . . . But drama [*Drama*] seeks to explore emotional possibilities more deeply and to give an enjoyable shape even to forebodings of misfortune; for this reason it depicts the hero in his struggles, or rather (with masochistic satisfaction) in defeat. This relation to suffering and misfortune might be taken as characteristic of drama, whether, as happens in serious plays, it is only *concern* that is aroused, and afterwards allayed, or whether, as happens in tragedies, the suffering is actually realized.[16]

It is clear that the reference to masochism does not invalidate the *economic* nature of tragic pleasure (we find proof of this later in the exclusion of physical illness from the theatrical space, an exclusion that follows directly from the law of compensation for suffering that governs theatrical identification and therefore, normatively, dramatic form itself).[17] The economic system deployed here is, however, not simple — there already begins to emerge a paradox that we know will have serious consequences when the question of masochism (and narcissism) comes metapsychologically to inform the doctrine of drives. This is the whole question of the role assigned to "supplementary yield," to *Nebengewinn*, in the "economy" of "pleasure."

Indeed, Freud explains that "to purge the emotions (the passions)" means to open wide "sources of pleasure [*Lust*] and enjoyment [*Genuß*]" in our emotional life — immediately adding (he was at this time in the process of writing *Jokes* . . .): "just as, in the case of intellectual activity, joking or fun open up similar sources, many of which that activity had made inaccessible." The dissymmetrical nature of the comparison ("intellectual activity" here appears as an agent of repression) should come as no surprise: the reference to jokes in fact begins the process of introducing what the last paragraph of "Psychopathic Characters" will identify as the "forepleasure" (*Vorlust*) of *Three Essays* and *Jokes*,[18] that is, the "supplementary yield" acting as an "incentive bonus" (*Verlockungsprämie*)[19] that, far from referring back to some "anesthetizing power of form," as Lyotard would have it, on the contrary presupposes a specific pleasure linked to "surplus tension" (*Höherspannung*), or, if you will, a "surplus tension" (an increase in pain) sought for its own sake:

> In this connection the prime factor is unquestionably the process of get-
> ting rid of one's own emotions by "blowing off steam" [*das Austoben*];
> and the consequent enjoyment corresponds on the one hand to the relief
> produced by a thorough discharge [*Abfuhr*] and on the other hand, no
> doubt, to an accompanying sexual excitation; for the latter, as we may
> suppose, appears as a supplementary yield [*Nebengewinn*] whenever an
> affect is aroused, and gives people the sense, which they so much de-
> sire, of a surplus tension [*Höherspannung*] in their psychical state.[20]

Theatrical pleasure, in other words, is *thoroughly* masochistic: the only pleasure that comes from suffering is prepared—*formally*—by this supplement of
pleasure which itself, however, implies pain. As in Nietzsche, or Goethe, the
"deepest pathos" is consequently only "aesthetic play" (could this be a possible definition of masochism?). And this, furthermore, explains, again as in Nietzsche,
the superiority of Greek tragedy over the drama of the Moderns:

> Suffering of every kind is thus the subject-matter of drama, and from
> this suffering it promises to give the audience pleasure. Thus we arrive
> at a first precondition of this form of art: that it should not cause suffer-
> ing to the audience, that it should know how to compensate, by means
> of the possible satisfactions involved, for the sympathetic suffering
> which is aroused. (Modern writers have particularly often failed to obey
> this rule.)[21]

This is why the second analytic "translation" that Freud proposes here is that
of the relation between Greek and modern (Shakespearean) dramaturgy, in keeping with the perpetual contrasting of *Hamlet* with *Oedipus* that this text, despite
appearances, does not belie.[22] Genealogically, the modern "break" occurs with
the introduction into the tragic conflict of the unconscious, that is, of the difference between the repressed and the nonrepressed. Up to and including psychological drama—which, in Freud's typology, means (beyond "character" and social
drama) "love tragedy" and opera—the theater still falls within the scope of the
Greek representational system. But once what the *Traumdeutung* calls the "secu-
lar advance of repression"[23] has come about—once the general space of neurosis
has therefore been established—we enter the truly modern period of drama:

> But the series of possibilities grows wider; and psychological drama turns
> into psychopathological drama when the source of the suffering in which
> we take part and from which we are meant to derive pleasure is no
> longer a conflict between two almost equally conscious impulses [which,
> of course, was the case in *Oedipus*] but between a conscious impulse and
> a repressed one. Here the precondition of enjoyment is that the spectator

should himself be a neurotic, for it is only such people who can derive pleasure instead of simple aversion from the revelation and the more or less conscious recognition of a repressed impulse. In anyone who is *not* neurotic this recognition will meet only with aversion and will call up a readiness to repeat the act of repression which has earlier been successfully brought to bear on the impulse: for in such people a single expenditure of repression has been enough to hold the repressed impulse completely in check. But in neurotics the repression is on the brink of failing; it is unstable and needs a constant renewal of expenditure, and this expenditure is spared if recognition of the impulse is brought about.[24]

And this, in point of fact, explains why, in order to maintain—apparently as is—the thesis of catharsis, it was necessary to modify the Aristotelian schema of "recognition" by taking into account identification: only the principle of identification allows for recognition of the repressed. But that in no way prevents modern catharsis from being as "economical" as that of the ancients (with some rules inevitably subtler and trickier to handle, such as the rule of *averted attention* that Freud sets forth regarding *Hamlet* and whose purpose is to weaken the resistances intrinsic to neurosis).[25] Besides, as before, the installation of the system implies an exclusion, which is no longer just that of physical suffering and illness but that of mental illness as well, of neurosis that is realized, constituted, and "foreign" (and thus resistant to recognition). One could doubtless go so far as to say that the exclusion pertains to *insanity* or *madness*.

Obscene Death

The entire operation is consequently without mystery—if not without difficulty. Here we find, in condensed form, the "economically oriented" aesthetics whose development Freud will later, in *Jenseits des Lustprinzips*, still feel obliged to recommend.[26] But we know that he will in fact only bring the subject up again in order to deny that it has any relevance to a far more serious and difficult question, the question of what is prior to the "pleasure principle" or beyond it—"independent" of it, in any case, "and perhaps more primitive." We know as well that when this question arises it is precisely *in* the space opened up by the breakdown of the Aristotelian analogy previously maintained between (children's) play and the *Schau-Spiel*. The allusion to Aristotle is even perfectly explicit: "Nevertheless [that is, whatever the insurmountable difficulty presented by the *undecidable* nature of play], it emerges from this discussion that there is no need to assume the existence of a special imitative instinct in order to provide a motive for play."[27]

But that is not all. For we know, finally, that if play is thus to be dissociated from "artistic play and artistic imitation," it is essentially for two reasons. The first is that play does not involve the representational mechanism, or, to be more exact (and because one will always argue the opposite by referring to the bedstead of the *fort/da-Spieler*), the *spectacular* mechanism. If play is mimetism, it is effective, direct, *active* mimetism, comparable to the actor's (not the spectator's), and thus presupposes a more immediate identification. But this mimetism is at the same time more compromising than the actor's, the difference constitutive of the stage having disappeared (or being still just embryonic) and hence (to some extent at least, assuming one must allow for a *primal* internalization of the representational split) the derealizing closure of the theatrical site not yet being really instituted. The other reason is that since play is, in the last instance, still necessarily included in a *libidinal economy* (but is there any other kind, and what would an *economy* that is not "erotic" be?), it therefore, by virtue of being reproductive (of the "disagreeable") and repetitive, and by virtue of its "abreactive" and mastering function, presupposes pleasure as an *indirect* goal (unlike theatrical participation). In other words, whether it occurs in the form of a renunciation of pleasure (however provisional) or of a reiteration of suffering (however transient and simulated), play in one way or another presupposes the breakdown — perhaps brief, furtive, barely suggested — of the economic system. There is in play, at some strictly unspecifiable point, a *loss*. And so a risk. One must lose (and risk oneself) in play in order to win (regain oneself) there. This is, but taken the other way around, the whole problem of the *general economy* in the Bataillian sense. The economy of play is not a simple economy like that of the theater or spectacle (at least according to the Aristotelian interpretation); it is rather a *deferred* economy. What is missing, finally, is the purely anesthetizing *form* (supposing at any rate that such a thing exists), even if play is in reality the birth of form. And there can be no doubt about what this *différance* — in the Derridean sense — at the same time reveals and conceals concerning profit, pleasure, security, and even life (survival); what it indicates without ever showing: nothing other than (the) death (drive) "itself."

Precisely, and yet — through a kind of chiasmus in which analysis becomes disoriented and which reveals at least the stubborn complexity of the question — in relation to dramatic mimesis itself and not play, this is, as we have seen, what Freud, in "Psychopathic Characters," begins to touch upon when he introduces masochism in order to account for tragic pleasure. The introduction of masochism is all the more problematic at this time as it is situated on the very border between stage and "audience," actors and spectators, and as "masochistic satisfaction" is already opposed here to "direct enjoyment" (a contradiction that explains the necessary theatrical — which is to say also epic — "magnification" of the victim): "Heroes are first and foremost rebels against God or against something divine; and pleasure is derived, as it seems, from the affliction of a weaker being in the face of divine might — a pleasure due to masochistic satisfaction as well as to direct enjoyment of a character whose greatness is insisted upon in spite of everything."[28] But this is still what Freud betrays when he submits to the systematic, uninterrupted constraint of excluding both illness and madness. In each case, the very ambivalence of *identification* is at issue, an ambivalence around which will be reorganized—although not without difficulty and only after the duality of drives has been established and secured—both the description of the Oedipus complex and the construction of that "scientific myth" here in embryo which is the hypothesis of the "primal horde."[29]

In a brief overview such as this it is clear that one can hardly allow oneself the luxury of tracing, in all of its complexity, the textual network in which the Freudian doctrine of death is fragilely elaborated and in which are inscribed, as Freud always indicated in his many historical recapitulations of the *Trieblehre*, the interimplicated questions of masochism, narcissism, identification, etc. But as for what interests us most particularly here, that is to say the question of theatricality itself, we can at least retain what this text of 1906 does not manage to say (though it does start in that direction—going just far enough, in short, to remain aporetic),[30] which is quite simply what a text of 1916 will say directly: namely, that the representational break does not come *in* the libido but *between* the libido (desire) and death, and that it is, therefore, in other words, the very *limit* of the economic mechanism in general:

It is indeed impossible to imagine our own death; and whenever we attempt to do so we can perceive that we are in fact still present as spectators. Hence the psycho-analytic school could venture on the assertion that at bottom no one believes in his own death, or, to put the same thing in another way, that in the unconscious every one of us is convinced of his own immortality.[31]

Death cannot—any more than can the woman's or the mother's sex—present itself as such, "in person," as Lyotard would say. Just as there is an *apotropaic* structure to the feminine abyss (to obscenity),[32] there is an unavoidable *necessity* to the re-presentation (staging, *mise en scène*, *Darstellung*) of death, and consequently to identification, to mimetism:

We . . . seek in the world of fiction, in literature and in the theater compensation [*Ersatz*] for what has been lost in life. There we still find people who know how to die. . . . There alone too the condition can be fulfilled which makes it possible for us to reconcile ourselves with death: namely, that behind all the vicissitudes of life we should still be able to preserve a life intact. . . . In the realm of fiction we find the plurality of lives which we need. We die with the hero with whom we have identified ourselves; yet we survive him, and are ready to die again just as safely with another hero.[33]

If we may be permitted to play on a "popular" etymology, we could say that death is *ob-scene*. What Freud knows, at least, is that death "cannot be looked at straight on" and that art (like religion) has the privilege of inaugurating economic representation—that is, libidinal representation. Death never appears as such; it is strictly *unpresentable*—it is the unpresentable itself, if that expression can have any meaning: *The death drive works in silence; the whole commotion of life emanates from Eros.* "It" ["Ça"] works, "it" disturbs manifestation, but "it" does not manifest itself, and if "it" comes to "manifest" "itself," it is *already* and always already "eroticized"—as in art, including modern art, and regardless of the devastation of form and of the work in which it may engage or risk itself. We never apprehend anything more than the *ebb* of death.[34] Whence the "economic problem of masochism." This is why representation, the representational mechanism, is not an enclave within the libidinal, but the libidinal itself—that is, the *economy of death* (in both senses of the genitive, of course). And there would be no point here in opposing, as does Lyotard following Ehrenzweig, the primary and secondary processes. On the contrary. It is the unconscious itself that is unaware of death (negation), or that, in other words, does not wish to hear about it (denial, *Verneinung*).

Theatricum Analyticum

All of this, in short, defines Freud's thought as "tragic thought." There is certainly nothing new about this. Except, perhaps, if we examine the precise relationship between *modern* tragedy (as well as that of Nietzsche) and the philosophy that it (unlike ancient tragedy) comes from, or, if you prefer, comes after. What tragic thought in fact reveals is that the *necessity of representation* goes beyond just art or religion: "thinking" itself is condemned to representation—which furthermore explains (the consequence is immediate) why philosophy and science are themselves to be understood (for Freud as for Nietzsche, though for different reasons) as "works of art," indeed as myths or rational fictions. "Thinking" is condemned to representation because death is in the end precisely that of which the "life of the Spirit" is afraid, that in which the Spirit, whether it likes it or not, proves incapable of "maintaining itself." The unconscious—Hyppolite and Lacan have shown this using the famous example of *Verneinung*[35]—obeys a logic that is comparable to Hegelian logic: it "sublates" (*aufhebt*) death, (de)negates it, and only agrees to speak of it or to "know" anything about it on the condition of believing itself in advance to be safe from it or of not "believing in it." It is also the case, reciprocally (and even if the reversibility here is not absolute), that the logic at work in philosophy is in its own way unaware of death—and is all the more unaware of it as it claims to have internalized it. But death is precisely what cannot be internalized, and maybe this is what defines the tragic (what Bataille called *dramatization*): the "consciousness" or even (it comes down to the same thing) the *admission* that there is nothing to do with death but dramatize it. And it is in any case certain that by protesting in the name of a supposed vocation for art of looking death straight in the face,[36] one has not only failed to find anything but a pre-Hegelian reply to Freud's supposed Hegelianism (which hardly gets us anywhere), but one is also running the risk of failing to recognize the very place in Freud where the function of theatricality as a matrix asserts itself in a decisive way: namely, beyond the constitution of the *analytic scene* (and a fortiori beyond the beginnings in the "cathartic method"), in metapsychology itself, in the irreducible dualism of drives.

The fact obviously remains that the fundamental theatricality of analysis is virtually indistinguishable from philosophical theatricality itself. This is even the most reliable indication of the fact that analysis *also* belongs to philosophy, depends upon it, is subordinate to it. In no case does "tragic thought" transgress the closure of philosophy. And up to a certain point, in fact, one cannot deny that all of analysis has been built on the representational mechanism of philosophy, that is, in the space marked off by Plato's (political) scenography. It is also true that, *belatedly* [*après coup*], analysis allows one to recognize and deconstruct this scenography by showing clearly, in the philosophical deviation of tragedy, the anticipation of royalty and mastery, the "basileic"[37] desire it conceals.

But that is perhaps not what is most important. For without even taking into account the detailed and "systematic" disturbance to which Freud, practically and empirically, subjected the representational mechanism,[38] one can find evidence throughout his text of the uneasiness that in fact and *in spite of everything* (and in Freud's case, this "everything" is impressive) troubles the philosophical and medical desire for mastery. Let us cite a single example, since it is very closely related to one of the major themes of "Psychopathic Characters." We have seen that modern dramaturgy presupposed the cultural or social establishment of neurosis. A quarter of a century later (which is to say fairly late), ruminating once again the same hypothesis, Freud asks himself exactly to what extent, and above all how, one can speak of a neurotic society or civilization. The question might appear anodyne, but all of medical authority itself (in the Nietzschean, philosophical sense of the "physician of civilization") is here suddenly and violently shaken in diagnosis as well as in therapy.

This happens in *Civilization and Its Discontents*, and it is not too hard to imagine what such a text might have meant in 1930:

> But there is one question which I can hardly evade. If the development
> of civilization has such a far-reaching similarity to the development of
> the individual and if it employs the same methods, may we not be
> justified in reaching the diagnosis that, under the influence of cultural
> urges, some civilizations, or some epochs of civilization—possibly the
> whole of mankind—have become "neurotic"? An analytic dissection of
> such neuroses might lead to therapeutic recommendations which could
> lay claim to great practical interest. . . . But we should have to be

very cautious and not forget that, after all, we are only dealing with analogies and that it is dangerous, not only with men but also with concepts, to tear them from the sphere in which they have originated and been evolved. Moreover, the diagnosis of communal neuroses is faced with a special difficulty. In an individual neurosis we take as our starting-point the contrast that distinguishes the patient from his environment, which is assumed to be "normal." For a group all of whose members are affected by one and the same disorder no such background could exist; it would have to be found elsewhere. And as regards the therapeutic application of our knowledge, what would be the use of the most correct analysis of social neuroses, since no one possesses authority to impose such a therapy upon the group?[39]

It goes without saying that these few remarks are too brief to be "decisive." Moreover, this was not their goal, as the intention that dictated them was rather to mark the "constitutive" *undecidability* of the Freudian treatment of representation. The critical undermining of medicophilosophical discourse does not prevent the critique itself from being translated, as often happens, into "conservative" terms. But one must not *relinquish* its power of disturbance in order to offer to just anybody the possibility of *retrieving* it, that is, of picking it up [*relever*]. Freud himself does not pick up anything. His "academicism," his economico-libidinal formalism, however questionable they may be, paradoxically have their reason, a reason whose boldness surpasses the prudence or narrowness from which they seem to derive. Which does not mean—and on this point, at least, we agree with Lyotard—that they do not pose problems.

The Ethical Trial of the Abyss

This is why—since under no circumstances could there be any question of *reinforcing* "Freudianism"—we end up here with a *question*.

In the text with which we began, Lyotard speaks of "Freud's belief in . . . the Sophoclean and Shakespearian *scenarios*."[40] We recognize in this a criticism that Nietzsche, at the time of writing *The Birth of Tragedy*, had leveled at the whole body of Western commentary on Greek tragedy and at "opera culture." But Lyotard says nothing more about it. Yet there is a symptom here that we cannot ignore. It is no accident that Freud on several occasions admits to being insensitive to music and to finding himself incapable of taking an interest in it. In so doing, he is perhaps merely carrying out, through philosophical obedience, the Aristotelian (as well as Platonic) elimination of *musical* catharsis—that is, as Rohde has shown, of Dionysian (and feminine) Corybantism. Nietzsche himself had, as they say, "hesitated" on this point. For instance, he had a certain distrust (and not only out of prudishness or "Protestant" uptightness) of the supposedly free and wild, "barbarian" experience of the Dionysian. But that is because he *also* knew that the Dionysian *itself* is inaccessible, or, which amounts to the same, that music *itself* is always already plastic, figural—Apollinian. Would Freud, if he had not refused to read it, have *recognized* something in a text of this kind?

> We need not conjecture regarding the immense gap which separates the *Dionysian Greek* from the Dionysian barbarian. From all quarters of the ancient world—to say nothing here of the modern—from Rome to Babylon, we can point to the existence of Dionysian festivals, types which bear, at best, the same relation to the Greek festivals which the bearded satyr, who borrowed his name and attributes from the goat, bears to Dionysus himself. In nearly every case these festivals centered in extravagant sexual licentiousness, whose waves overwhelmed all family life and its venerable traditions; the most savage natural instincts were unleashed, including even that horrible mixture of sensuality and cruelty which has always seemed to me to be the real "witches' brew." For some time, however, the Greeks were apparently perfectly insulated and guarded against the feverish excitements of these festivals, though knowledge of them must have come to Greece on all the routes of land and sea; for the figure of Apollo, rising full of pride, held out the Gorgon's head to this grotesquely uncouth Dionysian power—and really could not have countered any more dangerous force.[41]

This rectification or "rigidification" (which is that of Doric art) before the Dionysian—this apotropaic gesture marks the moment in the history of Greek culture that precedes the "reconciliation" of the Apollinian and the Dionysian, a reconciliation that only Greek "great art" (tragedy) proved capable of carrying out.

One can think what one wants about such a reconciliation. For us, it is certainly there to be *deconstructed*—if only in its (still) dialectical aspect, which is to say, precisely in everything about it that continues to mask the recognition of the ineluctability of representation, which, however, it already clearly implies. No need, it is true, to mobilize Apollo—and besides, Nietzsche himself ends up dispensing with him: it is within the Dionysian that presence is in fact *precluded*. Or, to put it another way (using the language that Freud used, in an enigmatic text, to justify the desire for art),[42] death *swallows up [abîme]* and tirelessly and irreversibly carries off "presence," dooming us to repetition.

We would be wrong to dismiss this thought as something bothersome, to accuse it of being symptomatic of nihilism or "pious and depressed thinking." For it is rather what Nietzsche termed "heroism"—and it should not be assumed that heroism, that is to say the impossible ethical (and non-"pathetic") trial of the abyss, has ever signified nihilism.

Translated by Karen McPherson

Chapter 6
The Unpresentable

1. Program

Let us say: *literature and philosophy* . . .

The program we will follow here was in fact sketched out by Maurice Blanchot. This acknowledgment will not—or should not—surprise anyone, but for the general tendency nowadays compulsively to deny this kind of indebtedness. In a text entitled *The Athenaeum*,[1] dealing with German romanticism, with Jena romanticism and the elusive ambiguity of its historical position and significance, Blanchot quotes this fragment (of a fragment) by F. Schlegel: "The romantic kind of poetry is still in the state of becoming; that, in fact, is its real essence: that it should forever be becoming and never be perfected. It can be exhausted by no theory. . . . It alone is infinite, just as it alone is free."[2] Blanchot then proposes this brief commentary:

> This seems to endow it with a happy and temporal eternity, and it does so in fact, but under the threat of an immediate disappearance, as we shall see with Hegel, who draws disastrous conclusions from this tendency of romantic art to universalize itself historically when he decides to call *romantic* all art of the Christian era and, on the other hand, acknowledges in romanticism proper only the dissolution of the movement, its fatal triumph, the moment of decline when art, turning against itself the principle of destruction which is at its center, coincides with its interminable and pitiful end.
>
> Let us acknowledge that, from the start and well before Hegel's *Lec-*

116

tures on Aesthetics, romanticism—this is its greatest merit—was not un-aware that such was its essence.[3]

This will be our starting point. Not that we will then say "something else" or "express" ["faire dire"] something else by these few lines. We shall start here be-cause it is probably "here," in this "moment" designated by Blanchot, that what is essential in the relation between *literature* and philosophy occurred and was determined (but perhaps did so, strictly speaking, without *occurring* and without *being determined*); because it is "here" that the *question* of this relation was, in the same movement, opened and closed, immediately carried to its point of rup-ture, exposed, exceeded, *passed* (even though it is, in a certain way, still to come). This is, as we know, what Blanchot has tirelessly repeated. But perhaps it is urgent to make it heard *again*.

Here is, then, very schematically, the program:

1. When (beyond Valéry, for example, but following Heidegger) we ask the question of the relation between literature and philosophy—when, at the very least, it comes to asking the *question* of literature in order, by treating literature as a "philosopheme," to dismiss, evade, or deflect the always obscurely or para-doxically emerging suspicion of a possible literary *filiation* of philosophy, we are probably doing nothing but asking in the Hegelian mode (but not in Hegelian terms) a question that Hegel himself never asked as such. A question that, in all probability, he even refused to ask. Or that he "asked" in such a way that it would not really amount to a question and would be "resolved" de facto before even be-ing properly established as a question. Here, but not quite in the same way as else-where, we are (strangely) subject to Hegel: to the thought (or the "system") at-tributed to Hegel as well as to the philosophical era that this thought constitutes and summarizes, that it *destines*.

This, at least, will be the hypothesis—a predictable one, although it is also dis-concerting: our question is the echo *after the fact* [*après coup*] of a question never asked or of an "answer" given to the absence of a question—in short, of a question that has never occurred anywhere originarily, even though it is marked, in-scribed, legible in the philosophical discourse that has thus "blinded" it (and that, as we know, is precisely the discourse claiming to be the sum and the truth of all [philosophical] discourse in general).

2. This is an impossible situation, which may not be surprising at all given that the topic under discussion is "literature." More precisely, there would be an in-comprehensible impossibility here if the Hegelian refusal were not in its turn the *repercussion* of a sort of question—or answer—of an *affirmation* in any case, hav-ing as it were emerged with and *as* the very birth of literature. Having thus emerged (we must immediately add) in the space entirely constituted (according to the same rigorous logic of the *aftereffect* [*après-coup*]) by the repercussion of philosophy, and in this case, primarily of Platonic-Aristotelian poetics, since

such an affirmation arose at the very center of *critical* and (or) *aesthetic* discourse —an affirmation to the effect that the end (in all senses) of philosophy is, under whatever name, literature. (A completion, an accomplishment in which, no doubt, literature must also disappear as such.)

3. This affirmation without the slightest autonomy, and hence without the slightest privilege, in relation to philosophy is, in all possible respects, that of *romanticism*. By "destroying" it, that is, in fact, by not mentioning it and at the same time slyly and massively opposing to it the idea of a philosophical accomplishment of philosophy, Hegel was obviously not simply attempting, through some movement of retreat or fear, to avert the danger it represents in order to "save" philosophy. In so doing, he also plainly put back in its place the advent of literature, whose logic—which was indeed, as Blanchot indicates, a logic of *dissolution*—he basically pushed to the limit.

With this slight difference, however, that he never took this step openly, that he neither said nor showed anything about it—and that, to a certain extent at least, he perhaps did not even really know that he was taking it. To be sure, he never failed to exhibit his hatred of or his contempt for romanticism, which he largely "mastered," and whose ontology, for example, or whose "philosophy of history," he "sublated" without difficulty. But on the subject of the "aesthetics" or the "poetics" of romanticism, on the subject also of its "literary practice," it seems that, each time, he avoided confronting its major ambition, which, however, beyond the projects of "absolute poetry" or of "new mythology," gave itself the title of the *concept* of literature (a title about which it turns out that Hegel never breathed a word).

4. This furtive, half-voluntary (and almost immediate) murder of the newly born "pretender" (this could indeed have been enacted as an obscure case of royal succession) has, as is always the case, left traces. Or, if the metaphor of murder appears at once too "active" and too brutal (not to mention—even though it is certainly legitimate, as we shall see, to call up here the semes of birth and death—that one might have to ascertain whether literature had ever *in fact* been born), let us say that, between Hegel and alchemy, the (silent and secret) dissolution or *Auflösung* of literature has left a remainder, a residue—an *abortion*: to begin with—though this is an hypothesis that almost goes without saying today—Hegel's *text*; but also, *before* Hegel's intervention (the logic of the *aftereffect* does not preclude it), "literature itself" to the extent that it has resisted, *in its "own" dissolution*, philosophical dissolution. It is well known that the abortion of the Masterpiece is the failure of this total dissolution which, moreover, fascinated the romantics (who never got enough of chemistry and *menstruum universale*) and which marks the transition to the organic—to the work and to the living (to the one *as* the other), to the *Organon* as such. It might thus be in this incompletion of the process of dissolution—in this *worklessness* [*désœuvrement*], if we may thus borrow the word from Blanchot—that we must look for the obviously undis-

coverable essence of that which, strictly speaking, we can no longer call literature, nor, any more justifiably, philosophy. There must be (have been) an *abortion* of literature. And probably (alchemy and chemistry were never anything but *secondary* metaphorical reserves) in the most "literal" sense. Consequently, to parody or divert a famous title, which is, however, not in the least alien to the *aftereffect* with which we are dealing, the least erroneous title that one could perhaps suitably give to all this would be something like (this is a "translation"): *The Abortion of Literature, Spiritual Daughter of Philosophy.*

5. In order to attempt to verify and partly to fulfill this program, we shall use an example. It will be F. Schlegel's *Lucinde* (1799).

We shall begin by asking ourselves — this is the least we can do — what Hegel must have thought of it.[4]

2. "The Era of *Lucinde*"

To touch briefly on the course of the further development of the subject, alongside the reawakening of the philosophical Idea, A. W. and Friedrich von Schlegel, greedy for novelty in the search for the distinctive and the extraordinary, appropriated from the philosophical Idea as much as their completely non-philosophical, but essentially critical natures were capable of accepting. For neither of them can claim a reputation for speculative thought. Nevertheless, it was they who, with their critical talent, put themselves near the standpoint of the Idea, and with great freedom of speech and boldness of innovation, even if with miserable philosophical ingredients, directed a spirited polemic against the views of their predecessors. And thus in different branches of art did they introduce a new standard of judgement and new considerations which were higher than those they attacked. But since their criticism was not accompanied by a thoroughly philosophical knowledge of their standard, this standard retained a somewhat indefinite and vacillating character, so that they sometimes achieved too much, sometimes too little.

Hegel, *Aesthetics*, 1: 63

There are only, in all of Hegel, three or four allusions to *Lucinde* — and most of the time, these allusions are not even accompanied by any explicit reference. This is as much as to say that Hegel never referred to it and that, on the contrary, everything leads us to believe he was practically unaware of it. Under such circumstances, the pertinence of the kind of "confrontation" we seem to have included in our program is difficult to see. All the more so, in fact, as nothing allows us to think, at least apparently, that this quasi silence might have been motivated by reasons other than indifference or contempt: there are no traces here—whereas elsewhere they abound—of a deliberate or "systematic" will to ignorance. *Lucinde* does not, it seems, belong to the range of Hegelian references—whose claims of exhaustiveness are otherwise well known. Unless, therefore, this lack of interest is raised to the status of hermeneutical criterium, out of complacency or a slightly futile taste for paradox, it is difficult to discern, from the point of view that concerns us here, what could confer any value of exemplarity upon this text. We are rather in the very midst of insignificance.

But of course this is not the case. At least two of these allusions deserve attention—and even if only, at first sight, because of the position they occupy in the texts in which they appear. No doubt Hegel did not think much of *Lucinde* and never considered it, even within romanticism, as a major work; this is the least we can say. But as we shall soon understand, he had good reasons for this (reasons unequivocally betrayed by these allusions), and if his (relative) discretion does not really seem, at first sight, "systematic," we cannot say that it is simply accidental or fortuitous either. There is here, in a discourse as concerted and controlled as this one, something arresting and intriguing, something we can all the less afford to let pass as precisely in it may be woven, quietly but solidly, a certain complicity with this "avoidance" of the question of literature with which we are dealing.

The first of these allusions is to be found in the historical part of the *Aesthetics*, in the chapter on "The Dissolution of the Classical Form of Art." Or more precisely—because precision is necessary here—in the second paragraph of this chapter (which of course is the third and last of the section devoted to classical art): "Dissolution of the Gods through their Anthropomorphism, b) The Transition to Christianity is only a Topic of Modern Art." *Lucinde* thus appears, is at least named (if only, as we shall see, in an apparently oblique way, "in passing") at the most decisive "moment" of the historical, which is also to say systematic, articulation between classical and romantic art. Right in the middle, architectonically speaking, of Hegel's exposition of this articulation (which may, as we know, represent the most decisive moment of the whole history of art in general). This is not a slight privilege. It is necessary, therefore, before turning to the text, to dwell for a moment on this situation. No doubt this detour runs the risk of being a little long. But this is because nothing here—especially here—is as simple as it appears.

As is well known, the transition to Christianity is the moment when what the *Phenomenology* called "aesthetic religion" (which, in Greek classical art, "creator of its gods," is identified with art proper) disappears in favor of revealed religion, which is the true religion—faith as the consciousness and certainty of truth—and which, consequently, as it is originally independent and free of any link with any *aesthetic* representation (which does not mean with any *representation*), already insures the sublation, the *Aufhebung* of art—even though it must also necessarily produce, in its historical wake, the unfolding of a Christian art (romantic art, as Hegel understands it), in which, although it has ceased to appear as the highest and most essential manifestation of the life of the Spirit, art still manages to *survive itself*. The transition to Christianity thus does not mean what is usually called, erroneously, the "death of art." How could anyone imagine that anything could *die* in such a system? But because art, in Greek classical art, attained what Kant already thought of as its *limit*, because classical art is "pure art"—"the perfection of art," the "conceptually adequate representation of the Ideal," "the consummation of the realm of beauty," etc. ("nothing can be or become more beautiful")[5]— the dissolution of classical art represents, in theory if not in fact, the dissolution of art in general. Moreover, the development that interests us here immediately precedes the famous analysis of Roman satire of which we can assume, for more than one reason, that Hegel considers it the matrix of the "final" dissolution of art. That Greek art could have concealed in itself the principle of its own dissolution, that there might already have been—in comedy, in the epigram (but also with Socrates)—a Greek dissolution of Greek art (a "dissolution of classical art in its own sphere") does not alter the fact that it is in reality Rome—this strange *fourth* "station" in the historical-geographical-ontological route, in the *theoretically* tertiary "calvary" that leads the Spirit of the Orient to *its Europe*—that had as its historical mission and perhaps, to a certain extent, as a "transhistorical" ("transsystematic"?) function, to destroy what was "genuinely true and living" in art, "its former actuality and necessity." In sum, there is only *one* proper dissolution of art, which the romantic dissolution will doubtless have to *accomplish*, but which it will also merely repeat (even parody) and *hasten* by degradation.[6]

We shall therefore have grounds to say that there is nothing surprising, from this point of view at least, in the fact that *Lucinde* (that is, any romantic text) appears at this moment in the *Aesthetics*, even though, if it is to have any place at all, it probably would have found a better one in the next paragraph among the considerations on satire. But this is not the problem. *Lucinde* is not here to *represent* anything. More precisely, it appears here only to represent that which, in fact, does not "represent" anything. Or hardly anything. The allusion would remain undecipherable (or anecdotal) if we hastily suspected in it a direct, explicit—if not justified—targeting of romanticism. We must therefore look at things a bit more closely.

The text in which *Lucinde* appears (or rather, as we shall see, its era) is actually a text devoted to Schiller. It is even a commentary on one of Schiller's great "philosophical poems," "The Gods of Greece." Hegel has just explained that the dissolution of classical art is the dissolution of the Greek pantheon precisely insofar as it manifests itself *as* and *in* art, and more particularly, as and in *statuary*, which is the art of the classical ideal par excellence, the highest possible adequation between the spiritual and sensuous form. This dissolution of the Greek pantheon is necessarily implied by the contradiction it comprises, the contradiction between, on the one hand, the submission of the gods to the superior substantiality of fate (or, in other words, the gods' lack of an "inner necessity"), and, on the other hand, the correlative anthropomorphic desubstantialization, that is, the dispersion of substantiality that these gods manifest in their very multiplicity. What the Greek pantheon lacks and what provokes its dissolution is consequently that of which Christianity alone has a sense, namely, the substantial or the spiritual as *subject*: "Therefore the plastic Ideal lacks the aspect of being represented as inwardness knowing itself as infinite."[7] For this reason—and it is fundamental—Greek art (the Greek pantheon) dissolves purely and simply, without confrontation, without struggle, without violence—without the "war of the gods," the "battle between the old gods and the new," which had marked the brutal dislocation (rather than the dissolution) of symbolic art and its sublation in (classical) art. The end of Greek art, the "transition" ["passage"] of art, is accomplished without tragedy.[8] Sublation—*revelation*—occurs outside of art; it comes from elsewhere:

> This transition could not have taken its starting-point from art; the clash of old and new would have been too disparate. The God of revealed religion, both in content and form, is the truly actual God; precisely for this reason his opponents would be mere creatures of men's imagination and they could not be matched with him on any terrain. On the other hand, the old and new gods of classical art both belong explicitly to the ground of imagination . . . and their opposition and battle is a serious matter. But if the transition from the Greek gods to the God of Christianity had been brought about by art, there would immediately have been no *true seriousness* in the portrayal of a battle of the gods.[9]

This is why, Hegel immediately adds, "this strife and transition has only in more recent times become a casual and distinct topic for art, a topic *which has been unable to mark an era* [*Epoche*] or in this form to be a decisive feature in the entirety of the development of art" (my emphasis). There follows, "in this connection," the analysis of "The Gods of Greece," taken here as a major testimony (and major precisely in that Schiller does not fall into the ridiculous or frivolous trap of representing an actual "battle") to that "nostalgia for Greece," to those "laments" about the "disappearance of the Greek gods and heroes" for which modern art holds Christianity responsible.

We shall obviously not follow this commentary, even though we should, if only to see the dividing line traced between the serious and the nonserious (a *certain* frivolity), less in Schiller himself than, discreetly, between the Greeks and Christianity, that is, between art and revelation. For the moment, it will suffice to indicate that this rehabilitation, against Schiller, of Christianity (which it would be an "error" to claim is "totally incompatible" with art) is accompanied, to an equal degree at least, by an homage to Schiller himself, whose pathos, Hegel says (and this justifies the place he reserves for "The Gods of Greece"), "is always both truly and deeply thought."

Therefore, we shall simply deal with the place reserved for Schiller; for it is on him, in fact, that the meaning and value of the allusion to *Lucinde* depend, if only by simple contrast. Indeed, no sooner has the critical analysis of "The Gods of Greece" been completed than Hegel adds—and here we have it at last:

> In another way, Parny, called the French Tibullus on the strength of his successful Elegies, turned against Christianity in a lengthy poem in ten books, a sort of epic, *La guerre des Dieux*, in order to make fun of Christian ideas by joking and jesting [*Scherz*] with an obvious frivolity of wit [*mit offener Frivolität des Witzes*], yet with good humor and spirit [*Geist*]. But these pleasantries went no further than frolicsome levity, and moral depravity [*Liederlichkeit*] was not made into something sacred and of the highest excellence as it was at the time of Friedrich von Schlegel's *Lucinde*. Mary of course comes off very badly in Parny's poem; monks, Dominicans, Franciscans, etc. are seduced by wine and Bacchantes, and nuns by fauns, and thus it goes on perversely enough. But finally the gods of the Greek world are conquered and they withdraw from Olympus to Parnassus.[10]

This, then, is the allusion. We must admit that it is a little thin, despite the astonishing silence about *Lucinde* itself, that is, despite the incongruity of the comparison or "association." For it goes without saying that the "content" of *Lucinde* has strictly nothing to do with that of *La guerre des Dieux* and that only a certain aura of moral licentiousness or dissoluteness, only, at bottom, the "scandalous" character of the two texts authorizes this strange "amalgamation." We shall come back to this point. There is woven, however, under this apparently arbitrary and gratuitous moral accusation—nevertheless preparing it, or, more precisely, justifying it—a completely different discourse, which a certain number of clues allow us to reconstruct without too much difficulty. Three motifs are indeed combined here, *between* which, so to speak, what is essential for us should allow itself to be progressively delimited:

1. There is, first of all, what we have just mentioned and which is indeed decisive, namely, *Schiller's position*. If, in fact, "The Gods of Greece" (even if we otherwise think the world of it) *does not mark an era*, if it can even be given, in a certain way, as the illustration of that "absence of era" which characterizes the whole art of the Moderns (and its unseasonable nostalgia for its past era), to what concept of era does *the era of Lucinde* correspond, if not to the most trivial and contemptible—a fortiori when the said era is characterized, as it is here, in a way that says a great deal about what we should think of it. But that naturally

also says a little too much. For it is hardly necessary to be a particularly clear-sighted scholar to detect here the clearest recognition of the capacity of *Lucinde* to have *marked an era*, regardless, once again, of our opinion concerning it. The era-argument—and this is one of them—is a double-edged sword. Or, if one prefers, it is perfectly "ambivalent." Of course, if we try to follow its logic to the end, this ambivalence both signifies and doubtless does not signify something other than the deliberate *epokhe* of *Lucinde* itself, its "bracketing," all the more impressive here as the allusion is not accompanied by the slightest explicit justi-fication. *Lucinde* is a book about which we must keep silent if we wish to vilify it and to set it up as an "example of the worst." Underlying all this is a quasi denial.

This quasi denial is confirmed and reinforced by the indisputable privilege granted to Schiller. As we know, Schiller is a Hegelian "character." He could al-most be a "figure." In any case, he never fails to appear in the most decisive places—beginning with (this is the major instance) the last page of the *Phenome-nology*, where the transition to the Concept, the return of the Absolute to its proper element, the very crossing over the threshold of the *Logic* are "illustrated," contrary to all expectations (but, as we shall see, quite coherently), by two lines, albeit badly quoted, from "Friendship." He appears again—and mutatis mutandis, this is no less important—in the very first pages of the *Aesthetics* itself, precisely where it is a question of grounding in the "era" (or more rigorously, in the closure) of art the justification of aesthetics, of the science or the philosophy of art. Count-ing all these "summonses" ["convocations"] would prove an endless task; it would require, as we say, an entire study. But why such a privilege?

There are at least two essential reasons for Schiller's exemplarity. First, the role that Schiller played *theoretically* in the philosophy of art. Let us reread, in the third chapter of the introduction to the *Aesthetics* ("Historical Deduction of the True Concept of Art"),[11] the second paragraph ("Schiller, Winckelmann, Schelling"): all the credit "for breaking through the Kantian subjectivity and ab-straction of thinking and for venturing on an attempt to get beyond this by in-tellectually grasping unity and reconciliation as the truth and by actualizing them in artistic production"[12] goes to Schiller—so that we can say without exaggeration that he led to the very threshold of its speculative return to the Idea, "the concept of the beautiful and of art" which, once the perspective of the Absolute has been adopted (that is, the principle of sublation), will be the Hegelian concept of the beautiful and of art (which is, as we know, the union or inner—and thus objective, actual—"fusion" of the rational and the sensuous, the spiritual and the natural, the Idea and individual appearance, etc.). Neither Goethe, nor even Schelling (who proceeds from Schiller and hardly goes beyond an "attempt" to rise to "the abso-lute standpoint of science"), is, from this point of view, comparable to him. But there is more than this—even much more: for Schiller did not merely take the aes-thetic a decisive step forward *within* aesthetics; he was also able to relate to phi-losophy itself this premonitory conception of art, thus accomplishing—Hegel almost says so outright[13] — what *had* to be accomplished in order for the speculative as such to be established, namely, the unity of sense and the sensuous without the presupposition of which, it is easy to understand, no phenomenology of the Spirit, no absolutizing of the phenomenon (and hence none of what Heidegger calls the *onto-theio-logical*) would have been conceivable. But this relating of philosophy and the question of art was made possible by Schiller's very (artistic and poetic) *practice*. In other words, this theoretical and practical unification of philosophy and art (poetry), this *philosophical poetry* which Schiller embodies (whatever its difficulties and limitations), was necessary in order for the speculative to come onto the scene and (re)present itself (*sich darstellen*). *Gedankenlyrik* was necessary to prepare the way for science. We have yet to realize the full consequences of this.

Schiller is thus, within the indissoluble unity (a unity threatened, however, with instability) of a sort of "theoretical practice," both the completion of aesthetics and, if we may say so, the "eve" of the speculative.[14] In other words, Schiller de-limits the prespeculative moment that precedes the philosophical *elevation* [*levée*] (the philosophical sublation of philosophy), that fringe (not indecisive, but contradictory and thus "fertile") where a certain poetic truth of philosophy (and a philosophical truth of poetry), insofar as it takes itself as object, *calls for* the supervention of the absolute Idea as the truth of *the identity of identity and difference*, of the sensuous and the intelligible. It is still too early to clarify what this truth — let us call it *poïetic* — is. The important thing is that nothing within romanticism ever had access to it, and especially not — this bears repeating — the Schlegels. The reason for this is quite simply that romanticism is *more* than the negative of Schiller: it is that corrosive "milieu" in which art, having (at last) understood, but stubbornly continuing to deny, that it is no longer *as such*, and has not been for a long time, *of the era* [*de l'époque*], is dissolved indistinctly and without any hope that in it philosophy will recognize and "retain" anything of its own. This leads us to the second of the three themes we mentioned above.

2. If Schiller, indeed, represents or illustrates the contradiction of a *philosophical poetry*, or, more generally, a *philosophical art* (not of an "artistic" philosophy, although the "philosopher artist" is not so farsighted), if his powerless nostalgia is the mark of the work [*travail*] of the negative and the sign that history is at work, it is because he corresponds somewhat — in the modern age and in view of what we shall rigorously be compelled to call the *transfiguration* of philosophy — to what was the " dissolution of classical art in its own sphere." And, in fact, his inclinations toward the restoration of Greece are not devoid of a certain politico-philosophical opposition (both to the *Aufklärung* and to Christianity), which, because it supposes a subjective withdrawal and a claim for "individual freedom," recalls, for example, with all due allowances, Socratism in its opposition to Sophism and the Athenian State. It is an artist's Socratism, more or less inverted and properly reactionary, even if — or all the more so as — it does not fail

to inscribe itself in the (totally relative) "progressivism" of Kantianism and Rous-seauism. The very organization of the chapter on the "Dissolution of the Classical Form of Art" revolves—yet without ever making it explicit—around an "intuition" that Nietzsche, who probably never read a single line of the *Aesthetics*, will not fail to exploit.

In contrast (that is the least we can say), Parny and romanticism—*Lucinde* and its era—represent the insignificant, superficial, frivolous, sneering (and de-bauched) side of this "moment." Hence, they correspond—once again, with all due allowances—to something *even worse* than what Roman satire must have rep-resented in relation to the Greek dissolution of Greek art. Here again, the organi-zation of the chapter impeccably inscribes what the text itself feels no need to make explicit—and feels it all the less, in fact, as elsewhere in the *Aesthetics* the lesson is clear. In chapter III[B] of the introduction, to which we just referred (paragraph 3: "Irony"), as in the whole development on the dissolution of roman-tic art that concludes the historical part of the *Aesthetics*, there is, under the (official) name of *romantic irony* (or under the Hegelian name of *subjective hu-mor*), an accumulation of all the features that delineate the face of this kinship between Rome and Jena. It goes without saying that Hegel is aware of the roman-tic claim to Romanism. He probably also knows, even though he never says any-thing about it, how this claim is connected, through a theory of poetic genres that Schlegel would call "transcendental," with the establishment of the *novel* (the name marks an era—and a concept) as the genre of the mixture (*satura*) of all the genres and "sublation" (before the spirit, if not before the letter—although nothing is less certain) of the very poetics of genre (including satire).[15] For whatever in-terpretation he may give of the novelistic (and we could easily show that this in-terpretation is not unrelated to the Schlegelian theory), Hegel indeed sees the novel—the "carnivalesque" or "comic" novel, *Don Quixote* in particular[16]—as the determining moment of the "final" dissolution of art.[17]

The great principle of this dissolution—as the whole "theory of the novel" in-spired by Hegel (from Lukács to Goldmann, or even Girard) has repeatedly shown—is, in fact, the rupture of the totality (that very totality of which Schiller had a sense), the dissociation of "external actuality" and "subjective inwardness," the loss of the (classical, Greek) adequation between content and form,[18] and—this is the essential point—the accidental, external contingency of the "material which artistic activity grasps and shapes" (a generalized accidentality in the midst of which "is presented the collapse of romantic art"). The necessary consequence is twofold:

> On one side, in other words, there stands the real world in, from the
> point of view of the ideal, its prosaic *objectivity*: the contents of ordi-
> nary daily life which is not apprehended in its substance (*in which it
> has an element of the ethical and divine*) [my emphasis], but in its

mutability and finite transitoriness. On the other side, it is the *subjectivity* of the artist which, with its feeling and insight, with the right and power of its wit, can rise to mastery of the whole of reality; it leaves nothing in its usual context and in the validity which it has for our usual way of looking at things; and it is satisfied only because everything drawn into this sphere proves to be inherently dissoluble owing to the shape and standing given to it by its subjective opinion, mood, and originality; and for contemplation and feeling it *is* dissolved.[19]

All this, at least as far as the "formal framing" is concerned, is Roman. The formal framing is *dissociation* itself, a kind of immobile, frozen (sterile and dangerous) "schism" ["schize"] between the prosaic nature of reality and the (more or less great) poetic richness of subjectivity. In the best of cases, it provokes anger: it is Rome.[20] In the worst of cases, when a certain repetition (which must be regarded as an aberration) tends to reestablish the schism, there remains only irony or humor, or else the *delectatio morosa* of the "beautiful soul." Only *mockery* is common to them—or even to all three, if between Rome and Jena we introduce the novelistic derision of chivalry (Ariosto, Cervantes). A long detour would be necessary here in order to compare all of these texts and, above all, to bring out, in this history (of art) which perhaps does not obey as blindly as it should the laws of (dialectical) historicity, the fact and the value of these strange resurgences of Rome. It would even be necessary, while following as closely as possible the trace of the Hegelian interpretation of irony, to go so far as to relate this (equivocal) depreciation of Romanism to the idea of a degradation or a perversion of Socratism, which, indeed, contains the germs of the dissociation, the cleavage of the prosaic through which subjectivity (consciousness) and philosophy (which establishes itself with prose) begin at the same time to free themselves, but which, "on the side of art" (especially when the cleavage is transplanted, by servile mimetism, onto the barren soil, that is, the natural prosaicness, of Rome), basically aggravates, and without allowing any rectification of the negative, the decomposition of totality. A fortiori when, as in romanticism, imitation operates on two levels (and Rome has, in the meantime, been transformed into the Vatican . . .). For what is then lost, degraded, and might very well escape all control if it happened by chance to *mark an era*, is the only thing that, in spite of everything, recognizably constituted still the (abstract) greatness of Rome—of ancient Rome at least: *the ethical sense*. And this ethical sense is precisely, as we have seen, the major objection to the era of *Lucinde*. This is the last motif we must remember here, for—

3. This is also by far the major objection to romanticism as a whole: all aesthetic or "literary" mediocrity, all philosophical (speculative) shortcomings aside, romanticism is properly—and profoundly—*scandalous*. The paragraph in the introduction devoted to the Schlegels—which, notwithstanding its injustice and violence (even its cantankerous and bitter character), is doubtless the best account

of romantic aesthetics, insofar as there is *one* homogeneous and systematic aesthetics of romanticism[21] — associates, for example (and this time, "systematically"), with each constitutive moment of "romantic irony," an accusation of *immorality*. Thus, the "application" to art of the Fichtean principle of the absoluteness of the (abstract) self means that "everything appears to it as null and vain, except its own subjectivity."[22] Similarly, the transformation, the shaping [*mise-en-forme*], the figuration, or even the fictioning [*fictionnement] (Gestaltung, Bildung*, etc.) by the romantic artist of his life into a work of art[23] means that one cannot "take seriously" any content nor "its expression and actualization," "for genuine earnestness enters only by means of a substantial interest, something of intrinsic worth like truth, ethical life, etc."[24] This is a by now classic problem of "axiology": subjectivism equals immoralism. This whole playful absolutizing of subjectivity, this "virtuosity of an ironical artistic life," this "divine creative genius," and this "self-enjoyment" (as well as the "entrenchment" of abstract and unsatisfied inwardness, the *"morbid* beautiful soul") — all of this invariably produces one and the same result: the desubstantialization of the substantial, the "self-destruction of the noble, great, and excellent," in short, desacralization and sacrilege. For example — here we have it again — the "representation of the Divine as the ironical."[25]

As we can see, the allusion to *Lucinde* only condensed the accusation — but without at all preventing it from remaining perfectly legible. The allusion even implied the questioning of what the repetition, on a second level, of the dissolution of classical art makes inevitable, namely, the degradation of the *comic* as such, and at the same time — if only in contrast with Rome (let us not mention Aristophanes or Lucian) — the absence of all subjective solidity, of all *character*, in this "destruction of content" which would be an art but which is nothing but a way of elevating the *nonartistic* itself into a "creation." Indeed, "taken abstractly," irony "borders nearly" on the comic; but Hegel says:

> Yet in this kinship the comic must be essentially distinguished from the ironic. For the comic must be restricted to showing that what destroys itself is something inherently null, a false and contradictory phenomenon, a whim, e.g., an oddity, a particular caprice in comparison with a mighty passion, or even a *supposedly* tenable principle and firm maxim. But it is a totally different thing if what is in fact moral and true, any inherently substantial content, displays itself in an individual, and by his agency, as null. In such an event the individual is null in character and contemptible, and his weakness and lack of character is brought into his portrayals also.[26]

In other words, the scabrous jokes of *Lucinde*, its tendentious apology for misbehavior, the confusion it aimed to create between the libertine and the sacred, only betrayed the foulness and perversity of its author. The era of *Lucinde* is also that of Schlegel—with everything this implies.

In any case, the condemnation is irrevocable. It is a regular "lashing" ["éreintage"]—from which, as we know, romanticism, in the philosophical tradition, never "recovered." But the point is perhaps that, in its very principle, the fundamental objection—which, moreover, is linked to the accusation against the exorbitant (philosophical) privileges granted to subjectivity—is an *ethical* objection, and not a forthrightly aesthetic (even less a "poetic") one. More precisely, ethical objection and aesthetic objection are one and the same to the precise extent that it is the *nonartistic* character of romanticism that constitutes its immorality. What we can forgive Jean Paul (as to humor), Solger and Tieck (as to the theory of irony), or even the Frenchman Parny (who after all is very witty), we do not forgive the romantics: their aesthetic-ethical "nihilism" (the word is already circulating) does not "pass"—or *passes too much*, that is, escapes or eludes controlling sublation. This actually means two things: on the one hand, it means that when art thus turns back against itself, it carries along with it, in this "self-negating" fury (as Schlegel says), all the substantiality that gave it shape and content (religion and the divine, the ethical, the law, the seriousness of existence, etc.) and that destined or predisposed it to its sublation in (revealed) religion and philosophy. But on the other hand, it means that, by dissolving on its own initiative, so to speak, by claiming dissolution to the point of proposing its theory—and a practical theory that, itself, goes so far as to contest the theoretical as such and to implicate, in an *ab-solute* generalization of art, the (subjective) subject and *its* reality, which is *the whole*—romantic "art," even in the best of cases (Solger), does not attain to the truth of dissolution, that is, to the speculative, reconciling truth of *determined* negativity.

It would be premature, for now, to draw the necessary conclusions about the "question of literature," even though it is already possible to see that literature, about which Hegel never stops talking without saying a word, is not unrelated to this nondialectical or predialectical, insufficiently speculative "aesthetics" which the *Aesthetics* itself proposes to correct and to *redress*, be it on the basis of a firm and salutary "return to Schiller." We must still ask ourselves exactly what this heavy and systematic *ethical* drifting [*dérive*] of the aesthetic objection covers and conceals. The second allusion that we find necessary to mention [*convoquer*] here should enlighten us on this point.

3. Shamelessness: The Veil and the Figure

What is hidden behind this veil?
"Truth" was the answer.

> Schiller, "The Veiled Image of Saïs," Stanza II.

On the form and details of the Greek manner of clothing, clas-
sical scholars have written ad infinitum; *for although men have*
otherwise no right to talk about fashion in clothes, the sort of
materials, trimmings, cut, and all the other details, neverthe-
less research has provided a more respectable reason for treat-
ing these trivialities as important, and discussing them at
length, than what women are allowed to have in this field.

Hegel, *Aesthetics*, 2: 747

Mysteries are female; they like to veil themselves but still want
to be seen and discovered.

F. Schlegel, *Ideas*, 128.

This second allusion is, if possible, even more discreet than the first—to the extent
that we cannot even say that it really belongs to the Hegelian "text." It is, in fact,
a marginal note handwritten by Hegel beside a passage in *The Philosophy of Right*
and intended to support one of the improvised oral digressions with which he used
to comment on his own books when teaching. The passage in question is the Remark to §164 of *The Philosophy of Right*—a paragraph which itself belongs to
the first development (A. Marriage) of the first section of Ethical Life (The Family). In the margin, then, simply (but among other annotations), Hegel has written
(and underlined): *Lucinde*.[27]

What does this Remark say? §164 is devoted to the "solemn declaration of consent to the ethical bond of marriage." Just as, says Hegel, "the stipulation of a con-
tract in itself contains the genuine transfer of property," so—that is, through an
identical substantiality of form—"the solemn declaration . . . and its recognition and confirmation by the family and community constitute the formal *conclusion* and *actuality* of marriage." This amounts to saying that this bond, or this sensuous, natural (affective, sexual) union, which marriage (also) is, is "ethically
constituted . . . only after this ceremony has *first taken place*, as the completion of the *substantial* [aspect of marriage] by means of the *sign*—i.e. by means
of language as the most spiritual existence of the spiritual." There is here, therefore, a genuine necessity: the sanctioned, legitimized—one might say, civilly
consecrated—union alone is ethical and hence actual. Then comes the Remark,
which, predictably, has practically no other object than to attack those who consider this formal necessity constitutive of actuality as a simple external "formality" or as a contingent and optional requirement. The defense of free union, especially when it legitimizes itself through or claims to derive from the purity and
authenticity of love, is immoral. It is an error, or rather a deception, of the understanding. But we must read, at least in part, the text itself:

If the *conclusion of marriage* as such—i.e. the ceremony whereby the
essence of this bond is expressed and *confirmed* as an ethical quality

exalted above the *contingency* of feeling and *particular inclination* — is seen as an *external formality* and a so-called purely *civil precept*, nothing remains of this act except perhaps the purpose of edification and of attesting the civil relationship [of the marriage partners]. Or indeed, it is the merely positive, arbitrary enactment of a civil or ecclesiastical precept, which is not only indifferent to the nature of marriage, but also — in so far as the emotions are inclined by this precept to attach a value to the formal conclusion [of marriage] and to regard it as a condition which must be fulfilled before the partners can commit themselves totally to each other — brings disunity into the disposition [*Gesinnung*] of love and, as an alien factor, runs counter to the inwardness of this union. Although such an opinion claims to impart the highest conception of the freedom, inwardness, and perfection of love, it in fact denies the ethical character of love, that higher suppression [*die höhere Hemmung*] and subordination of mere natural drive which is already naturally present in *shame* and which the more determinate spiritual consciousness raises to *chastity* and *purity* [*Zucht*]. More particularly, the view just referred to casts aside the ethical determination [of marriage]. This consists in the fact that the consciousness emerges from its naturalness and subjectivity to concentrate on the thought [*Gedanke*] of the substantial. Instead of further reserving to itself the contingency and arbitrariness of sensuous inclination, it removes the marriage bond from this arbitrariness and, pledging itself to the Penates, makes it over to the substantial; it thereby reduces the sensuous moment to a merely *conditional* one — conditioned, that is, by the true and ethical character of the relationship, and by the recognition of the marriage bond as an ethical one. It is impertinence [*die Frechheit*] and its ally, the understanding, which cannot grasp the speculative nature of the substantial relationship; but both the uncorrupted ethical emotions and the legislations of Christian peoples are in keeping with this speculative nature.[28]

By inscribing *Lucinde* in the margin of this text — and more precisely beside the last lines[29] — it is obvious that, as previously in the *Aesthetics*, Hegel echoes, more than twenty years later, the "*succès de scandale*" of *Lucinde* around 1800, and thus confirms, if it were necessary, the reality of the *era* of which this book had been the emblem. Here is a new indication, therefore, of Hegel's ambiguous desire to reduce its scope and to minimize its interest, that is, to avoid its "intrinsic content" in order to retain, without the slightest thoughtlessness, only its apparently "superficial" side and to consider it finally, each time, as a kind of negative example or symptom.

What is Hegel, in effect, aiming at? First of all — we know the objection — at the licentious, amoral, indecent, perverse character of the book in question. *Lucinde* is definitely a model (and yet, the "era" had seen several others). But also, the ethical objection finds its real justification in the kind of apology or plea *pro domo* for the revelation of love and its absolute accomplishment "outside of marriage," in "free union,"[30] which *Lucinde* seems to constitute. This is why *Lucinde* raises unethical conduct to the level of "something sacred and of the highest excellence." Impertinence, says Hegel, a corruption of ethical purity of heart, especially *misapprehension* — and without innocence — of the understanding, which does not understand or does not want to understand, which in any case does not *conceive* "the speculative nature of substantial conduct" and hence obscurely works toward the regression of consciousness and of the spiritual even beyond its simple natural level (which, itself, is not unaware of shame). As in the underhanded confrontation with Parny and Schiller, there is, in the philosophical task assigned to criticism — the mobilization of the speculative — nothing "mechanical" or "routine." No more than in the ethical *surcharge*. Thus, it would certainly be a gross misapprehension to acknowledge in this "piece" only the compulsively accumulated signs of a conservatism or conformism, of a tense and slightly foolish prudery. There is undoubtedly some of that — it would be utterly absurd to deny it. But this is not at all what is essential. What is *really* at stake is elsewhere. For — we have been sufficiently warned — if a novel, *this* novel, being such an ethical (and philosophical) scandal, can here, for the second time, serve as a lone reference, it is probably not with the status of a simple "illustration." No more so, as we shall see, than Greek tragedy (*Antigone*) simply "illustrates" the substantiality of marriage. The odds are, on the contrary — and everything in the very position of the first allusion confirms this suspicion — that the scandal in this case is rather, if not the novel itself in general, then at the very least the configuration, the function, and the finality that *Lucinde* aimed to attribute to this "genre," which must remain the genre of a certain very precise and very precisely oriented dissolution. Perhaps indeed the ethical-speculative claim is more closely related than it seems to the "question of literature." That is, in fact — but it is quite obviously always here(by) that the question of literature is *done away with* [*saute*], so to speak — to the *question*, tirelessly foregrounded, of the essence of the beautiful and of art, or, which amounts to the same, as we shall gradually learn, to the *question* of art (and in particular of *poetry*) in its relation to philosophy. This is what we must now attempt to demonstrate.

Thus, impertinence, incapable as it is of grasping "the speculative nature of the substantial relationship," ridicules marriage. This is, explicitly at least, the scandal of *Lucinde*. Hence the first question: What is this substantial relationship? How is its speculative character defined? More briefly formulated, what does the *substantiality of marriage* consist in?

§§165 and 166, which immediately follow the Remark, answer this question. By "substantiality of marriage," we should not basically understand anything other than the "intellectual and ethical" assignment to both sexes of their respective roles, that is, the sublation — the cancellation, the preservation, the elevation, the spiritualization, and the humanization of the natural difference between the sexes in a significant and living unity: "The *natural* determinacy of the two sexes acquires an *intellectual* and *ethical* significance by virtue of its rationality. This significance is determined by the difference into which the ethical substantiality, as the concept in itself, divides itself up [*an sich selbst*] in order that its vitality [*Lebendigkeit*] may thereby achieve a concrete unity." In other words, marriage *sanctions* the sensuous and natural union of the sexes as their spiritual difference, a difference from which *alone* the sensuous union (coitus or copulation, "sexual intercourse") can be accomplished as non-such, humanly, and thus be promoted to the rank of *concrete unity*. There would thus be, between the sexes, no possible unity (or, which amounts to the same, no possible difference) without the matrimonial sanction. Hence marriage, conjugality, *destine* man and woman in their essence and their function. Masculinity and femininity are constituted *by right*, are ordered by and subordinated to the prior (that is, always anterior) legality that founds the human community as such. For this reason, the difference between the "sexes" is a distribution of *roles* and *characters*. The *speculative distribution* itself:

> The *one* [sex] is therefore spirituality which divides itself up into personal self-sufficiency with being *for itself* and the knowledge and volition of *free universality*, i.e. into the self-consciousness of conceptual thought and the volition of the objective and ultimate end. And the *other* is spirituality which maintains itself in unity as knowledge and volition of the substantial in the form of concrete *individuality* and *feeling* [*Empfindung*]. In its external relations, the former is powerful and active, the latter passive and subjective. Man therefore has his actual substantial life in the state, in learning, etc., and otherwise in work and struggle with the external world and with himself, so that it is only through his division that he fights his way to self-sufficient unity with himself. In the family, he has a peaceful intuition [*Anschauung*] of this unity, and an emotive and subjective ethical life. Woman [*Frau*], however, has her substantial vocation in the family, and her ethical disposition [*Gesinnung*] consists in this [family] *piety*.[31]

Activity and passivity, of course: it's a sure thing. But also, and especially, duplicity and unity. Man is first *double*: marriage sanctions his external destiny, his actual belonging to the outside, his self-sufficiency, and the simultaneously "conflictual" and "projective" character of his (always) future unity. As Lacan would say, man *ex-sists*. He "is" difference, anxiety, opposition, work. He "is" the negative, the power [*pouvoir*] (knowledge and volition) of the spiritual, the very power [*puissance*] of the concept: something like the *power* [*force*] of sublation (of speculative rectification, stiffening, erection). Man "is" the speculative. Woman, on the other hand, is indivisible, without difference. She does not exsist, she *in-sists*. She is, in marriage, its substantial inwardness—"pregnant," in fact, with this (her) difference which is man—economy in the strict (and restricted) sense of the word, closed appropriation, closed familial piety. She is the inside (the crypt, of course) in which is accomplished—but obviously without appeasement—the union of the spiritual and the sensuous within subjective individuality itself.

One recognizes here the major tenets of "phallogocentrism."[32] And, as far as Hegel is concerned, a whole discourse constituted at least since the *Phenomenology of Spirit*. But whatever its interest—whatever its interest regarding the question with which we are dealing—it is hardly possible for us to refer to it here. We should simply remember that this distribution of roles, this speculative differentiation between femininity and masculinity, insofar as it relies on the analysis of the Greek city, that is (as the Remark to §166 will remind us), on a hermeneutics of *Antigone* (envisaged as the paradigm of tragedy), and insofar as it determines, in its very configuration, the whole structure of the "ethical order," in fact presents itself, or at least can be read, in the Hegelian text as the "formal" matrix of the transition to aesthetic religion, and from there, to revealed religion and to Science (to absolute knowledge). For what is at stake in this very differentiation is no less than the possibility of the philosophical as such. As we shall verify from other texts, nothing in the speculative is alien to what, for lack of a better word, we are compelled to call a "sexual" "symbolic" (in the most general sense),[33] constitutive, in the mode of a kind of *anthropo-phenomeno-logic*, of the "figuratic" in which emerging knowledge must necessarily (re)present itself, *sich darstellen*: masculinity—active duplicity struggling, working, and conceiving— therein *transfixes* and *sublimates* (literally, that is, *transitively*), insofar as it must emerge out of "particular determinacy" and establish itself out of the "appearance of being sullied by something alien which is only for it as another," the philosophical (discourse) itself. The concept is the (protruding and salient) *protrusion* [*saillie*] of the figure.[34] But what concerns us here, at least for the moment, is the fact that this speculative coitus (the concept of which has always already been "sublated" as the very possibility—we must think of the speculative as a fertile onanism—of its self-generation and its self-conception) finds in tragedy its entire symbolic reserve and something like its most primitive (re)presentation. This is why the tragedy par excellence, the (re)presentation of the tragic conflict itself—the tragedy that is *Antigone*[35]—"inclines" to phenomenology. *Antigone* (already) (re)presents (re)presentation, *Darstellung* as the *Darstellung* of emerging knowledge. The dialogue of dialectics, the "*dialeguesthai*" of natural consciousness and of self-consciousness, and hence of the concept and of the figure, is prepared in "conjugal" dialogue, in the split between the two laws, in the whole system of "ethical" oppositions (woman/man, night/day, dead/alive, house/State, home/ agora, etc.). Behind the mask of Creon, but first and foremost in the inward split, in the guilty admission and the resignation of Antigone herself — "the most sublime figure that ever appeared on earth" — the speculative is already at work.

Under these conditions, it is easy to understand that, by (re)presenting rebelliousness against marriage, *Lucinde* could be such a scandal for the speculative. However, we should not understand it too hastily or too easily. For if something more than a pure and simple ethical scandal is at stake here, if the ethical scandal also encompasses an aesthetic scandal (*essentially* encompasses an aesthetic scandal), the whole question remains as to what exact "symbolic" relationship there is between marriage and, say, the work of art. It is indeed tempting to think — but "legalism" aside, this would in fact be the romantic interpretation — that marriage, considered as the substantial union of the spiritual and the natural and as the crucible of "dialectical conjugality" itself, is the work of art or beauty insofar as it results, in the words of the homage to Schiller that we have already read in part, from "the mutual formation of the rational and the sensuous."[36] There would be nothing surprising, then, if, under the worst of its aspects, the (romantic) dissolution of art had necessarily to *re-mark* itself in ethical dissolution itself, in the satirical-novelistic apology (that is, also, in the "ironic" practice) of free union, in this crepuscular and decadent defiance of the ethical ritual which is but the misunderstanding of the ontological obligation.

In so doing, we would simultaneously make at least three mistakes: first of all, we would misapprehend the meaning of the speculative distribution of the masculine and the feminine. We shall come back to this point. We would then be compelled to regard the *Phenomenology* as a work of art — a sort of "narrative tragedy" or even, in the worst of cases, a novelistic "epos," a kind of "Odyssey of Consciousness," which at any rate the *Phenomenology* refuses to be, even though it needs, as a *Darstellung* preliminary to the "eigentliche Darstellung . . . in der spekulativen Philosophie" and an "anticipatory assurance" ("antizipierte Versicherung") of the concept, to pass through a "partly narrative exposition."[37] Finally, we would settle the question of the status of tragedy itself; we would *decide* that it belonged entirely to the "sphere of art," when everything *also* designates it, in the Hegelian text, as the art of the sublation of art.

All of this would in effect amount to misapprehending the significance of marriage itself. If marriage "calls for" the speculative (and not the work of art), if it lets itself be (re)presented in tragic dia-logism, it is not only because it is constituted by "the *sign* . . . language as the most spiritual existence of the spiritual," but also because the language to which it holds and of which, like tragedy, it mobilizes the *ethical* function, actually sanctions *difference*. Marriage is not union — even less fusion. What it sanctions is the consent to (union as) difference. It is thus always — and firstly insofar as man comes out of it and does not live in it (as the life of the Spirit is outside and not *zu Hause*) — division, that which "passes" union — the *analogon* (here, as elsewhere, the word is strictly unavoidable) of the conflict that, in tragedy (behind the still aesthetic [re]conciliation of tragedy), informs, without anything in it ever being able to escape, the "beautiful ethical totality" and prepares the rectification of politico-philosophical man.

In contrast, union as such, fusion, is *woman*. In the ethical and tragic order, woman doubtless represents essentially the law of the chthonic realm, the ancient gods, the whole nocturnal, fatal, chthonic closure out of which man must (re)emerge, be born or reborn, from which he must raise himself [*se relève*]. But woman is also, as we know, "spirituality which maintains itself in *unity* [my emphasis] as knowledge and volition of the substantial in the form of concrete *individuality* and *feeling*." It is she, consequently, who bears, embodies, *figures* this union of the spiritual and the sensuous which also defines the work of art and beauty. It is she, in sum, who, in tragedy, (re)presents the *aesthetic* part—which her ethical (male) destination sublates. In her, tragedy as a work of art is *engulfed* [*s'abyme*]. Nietzsche knew something about this: "Fear and pity: with these feelings man has so far confronted woman, always with one foot in tragedy which tears to pieces as it enchants."[38] This indeed is why it is a young girl, a virgin (and not a spouse), Antigone, who contradictorily supports the whole ethical conflict of (ideal) generalized conjugality in which is *ruined* [*s'abîme*], this time, the beautiful ethical totality and in which is engendered, but without any procreation or childbirth that has not already entered into ideality, something like philosophical speech. In the same way, if you will, that, without the slightest sacrifice to any "poetic" complacency, it is again a young woman who, in the first pages on "revealed religion" in the *Phenomenology* (VII, C), *appears* [*comparaît*] in order to insure the "transfer" of art:

> [The works of the Muses] have become what they are for us now—
> beautiful fruit already picked from the tree, which a friendly Fate has
> offered us, as a girl might set the fruit before us. It cannot give us the
> actual life in which they existed, not the tree that bore them, not the
> earth and the elements which constituted their substance, etc.[39]

All of this does not, of course, mean that woman is beauty. This would hardly make sense. On the other hand, however, beauty is feminine. Between woman and art, the "symbolic" equivalence, or the analogy, is rigorous and strong. It is so rigorous and strong, in fact, that Hegel presents it as such, or, more exactly, approves and recognizes its pertinence. Indeed, in the same "homage," hardly has he credited Schiller with having been able to determine "the concept of the beautiful," than he adds (and this is how the homage ends): "In general this view of Schiller's can be recognized already in his *Anmut und Würde* [*Grace and Dignity*, 1793], as well as in his poems, because he makes the praise of women his special subject matter, for in their character he recognized and emphasized just that spontaneously present unification [*die von selbst vorhandene Vereinigung*] of spirit and nature."[40]

Despite the slightly oblique quality of this acknowledgment, we shall soon have the opportunity to see that Hegel knows perfectly well what he is talking about. He knows, in any case, what strict constraint is at work in this "feminine" determination of art, and even more immediately, he knows the role that woman and femininity will have played, all through the century to whose closure he contributes, in the establishment and the constitution of aesthetics. He knows, in sum, as Nietzsche will later say (but turning it into an objection and hoping for a "reversal" of values), that "our aesthetics . . . has been a *woman's* aesthetics,"[41] and that something destines art, "the love of art," and the discourse on art, to femininity. Nevertheless, this "knowledge" is never, or almost never, acknowledged as such: it remains, on the contrary—and it is not too difficult to understand why—that "knowledge" which Knowledge itself must erase or at least justify. (The) Science (of art) is, for instance, the sublation (that is, also, in this case, the *critique*) of everything presented and developed (Schiller included) under the name of aesthetics. This, however, in no way changes the fact (this is, by now, a well-known law) that such a "knowledge," reverberated, echoed, manipulated, worked over, still circulates and resonates in the discourse that determines it, occasionally amplifying or "jamming" that discourse by some effect of fading.

This perhaps explains, in any case, why, in the Remark that interests us here, the accusation leveled against *Lucinde* is actually concerned less with the *question of marriage* than with the reasons or pretexts (philosophically) invoked in favor of concubinage: that is, the idea of an *actualizing* of love, of the truth and authenticity of love, in *illegality*. For this erotic "anarchism" or this libertarian "naturism," worse than instinctive nature itself, bears a name (or two names, if we do not lose sight of the *Aesthetics*): impertinence (*die Frechheit*) or depravity (*die Liederlichkeit*). But it also conceals a danger: the emancipation of woman (whom marriage, as is its function, must enclose and "domesticate"—*d'hommestiquer*, as Lacan would say—when it leaves man with his "substantial life" elsewhere). It represents, then, from the speculative point of view, a threat, a double threat: that of a disturbance, even a reversal, in the distribution of male and female roles; and that—correlative to the first—of a "bad" dissolution, of a "regressive," "downward" dissolution—the slightest affirmation of feminine auto-nomy being capable only of causing what marriage is meant to *inhibit* in accordance with the Law (of man), that is, the return to an animality or bestiality that, as everyone knows, will always lie in wait for woman more precisely and more immediately than for man, or that never surprises or takes hold of man except through the intervention of woman. The whole scandal about *Lucinde* lies here: in the *position* (literally, and in all the senses of the word, as we shall see) of woman. In other words, in the "displacement" of woman, in a certain tearing away of woman from the reserve that the law, if not nature, prescribes for her. In indecency, therefore. Like any breach of conduct [*atteinte aux bonnes mœurs*], *Lucinde* is an *offense against decency* [*attentat à la pudeur*].

But the sense of shame [*la pudeur*] is the essence of art.

As it turns out, Hegel explains himself at length on shame, on the necessity of shame (and above all the necessity of shame in *woman*). More important, he deliberately discusses it as an aesthetic question, even as the most central question of aesthetics. For—but this is not surprising—it is in relation to *statuary*, to *Greek* statuary, that the question of shame arises. That is—must we repeat this?—in relation to the classical (artistic) ideal par excellence. So that it is, in effect, a matter of no less importance than the determination of the beautiful, of the ideal, in general. The analysis is famous. But it is nonetheless necessary to give a broad outline of its movement. Hegel ponders the nude in classical sculpture, or, more precisely, the significance of the division in classical sculpture between nude figures and clothed, dressed, *veiled* figures. The question, then, is what nudity represents in relation to the "ideal destination" of classical art: "At first sight it may seem that the nude form and its spiritually permeated and sensuous beauty of body in its posture and movement is what is most appropriate to the ideal of sculpture and that drapery is only a disadvantage."[42] And this is purely and simply the question of the beautiful. But the reply is surprising. A few lines further on, after once more "challenging" the modern nostalgia for Greek art and all those who "complain nowadays" that sculpture is so often compelled to "clothe its figures," Hegel writes the following:

> In general it need only be said on this matter that from the point of view of sensuous beauty preference must be given to the nude, but sensuous beauty as such is not the ultimate aim of sculpture, and so it follows that the Greeks did not fall into error by [re]presenting most of their male figures nude but by far the majority of the female ones clothed.

The answer is surprising but, of course, "revealing." It is easy to understand that sensuous beauty does not constitute the end of art: the beautiful is the manifestation or the (re)presentation, the sensuous *Darstellung* of the spiritual and of inwardness. It is also easy to understand that nudity, the natural beauty of the body, is sensuous beauty. And finally, without the slightest difficulty, that clothes, while veiling sensuous beauty, might reveal, under certain conditions (that is, provided the bodily structure, the attitude, is shown and not masked, occulted, or distorted), the spiritual itself: for indeed, "the external human form is alone capable of revealing the spiritual in a sensuous way." And if it is true that there always remains in it "much of the general animal type," "dead and ugly things, i.e. determined by other influences and by dependence on them," it is "precisely the business of art to expunge the difference between the spiritual and the purely natural, and to make the external bodily presence into a shape, beautiful, through and through developed, ensouled and spiritually living."[43] This is also why drapery in Greek statuary emphasizes (*hebt . . . heraus*) that by which, apart from the face, the human form signifies the spiritual, namely the position (*die Stellung*), which is "a sign of the spirit."[44] So far, then, no problem. What is less easy to understand, on the other hand (unless it is too easily understood), is the way in which this difference between the nude and the veiled comes to intersect with the difference between the sexes itself; it is the division, as far as modesty is concerned, between masculinity and femininity. For if "the Greeks did not fall into error" in leaving the male figures nude and in veiling only, preferably, the female figures, we must conclude, not that male nudity is ugly, but that female nudity simply falls within the province of sensuous beauty—or, which amounts to the same, that male nudity is not really sensuous (or that it is less sensuous and more spontaneously beautiful, of a beauty that is not sensuous beauty). In other words, femininity is only beautiful, ideally, when veiled, clothed, partially withdrawn from the eye. Thus, woman expresses the spiritual only provided she does not show herself, provided she conceals in herself the sensuous (her body). Hence, the female nude does not quite (re)present that reciprocal belonging or "appropriation" of body and spirit, of meaning and manifestation, which the human form in general (re)presents (and which the human form alone [re]presents): "The spirit [does not] cross [entirely] this corporeal envelope [*Hülle*]."[45] Something in the female body eludes or does not yet attain to *humanity* as such, which it seems only the male body (re)presents (which body would in sum be—this, at least, is probably the last conclusion to be drawn—naturally veiled).[46]

Woman must, then, "take the veil" in order to enter art proper. But why exactly? What exactly does the veil veil? What must it conceal under the name of sensuous beauty? What is, in short, the function of clothing? This is where shame comes in. Clothing, Hegel says—"in general . . . apart from artistic purposes" —has a double function: on the one hand, the reason for clothing "lies . . . in the need for protection from the weather, since nature has given man this concern while exempting animals from it by covering them with fur, feathers, hair, scales, etc." On the other hand—and this is obviously, from the speculative point of view, what is essential—"it is a sense of shame which drives men to cover themselves with clothes." But what is shame? It is quite simply the refusal of animality, the very sign of the humanity of man, the first constitutive sign of his spiritual nature:

> Shame, considered quite generally, is the start of anger [*Zorn*] against something that ought not to be [*über etwas, das nicht sein soll*]. Man becomes conscious of his higher vocation to be spirit and he must therefore regard what is animal as incompatible . . . with his higher inner life, especially those parts of his body—trunk [*Leib*], breast, back, and legs—which serve purely animal functions or point to the purely external and have no directly spiritual vocation and express nothing spiritual. Amongst all peoples who have risen to the beginning of reflection we find therefore in a greater or lesser degree the sense of shame and the need for clothing.[47]

Consciousness thus emerges with the sense of shame. The Spirit invests man as the gesture by which man, covering himself, veiling himself, allows himself to be traversed by the difference between what is and what ought to be, and "represses" or "suppresses" the animal in himself.[48] The animal, that is, from the point of view of form, "the organs which are necessary, it is true, for the body's self-preservation, for digestion, etc., but for the expression of the spirit, otherwise superfluous."[49]

Despite the modest character of this designation, all of this seems perfectly clear. But in fact, things are not so simple. Indeed, the question remains why, in Greek statuary, the necessity for modesty affects practically only female figures. In other words, the question remains as to what destines woman, as a "privilege," to the "return" (in her—in humanity?) of animality. The problem here is the concept of animality—of animality in "man." And it is all the more a problem as, in the *Philosophy of Right*, shame is said, we recall, to exist as an "already naturally present" mode of inhibition. In fact, contrary to what we might think, the animality with which we are dealing here is not, let us say, the "physiological" kind. The physiological—and the physical, organic externalization of physiological functions—has, of course, a role to play in it. But its role does not amount to much; it hardly amounts to more, for instance, than the physical imperfections or peculiarities (hairs, warts, wrinkles, little veins, etc.) that recall the animal, that sully or disfigure natural nudity, and occasionally cause a certain repulsion. For animality as such—that which ought not to be and against which, therefore, the anger of consciousness growls—is quite simply *desire*. This is why, for the Greeks, (male) nudity, far from betraying any propensity to indecency or any lack of concern for the spiritual, expresses, on the contrary, indifference to desire—to sensuous and sensual desire, to what Hegel calls the "purely sensual [side of] desire [*das nur Sinnliche der Begierde*]":

> In the Greek national character the feeling of personal individuality just
> as it immediately exists, and as spiritually animated in its existence, is
> as highly intensified as the sense for free and beautiful forms. Therefore
> the Greeks were led to give form on its own account to the human
> being in its immediacy, to the body as it belongs to man and is per-
> meated by his spirit, and to respect above everything else the human
> figure as a figure, just because it is the freest and most beautiful one. In
> this sense of course they discarded that shame or modesty which forbids
> the purely human body to be seen, and they did this, not from indiffer-
> ence to the spiritual, but from indifference to purely sensual desire, for
> the sake of beauty alone. For this reason a great number of their sculp-
> tures are presented naked from deliberate intention.[50]

The division of the sense of shame is thus established on no other grounds than the motif of desire. If woman alone needs to be veiled, it is because she alone expresses—and arouses?—*sensual* desire. In accordance with what the whole philosophical tradition has always said or implied, there is, properly speaking, no *pudendum* other than female *pudendum*; or, what amounts to exactly the same thing, male homosexual desire (we should write: *hommosexuel* desire) is spiritual desire: the phallus is the "organ" of the Spirit. Whence the distribution of the veil in classical sculpture. It is unassailably appropriate:

> The Greeks exhibited in the nude (*a*) children, e.g. Eros, for in them the bodily appearance is wholly naïve, and spiritual beauty consists precisely in this entire naïveté and ingenuousness; (*b*) youth, gods of youth, heroic gods and heroes like Perseus, Heracles, Theseus, Jason, for in them the chief thing is heroic courage, the use and development of the body for deeds of bodily strength and endurance; (*c*) wrestlers in contests at the national games, where the sole thing that could be of interest was not what they did, or their spirit and individual character, but the body's action, the force, flexibility, beauty, and free play of the muscles and limbs; (*d*) fauns and satyrs and bacchantes in the frenzy of their dance; (*e*) Aphrodite, because in her a chief feature is the sensuous charm of a woman [*insofern in ihr der sinnliche weibliche Liebreiz ein Hauptmoment ist*]. Whereas we get drapery where a higher intellectual significance, an inner seriousness of the spirit, is prominent and, in short, where nature is not to be made the predominant thing. So, for example, Winckelmann cited the fact that out of ten statues of women scarcely one was nude. Among goddesses it is especially Pallas, Juno, Vesta, Diana, Ceres, and the Muses who are robed, and, amongst the gods, Zeus especially, the bearded Bacchus Indicus, and some others.[51]

From this taxonomic exercise—which, as always in Hegel (leaving aside youthful heroism and childish naïveté), is ordered around the difference between the Dionysian (fauns, satyrs, bacchantes) and the Apollinian (the Muses)—we shall retain the emblematic character of Aphrodite. It is in her that desire is properly "figured"; it is therefore she who (re)presents, in its essence, femininity. We shall have to remember this later. But what would a modest Aphrodite be? What would a veiled Aphrodite (re)present? If beauty is the veiling of the sensuous (of that which, in the sensuous, arouses desire), if modesty, in veiling the sensuous, unveils the spiritual, what then is the beauty of the classical ideal if not precisely veiled immodesty? In other words, if woman, except to (re)present what does not express the spiritual, is a figure only when veiled—if man embodies, except to (re)present strength and courage, the innocence of nudity and indifference to the sensuous—if man is always (already) the spiritual and woman always (still) the sensuous, what then is the figure itself, the beautiful unity (expressing the spiritual) of the spiritual and the sensuous, if not the veiled female figure? It is in female modesty, in the "aletheic" play (veiling/unveiling, manifestation/withdrawal) of woman that the beautiful is defined and the work of art—the figure—

figured. Modesty figures the figure: a sensuous veil thrown over the sensuous, a negation of the negation of the spiritual, through which the spiritual begins to appear. —Art itself.

This is the reason why we cannot really say of the male figure that it is, in the most rigorous sense, a figure. Masculinity is difficult to figure, or, ultimately, is figured only in being feminized. The great male spiritual figures of the Greek pantheon (Zeus, bearded Dionysus—manly or in drag?) are clothed. This is because man, insofar as he expresses more spontaneously the spiritual or as the spiritual in him predominates over the sensuous, (re)presents rather the very boundary of the figural, the moment when the spiritual already sublates the figure: the figure being sublated in the spiritual.[52] Strictly speaking, then, the figure unveiling itself. Not to reveal the sensuous, but to tear away or lift up the veil (itself sensuous) of the sensuous. This is why male nudity can be shown: masculinity is the unveiling of the spiritual. Besides, we know exactly where this logic leads: well beyond the philosophy of art—but allowing itself to be supported by the philosophy of art at least as much as the philosophy of art is supported by it (and this is true also of psychoanalysis)—to some determination of truth as truth-castration and truth of (truth-) castration. It is not by chance, therefore, that the Greek world (that is, the dawn of philosophy) is "figured" *also* in the father-brother of Antigone and is tragically ruined [*s'abîme*] in the one who, solving the riddle of the Sphinx, actually lifts up the veil of Isis, fills in the abyss [*abîme*] of truth, and gives the philosophical answer to the question concealed by the East.[53] For Oedipus, the figure of Greek art at its climax (that is, having already reached its limit) and the male figure of that art, already (re)presents—and will henceforth (re)present— *between* the (oriental) night of the symbolic (of the blurry, indistinct kinship between sense and the sensuous) and the luminous day of self-consciousness (of the reign of the Spirit establishing itself), philosophical anxiety, to the extent that it has emerged from the figural conflict itself and from the confrontation, in the work of art of the classical ideal, between the spiritual and the sensuous, signification and manifestation, the veil and unveiling, knowledge and desire. When, in the unveiling gesture, the knowledge of desire engenders the desire for Knowledge, everything is already ready for the *parousia* of Truth.

In this unveiling of the figure lies, of course, the whole history of truth. The *Phenomenology* "narrates" this history in its own way and stops where narrative stops in the West, where "fiction" becomes unnarratable because the figure itself, sublated, concealed, pierced and traversed, allows Sense, unveiled, to appear. In other words, where "Spirit . . . having won the concept, displays its existence and movement in this ether of its life and is *Science*."[54] Thus, in this unveiling of the figure lies the whole necessity of *Darstellung*, of (re)presentation; and in the necessity of this unveiling, the whole question of form and manifestation. The question of femininity, of the veil, of modesty. Hence, the question of the violation of modesty. A whole relationship to art is sketched out here: the very opposite of the relationship assumed by the immodesty of *Lucinde* (or Lucinde).

And this relationship is designated by Hegel. It is the relationship between philosophy and poetry (let us come back to this: two lines by Schiller—mistreated, massacred—that conclude the *Phenomenology of Spirit* in telling and figuring, in extremis, the overflowing of the figure [transfiguration] and the infinite actuality of the Spirit knowing itself). But why poetry?

4. The Subornation of Aphrodite: Poetry and Philosophy

> *When the picturesque veil of poetry was still gracefully floating around truth. . . .*
>
> Schiller, "The Gods of Greece"

> *The whole history of modern poetry is a running commentary on the following brief philosophical text: all art should become science and all science art; poetry and philosophy should be made one.*
>
> F. Schlegel, *Lyceum*, 115

> *So, e.g., in F. von Schlegel's poems at the time when he imagined himself a poet, what is unsaid is given out as the best thing of all; yet this "poetry of poetry" proved itself to be precisely the flattest prose.*
>
> Hegel, *Aesthetics*, 1: 296

Because the Hegelian *question* is the following: can what is to be thought, whatever it may be (being, truth, thought itself) present itself *as such*; can it appear *in its own element*? Would presenting itself as such, appearing in its own element, not ultimately mean, for what is to be thought, *not presenting itself at all*, *not appearing*? Is there not, in other words, a necessity of manifestation? And in this case, is there a possible revelation, a *parousia*, without loss or residue, of what is to be thought? Or is it not necessary, for a "presentation" in general, for an "appearance" to occur, that what must "present" itself not present *itself*, not appear *as* itself (that is, rigorously speaking, not *present* itself), but differentiate itself, alienate itself, externalize itself, transport itself [*s'extasie*], give itself (to be "seen" and thought, to be *theorized*), and, through giving itself, lose itself? Does not the necessity of manifestation entail the necessity of *loss*?

It is a well-known question. A well-known *economic* question. A question, then, of *form*—to the extent that it governs the whole problematic of *Darstellung*, of the properly philosophical (re)presentation of philosophy. That is, to the extent that it governs the whole problematic of *transfiguration*.

This question—as we have seen proven, not once but thrice—certainly has its answer. (This again is a trivial point: every question in the system always already has its answer.) And an answer that we know, since it suffices to know that there is one. The *Aufhebung* is infallible. Let us give the answer anyway, if only to go and look for it where it cannot fail to be found, that is, it goes without saying, at the very beginning of the *Aesthetics*, where it is a matter of assigning to art its (exact) place in the hierarchy of truth. The answer is found in two sentences that Hegel opposes to the reproach of "unworthiness" leveled against art under the pretext that its "element" is appearance and illusion (*Schein und Täuschung*). This reproach would be justified, says Hegel, if one could speak of appearance as of that which ought not to be (*das Nichtseinsollende*) and thus confuse it with illusion. However, first, "appearance itself is essential to essence [*der Schein selbst ist dem Wesen wesentlich*]. Truth would not be truth if it did not show itself and appear [*wenn sie nicht schiene und erschiene*], if it were not truth *for* someone [für *Eines*] and *for* itself as well as for the spirit in general." And second, "only beyond the immediacy of feeling and external objects is genuine actuality to be found. For the truly actual is only that which has being in and for itself [*das Anundfürsichseiende*], the substance of nature and spirit, which indeed gives itself presence and existence [*Gegenwart und Dasein*], but in this existence remains in and for itself and only so is truly actual."[55] In other words, if there is indeed a necessity of appearance or of appearing (of manifestation), if manifestation is a "moment," itself essential, of essence, then it is precisely only a "moment" that must therefore be followed by—or that must actually be comprised beforehand by—the "moment" (in which every moment is dissolved) of return, of reinternalization, of reappropriation *without loss*, without the *slightest* loss (not even that of sublated, and hence maintained, manifestation). This is why a (re)presentation as such, a manifestation "in its own element" of what is to be thought, is not only possible but also necessary—and of a necessity that is the very necessity of appearance or manifestation. Without manifestation, there is nothing—to think. But once there is manifestation (and this is how the introduction to the *Phenomenology* opposes Kant), the Thing itself—the *Sache selbst*—gives itself to be thought, reveals itself to be thinkable as such in its entirety, and necessarily proves to consist in thought itself knowing itself and certain of its absoluteness. What is to be thought must present itself as such to the extent that there is no presentation except of thought. Ideally (that is, leaving aside for the moment the "question" of language), philosophy (Science) is thus the manifestation and the (re)presentation of thought in its own element or its own form, in the (immaterial) element or in the (nonsensuous) form of thought itself: in the pure adequation or pure self-equality, that is, in the identified, *homologized*, self-difference of thought. To cite only one well-known example, this is what allows Hegel, in the introduction to the *History of Philosophy*, to condemn, in agreement with Aristotle, "mythical philosophizing" (that of Plato, essentially, but also that of all "returns to mythology")[56] and even to exclude (*ausschließen*) from the survey of the history of philosophy "myth as such and the mythical forms of philosophizing." Whence, among others, these three statements: "The truth rather is that thought is precisely self-manifestation; this is its nature, i.e. to be clarity itself. Manifestation is not like something which may equally be or not be, so that thought would remain thought if it were not manifest; on the contrary, manifestation itself is the very being of thought"; "The thought which has itself as its object must itself also be objective in its form; it must have raised itself [erheben] above its natural form; it must also appear in the form of thought"; "That which is thought must be expressed [sich aussprechen] in the form of thought."[57]

All of this is very clear — and definite, "decisive." None of it raises a question. However, this assurance (this certainty) does not fail to be doubled by a certain anxiety. Of course, the principle of transfiguration is never contested in itself. But here and there, something resists transfiguration enough to force the discourse that desires it and works toward its actualization, not only ceaselessly to reaffirm its possibility but also to engage in long procedural operations in order to circumvent what must indeed be understood as difficulties (if not, more brutally and obscurely, to ward off its impossibility).

And this is what happens, in an exemplary manner, in the case of poetry.

It happens, once again, in the *Aesthetics* — in the chapter on "The Poetic Work of Art as Distinguished from a Prose Work of Art." Hegel recalls, in the introduction to this chapter, that poetry (the art of speech), considered as a sublation of the (properly) plastic arts and of music, has its principle in spirituality, in "spiritual inner life": "Poetry . . . expresses directly for spirit's apprehension the spirit itself with all its imaginative and artistic conceptions but without setting these out [herausstellen] visibly and bodily for contemplation from the outside."[58] He has even assigned to poetry its position in the historical-systematic process of art (of truth): poetry is "that particular art in which art itself begins at the same time to dissolve and acquire in the eyes of philosophy its point of transition to religious pictorial thinking as such, as well as to the prose of scientific thought."[59] And yet, as surprising as it may seem, it is as such that poetry represents art in general, or, as Hegel says, that "the nature of poetry coincides [fällt . . . zusammen] in general with the conception of the beauty of art and works of art as such."[60] The question then arises, with regard to its difference from prose, of the proximity of poetry to speculative thought. The discussion starts as follows:

> This apprehension, formation [Gestalten], and expression [of the subject-matter] remains purely theoretical [rein theoretisch] in poetry. The aim of poetry is imagery and speech [Bilden und Reden], not the thing talked about or its existence in practice. Poetry began when man undertook to express *himself*; for poetry, what is spoken is there only to be an expression [das Gesprochene ist ihr nur deswegen da, um ausgesprochen zu sein]. When once, in the midst of his practical activity and need, man proceeds to collect his thoughts and communicate himself to

others, then he immediately produces a coined expression [*ein gebild-eter Ausdruck*], a touch of poetry.[61]

This is illustrated by the "distich which [Herodotus] has preserved for us and which reports the death of the Greeks who fell at Thermopylae." The content is "entirely simple" (that is, entirely prosaic), but its "interest lies in the preparation of an inscription to relate this event for contemporaries and posterity"; it "is meant to be a *poiein* which leaves the story in its simplicity but intentionally gives special form to its description [*das Aussprechen jedoch absichtlich bildet*]." It is thus through form, through this *Bilden*, that poetry distinguishes itself, that is, through its determination to give "the formation of the expression . . . more importance than mere enunciation." This is why, compared to prose (the prose of the understanding)—but how exactly would the prose of reason be defined?—the prose of understanding that is always depreciated by Hegel in the same way that, as we know, Rome is always declared inferior to Greece—compared to prose, then, poetry is not devoid of kinship with speculative thought. With the exception, again (but barely), of form itself, of *Bilden*:

> These deficiencies of the Understanding's categories and the ordinary man's vision are extinguished by *speculative* thinking which therefore is . . . akin [*steht . . . in Verwandtschaft*] to the poetic imagination [*die poetische Phantasie*]. Reason's knowing neither has to do with accidental details nor does it overlook the essence of the phenomena; neither is it content with those dissections and mere relations characteristic of the Understanding's outlook and reflections; on the contrary, it conjoins in a free totality what under a finite type of consideration falls to pieces into aspects that are either independent or put into relations with one another without any unification.
>
> Thinking, however, results in thoughts alone [*Das Denken aber hat nur Gedanken zu seinem Resultat*]; it evaporates [*verflüchtigt*] the form of reality into the form of the pure Concept, and even if it grasps and apprehends real things in their particular character and real existence, it nevertheless lifts [*erhebt*] even this particular sphere into the element of the universal and ideal wherein alone thinking is at home with itself. Consequently, contrasted with the world of appearance, a new realm arises which is indeed the truth of reality, but this is a truth which is not made *manifest* again in the real world itself as its formative power and as its own soul [*als gestaltende Macht und eigene Seele*]. Thinking is only a reconciliation [*Versöhnung*] between reality and truth within thinking itself. But poetic creation and formation [*das poetische Schaffen und Bilden*] is a reconciliation in the form of a *real* phenomenon itself [*Erscheinung*], even if this form be presented only spiritually.[62]

Of course, this is again the same answer. Of course, the "kinship" of speculative thought and poetry (that is, in fact, their common opposition to the understanding) is finally severed. And, of course, the separation is established along the dividing line between reality and the concept, between the world of manifestation and the realm of the spirit, between phenomenality and the element of thought. But this being said, what exactly is a reconciliation (of truth and reality) in the form of phenomenality, when this form is itself "[re]presented only spiritually"? In other words, what is a spiritual representation? What is the relation between spiritual representation and phenomenality? What connection is there between form and phenomenality, when form belongs to spiritual representation? What stage or intermediate register must we assume between phenomenality and thought, in which form would still be form (the figure still a figure) even though, strictly speaking, it no longer manifests itself? These are unavoidable questions, and they are not trivial: the whole status of poetry itself is involved and at stake in them. On them may depend, therefore, Hegel's whole attempt to force his way beyond (the question of) literature.

Poetry is in effect the locus, for Hegel, of a double difficulty. The first, which is architectonic in nature, concerns the position of poetry. A position as ambiguous as that, for example, of tragedy—and such, in fact, as to compel Hegel to highlight this "kinship" of the poetic and the speculative. This is again a double position. On the one hand, as Hegel never stops repeating, poetry is the oldest of the arts of speech: "Poetry is older than skillfully elaborated prosaic speech."[63] But on the other hand, poetry also comes after prose, defines itself against prose, and has as it were the task, after prose "has already drawn into its mode of treatment the entire contents of the spirit," of sublating, in prose, that which subjects language to mere understanding.[64] It is, therefore, as though there were two kinds of poetry, or more precisely, as though this double position somehow shook the unity of the historical and systematic process of truth—something in history (the primitiveness of the poetic) resists systematic determination (according to which poetry must be situated between the prose of the understanding and thinking reason manifesting itself in its own element). If we add to this that, from the point of view of philosophy, as we have seen, poetry—as the general locus of the dissolution of art—prepares the advent of scientific prose, we can see that the difficulty, far from being cleared up, only gets worse, and in such a way that no "decision" here seems able—however powerful the Hegelian "reserve" ["répondant"]—to insure its erasure.

And this first difficulty supposes another, which relates precisely to the strange determination of poetic form, that is, of the form of poetic *Bilden*. This *Bilden* is untranslatable. We must understand it at least as the formation [*le façonner*], the *Gestalten*, of the figure or fiction in general—and as the imaging [*l'imager*] of the image or the rhetorical figure. It corresponds, in sum, to *Dichten* in its most common and classical sense, and for which the best equivalents would be the *plastic* or the *fictional*, if we appeal at least to the broadest sense of the Greek *plassein* or *plattein* (*fingere* in Latin, *feindre* in seventeenth-century French) as it can serve, for instance in Plato,[65] to determine the *poiein* of "music" or of "poïesis" in general (a *poiein* to which, moreover, as we have seen, Hegel explicitly refers). Hegel relies on such *fictioning* [*fictionner*] with enough precision to remind us that speech, the element of poetry, is "this most malleable material [*dies bildsamste Material*, this material which is shapable to the highest degree], the direct property of the spirit, of all media of expression the one most capable of seizing the interests and movements of the spirit in their inner vivacity."[66] Fictioning, therefore, is *rein theoretisch*, purely theoretical, because it is *ganz geistig*, completely spiritual. Poetry is very precisely *theoretical fiction* (which does not mean *fictional theory*, nothing ever being "reversible" in this area).[67]

Poetic fictioning is indeed an inward fictioning; and if it is true that poetry is "actual *speaking*, i.e. audible words which in respect of their temporal duration as well as their real sound must be moulded [*gebildet*] by the poet, and this necessitates tempo, rhythm, euphony, rhyme, and so forth,"[68] it is no less true that "the words are only *signs* of ideas and therefore the real origin of poetic speech lies neither in the choice of single words and the manner of their collocation into sentences and elaborate paragraphs, nor in euphony, rhythm, rhyme, etc., but in the sort and kind of *representation*."[69] Hence the status of poetic *form*, that intermediate register between manifestation and the speculative, which destines poetry (theoretical fiction), in its very kinship with the speculative, to sublate (while dissolving) art in general: this is the status of representation (*Vorstellung*):

> What in the visual arts is the perceptible shape [*Gestalt*] expressed in stone and colour, in music the soul-laden harmony and melody, i.e. the external mode in which a subject *appears* artistically, this in poetry can only be representation [*Vorstellung*]. This is a point to which we have to recur continually. The power of poetic fictioning [*das dichterische Bilden*] consists therefore in the fact that poetry gives shape [*gestaltet*] to a subject-matter within, without proceeding to express it in actual visual shapes [*wirkliche Außengestalten*] or in series of melodies; and thereby it makes the external object produced by the other arts into an internal one which the spirit itself externalizes for representation [*für das Vorstellen*] in the form that this internal object has and is to keep within the spirit.[70]

Poetry thus occupies, if we may say so, that zero space or this nonlocus (but which constitutes perhaps all of space, that is, the whole "internal" spacing of language) which is the dividing line "itself" between the external and the internal, outside and inside, manifestation and thought. It is a plastic (fictioned) use of language (hence its strength and its liveliness, its animating power), but this figuration (this fictioning) is essentially already turned toward the inside, and affecting ultimately (that is, also, at the limit of the concept itself) the "signified" alone. The essence of poetry is therefore *figurative representation* [*représentation ima-*

gée]—nothing more, then, than figuration in the *rhetorical* sense of the term—a representation separated from the concept (from presentation itself) only by the distance separating the proper from the improper. The Hegelian determination of poetry is the classical rhetorical determination of poetry. This is why, all things considered, it is less a matter of sublating in Science the plastic use of language in its material aspect (the plastic use of the signifier) than the plastic use of the sign itself. The recourse to language is unavoidable, but not the recourse to figure (or to the effects of signification of the signifier alone). This is very precisely what romanticism never understood.[71] But this is also why, if the figure is this already internal externalization or this already spiritual manifestation, it is inevitable that, in phenomeno-logy, the (re)presentation of emerging knowledge—to the extent that therein is prepared the presentation of Knowledge itself as that which is—should be accomplished through figures and should lead the chain of figures to the figure of representation itself, which is (the) revealed representation (of revealed religion)—and, as such, should dispose to sublation (if we take for granted here that revealed religion is the revelation of representation). Phenomeno-logy as a poem? As theoretical fiction? It will be objected that *Gestalt* is not figure in the rhetorical sense of the word. But then why, once again, the poetic "slip" that concludes the *Phenomenology of Spirit*?

We shall not get into the question that arises here, which is none other than the now classic question entitled: *rhetoric and philosophy*.[72] Nor shall we ask what differentiates speculative *Gestalt* from rhetorical figure. For this, a whole commentary on the *Phenomenology* (at least) would doubtless be necessary. We shall simply ask what brings together in the same "logic" (of internalization, of spiritualization, of appropriation, in short, of sublation) all the possible Hegelian treatments of figure—from the properly plastic, external, phenomenal figure to the poetic or rhetorical figure (the internalized figure), or even to the "speculative figure." What is, then, the logic of transfiguration? Is it not a logic of revelation, that is, in each instance, a logic of unveiling? Would the operation we saw performed on Greek statuary not be repeated on poetry or on philosophical discourse itself? Such a question proceeds from a suspicion about the very nature of the figure: why indeed does Hegel attempt in all possible ways, even to the point of risking the indecision of the speculative division itself, to reintroduce the entire fictional determination of the poetic (and hence all of figurality in general) into the most classical problematic of *figurative discourse*? Why this classical gesture? Why even this classicism? Would it not be in order to identify the figure with the veil—phenomenality in general (form, manifestation, externalization, *Bild*, *Gestalt*, etc.) with veiling? To frame sublation within *parousia* and truth within *Offenbarung*? To embed adequation, identity, self-equality (all the forms of *homoïosis*) in *aletheia*, the play of veiling-unveiling? To *save* the possibility of unveiling—of adequation, of homogeneity, of presentation, of presence, of thought, and of knowledge (of the presence of knowledge as the knowledge of presence)? To insure the *onto-theio-logical*?

It is clear what such a suspicion cannot fail in its turn to conceal. Nothing less than the question known by the name of the *relationship to Kant*. Known by this name, that is, in general, *avoided* under this name. So we will not depart from this general rule. And as long as we are "avoiding" it, we shall even give up the ridiculous attempt to sketch its outline. Besides, one can imagine the tortuous, complex (perhaps topologically unrepresentable) path we would have to follow or trace, the strange "story" we would have rigorously to reconstruct—a story in which Kant, for instance, having read Hegel, would write, but in Nietzsche's hand, something like the Heideggerian text.[73] We shall thus be content with a shorter and more direct path. And, narrowing once more the angle of vision, we shall simply ask what, in figure or in fiction, is so threatening that it must always, so to speak, be reduced to the veil, hidden under the veil, considered only as veiled.

What, then, is so threatening in the figure? Nothing, obviously, if we keep to a (the) classical conception of figure or of fiction, that is, to a fictioning such as philosophy, from Plato to Christian allegorism, from Dante to Descartes and Leibniz, has always opposed, under whatever name, to the *e-vidence* of truth. This does not mean that it was ever a question of excluding fictioning (even less of "repressing" it). It has always functioned, on the contrary, either as a propaedeutic to the revelation of truth (this is the case, for example, in the medieval treatment of *figura*, *umbra veritatis*, as Dante and Renaissance Neoplatonism will use it),[74] or, as in Cartesianism, as an auxiliary to the presentation of truth, that is, as a supplement to evidence (which is limited by—among other things—its temporal punctuality). This is why fiction is never absolutely error (even in Spinoza) or lie (even in Plato), even if it is—and this is the price of its inevitable belonging to the sensuous, to subjectivity, to the imaginary—on the side of the shadow, of phenomenal darkness, of indistinctness, of confusion, of veiling, and of the veiled. And in the same way, rigorously, that, on the tenacious model of the erotic division established by "Plato" (Aristophanes) in the *Symposium*, there are, as Leibniz says, two kinds of eloquence—the heavenly and the earthly, the Uranian and the Pandemian[75]—there are two kinds of fiction, the "good" one, obviously, and the "bad" one; the one that leads to truth, effaces itself before truth or even heightens it—and the other one, the one that resists, that does not efface itself, does not lift [*ne se (re)lève pas*], the aberrant one. A double veil, two kinds of veil: transparency and the obstacle.[76] Fiction is always divided. But we must add immediately that the good one always has within it the wherewithal to touch up, correct, and master the bad one. At least by right. Philosophical discourse excludes nothing, especially not what it represents to itself as being of an "order" not its own. And even when it attempts to exclude (if ever it wants to), its "sublating" power is such that what is excluded never fails to return, so that not only must philosophy negotiate with it, but it can also claim it, (re)adopt it, or even, at the limit, pride itself on it. Philosophy divides, decides, and *criticizes*[77]: but what it severs, it also constitutes on both sides, and the whole as such (be it re-arranged) *returns*—in all senses[78]—to philosophy.

But if fiction and the figure thus belong to philosophy and have always belonged to it; if there is no theory of fictioning in general that is not fundamentally included in the very system of the most "primitive" philosophical oppositions (sensuous/intelligible, dark/clear, indistinct/distinct, particular/universal, improper/proper, imaginary/real, veil/unveiling, etc.), this in no way prevents this fictional order from having been the occasion or the pretext for a certain displacement that, without destroying this system of oppositions (it is indestructible) or breaking the deep bond between the fictional and the theoretical (it is unbreakable), nevertheless has posited the fictional in a different (displaced) relation to truth by dissociating it, at least up to a certain point, from the problematic of veiling/unveiling. This displacement is difficult to measure, if not to perceive. For the place where it occurs (the place it produces in order to occur) is very precisely everything that, in the eighteenth century, is called *aesthetics*—that complex, hazy, empirical-theoretical field about which, as we well know, Hegel does not want to hear anything, to the point that the *Aesthetics* itself (as the science both of art and of the discourse on art) can, in this respect and without the least difficulty, also be interpreted as a gigantic "war-machine" directed against aesthetics in general (from Boileau to the romantics) and intended, under the pretext of correcting its mistakes (its inability to grasp the beautiful in its *concept*), to contain the danger which its "establishment" represented (or could still represent).[79]

Why aesthetics? Because in a way, aesthetics cannot be defined otherwise than as a theory of fiction—aesthetics is the *theory of fiction*. That is, the locus where fiction, the fictional in general, becomes worthy of theory, becomes worthy of having its own theory—and in such a way that, if none of the privileges of the theoretical itself is questioned therein, the contagious effect of the fictional nevertheless makes itself felt in (its) theory and insidiously threatens its integrity, its autonomy, and its validity. The reason for this is that the domain invested by aesthetics and constituted by it as a theoretical domain is, under the name of "sensuous knowledge" (*cognitio sensitiva*), the previously nontheoretical domain par excellence, that is, the domain falling, in accordance with the great Platonic-Aristotelian divisions, under the joint jurisdiction of simple poetic and rhetorical *technai*: the general domain, as we know, of that about which there is only "sensuous discourse" (*oratio sensitiva*), that is, the domain of uncertain and probable knowledge, of veri-similitude (*verisimilitudo*), or, which amounts to the same, of the *analogon rationis*. Here, moreover, it is poetics—more than rhetoric proper—that plays a decisive role. Witness, in the first place, Baumgarten himself—whose terminology we were just using: the foundation of aesthetics as such, that is, as a science, occurs precisely in his poetics, in the *Meditationes philosophicae de nonnullis ad poema pertinentibus* of 1735, of which the *Aesthetica* will be explicitly given as an extension. For the concept of science is pertinent here, or, in the last instance, rigorously justified, only if the object promised to it (sensuous knowledge and discourse)—traditionally depreciated (which Baumgarten does not for a moment dream of contesting),[80] but depreciated to such an extent that it had disappeared from the theoretical or epistemic horizon as such— is susceptible, in its own order (that is, in its very inferiority), of a "perfection," or, following Bäumler's translation, of a "completion" (*Vollendung*).[81] And *oratio sensitiva perfecta*, perfected sensuous discourse, is poetry.[82] This is why it is the prerogative of poetics (whose task is precisely, through science, to lead *oratio sensitiva* to perfection),[83] rather than of rhetoric in the broad sense of the term (that is, the science of the *imperfect* exposition of sensuous representations),[84] to engender aesthetics proper.

It goes without saying—but we must insist—that Baumgarten does not at all overturn the Platonic, then Cartesian, hierarchy of the sensuous and the intelligible. On the contrary, the whole interest of the aesthetic operation stems paradoxically from the fact that it never supposes a "reversal" of the classical hierarchies and that it is content to apply to a presumably nontheorizable field an entirely traditional concept of science. The revalorization of the sensuous (of the *aïstheta*) is all the stronger and more powerful as it is not accompanied by any correlative devalorization of the intelligible (of the *noeta*) and of the science corresponding to it, that is, logic. It is, in general, the order of the *gnoseologia inferior* (and poetry in the first place) that enters, for itself, into the philosophical. It is "pure aesthetic intuition," says Cassirer, that we must "save."[85] And if what is covered, therefore, by such a "legitimation" of the "inferior faculties of the soul" is nothing other, according to the introductory definition of the *Aesthetica*, than the entire field of the *analogon rationis* (defined both as the domain of art and as that of "thinking beautifully"),[86] one can perhaps imagine the impact that this gesture will have (its future, the effect it will produce, the threat it will represent) when, from the locus constituted by it as "aesthetics"—but at the price of a then unforeseeable transformation—*ratio* as such will withdraw into a radical inaccessibility. Of course, Baumgarten is far from "containing" Kant (even if Kant is perhaps less far, in many respects, from being ruled and constrained by Baumgarten). Baumgarten is even further still from "prefiguring" Nietzsche. Yet something like a "break" in (the question of) truth, an irruption of heterogeneity, a revalorization of the "low," begins to take shape with him. With difficulty, in indecision and "hesitation." But in a clear enough way nevertheless to have awakened Hegel's anxiety.

For once aesthetics has been defined in the broadest terms—even once it has been defined more strictly as the science of beauty (*pulcritudo*) and of "the art of thinking beautifully" (*ars pulcre cogitandi*) – the essential part of the aesthetic operation bears on the determination of the *faculty* required by aesthetics itself. And it turns out – naturally – that this faculty is the *ars fingendi*, the art of fiction or of figuration, the art of fictioning, on which (what Baumgarten calls) "aesthetic truth" (*veritas aesthetica*), that is, verisimilitude itself, *verisimilitudo*,[87] entirely relies. Indeed, of all the inclinations that work toward forming the "natural inclination to think beautifully" in general – an inclination that, according to the Aristotelian concept applied, as we know, to the art of perceiving the similar (*to homoïon*) and of making good metaphors,[88] is an *euphuia*, an innate natural gift[89] – the *dispositio naturalis ad imaginandum*, the *fantasia*, to which the *ars fingendi* refers[90] (*Phantasie* as *Einbildungskraft*, in other words), bears, more than accuracy of judgment, perspicacity, memory, taste, etc., the whole burden, or almost the whole burden, of insuring the very *elegance* through which beautiful thinking[91] is determined and which is properly discovered or revealed in the *figure*, or, as Baumgarten once again says, in the *schema*.[92]

To be sure, in this fiction so allied with elegance, there is nothing that seems too threatening. For instance, we hardly leave the field of what we are compelled to call, after Plato, a *cosmetic* conception of beauty. The art of thinking beautifully is, quite simply, the art of decorating, of adorning, of making up, of dressing, of veiling, of "arranging" thought in order to make it, as we say, "presentable." And if it is a matter of elegance (or of ornamentation), it is not only because elegance is, as the old oratory rhetoric used to state, the indispensable condition of pleasing and persuading, but also (and especially) because elegance has the power of *animating* thought, of making it *alive* – of making up, in sum, for the deficiency of bare thought, that is, for "cold," "dry," or "dead" abstraction, for the bare rigidity of the concept. This is why thinking beautifully, fictioning thought, consists in fact in introducing *oratio sensitiva*, figurative discourse, into discourse itself, into theoretical discourse. This amounts to "poetizing" discourse. Thus, there is apparently nothing here that is not very classical. And it would be easy to show that everything in Baumgarten (as in aesthetics generally), including what is proposed more narrowly as a theory of fiction,[93] remains encompassed by (and subordinated to) the most traditional determination of truth: after all, fiction is defined here as being able only to cover it up (or to veil it), even if this capacity entails the *duty* of *heightening* it.

And it is precisely this function (this duty) granted to (demanded of) fiction that begins, in spite of everything, to displace truth itself, that is, to shake a whole relationship, at least willed or desired, between philosophy (philosophical discourse) and truth. Here we are on familiar footing. Or, more precisely, we broach the prehistory of a history itself well known: that of a certain denunciation of philosophy that goes, from Nietzsche to Valéry (the Valéry of *Léonard et les philosophes*, for example), through the sudden discovery that philosophy is perhaps after all only an "aesthetic phenomenon." This is, indeed, what the theory of *verisimilitudo* and of *ars fingendi* supposes, what the desire to heighten truth through fictioning requires: a certain practice of philosophy, that is, an "artistic" practice of philosophy. And what aesthetics prepares, that for which, so to speak, it "militates," is the "philosopher-artist." For not only, as Baumgarten says, is it not unworthy of philosophy to be concerned with art (with "sensuous things, phantasms, fables, emotional disturbances, etc."),[94] but it is also the philosopher's duty to perfect himself as an artist. This is what Aristotle and Leibniz, for instance, did by excelling "in both parts of the cognitive faculty" (the sensuous and the noetic) and by knowing how, without sacrificing one to the other, "to apply both in their proper places."[95] To speak, in this respect, of "humanistic conception," as Cassirer does, is insufficient. What manifests itself here—but the consequences of such a manifestation will, despite Hegel, doubtless be irreversible—is rather what may be the deepest desire in all of philosophy, which is not to *fail* either to be an art, and which requires the heightening of truth through fictioning. This desire, as we know, is so strong and so powerful in the *rivalry* it implies that it has resisted all attempts at "exclusion" or debasement—of the artistic, the poetic, the fictional, etc.—and that it has always *marked* the very discourse in which these attempts have taken place (beginning, of course, with Platonic discourse). In this sense, an artist has always inhabited the philosopher. And this is certainly what will allow one to say, once more, that there is nothing very new here: that this determination of art as ornament or as decoration, this conception of beauty as elegance, will never have produced, in philosophy—whatever the discursive register or the philosophical aim—anything but a concern for *beautiful presentation*. That is, quite simply, a *stylistic* concern equally noticeable in the recourse to set eloquence or to *Kunstprosa*, in the use of poetic resources (versification, figuration, rhetoric, exemplification, etc.), in dramatization and dialogue, and in narration—even in demonstrative rigor and in the choice of the *mos geometricum* itself (so great is also the aesthetic fascination exerted by mathematics). So there would be nothing here that exceeds the preoccupation with *speaking well*, or, which amounts to the same, *writing well*.

But the "novelty" here, and the threat, are in the *affirmation*. When aesthetics claims and theorizes the right for philosophy to be an art, for truth to be figured, etc., it hardly matters in fact whether a classical conception of art or of figure is involved. Just as it hardly matters whether, allowing for its inscription in a precise historical and sociological space (the eighteenth century of salons, Societies, the University, etc.), such a gesture rediscovers and "modernizes" the very old (philosophical) obsession with "popularity." The point is rather that a certain emphasis on the necessity of veiling truth (and, correlatively, of unveiling the sensuous), a certain *verification*, as it were, of the poetic, the figural, the fictional, etc., begins, without the need for any "reversal" of values, without any limit of the philosophical being even affected (the "philosopher-artist" is, as we know, an old story), slowly to pervert the "logic of truth," that is, the logic of (un)veiling, dis-

sociating (at least in part) the figural from "aletheic" play, displacing the play itself
and so preparing the paradoxical locus where truth could be *revealed* as undis-
coverable [*indévoilable*], unrepresentable: *un-(re)presentable, undarstellbar*.

It is easy to understand that this is precisely what Hegel would have liked to
avoid. And what, consequently, he fought against, openly or not. It is, in any
case, the reason for which he had to "redress" the figural, veil the figure, confine
the fictional, and compel poetry (the veiled discourse) to be opposed to philosophy. There was at bottom, in aesthetics (in the sense of the term that Hegel will
deem *empirical*)—there was perhaps, in a certain empiricism in general, the
opening of a possible *era* of truth. Hegel must have wanted to close it by *verifying*
it, that is, by revising the *verification* of the fictional, of the sensuous, of the
verisimilar, etc., that it implied. A closing all the more violent and brutal as the
said era, in the vagueness of its outline, in the contradictoriness of its postula-
tions, in its very *indecision*, not only (nor even, probably, essentially) included
Kant, but also as the whole disordered, confused, mixed, heterogeneous (philosophical and theological, mythographical, poetic, speculative and empirical, dog-
matic and critical, etc.) "ebb" of Kantianism—romanticism "itself"—had come to
inscribe and almost to establish itself within it.

And it is in such a conflict, in such a struggle within philosophy, that woman is
at stake. And of which Venus (Aphrodite) is the emblematic *figure*. An abyss
[*abyme*] in which the "logic" of figuration (that is, of analogy and of the "symbolic") perhaps overflows—leading it beyond itself—the Hegelian discourse of
figure.

Woman is at stake because she represents, not as Hegel through Schiller would
have liked, the sensuous itself in its opposition to the spiritual, or—which
amounts to the same once it has been rigged with a veil—the "inner fusion of the
sensuous and the spiritual," but the sensuous in *its* "truth," which is the "truth"
of figure and the fictional. Because, in other words, she represents or signifies
that there is a "truth of the sensuous" which is not beyond the sensuous, which
is not *verified* in trans-figuration and is not (re)presented in absolute (re)presenta-
tion. But, rather, in *fiction*, in (re)presentation as fiction.

A fiction of which Aphrodite is indeed the figure.

Not the Aphrodite who is unveiled in order to exhibit the purely sensuous in
its nudity or to arouse pure desire in its crudity. Even less to exhibit the animal
side in "man" and the absence, the *lack* of the spiritual—castration (speculative
castration—assuming there is another kind). Not the Aphrodite who must, therefore, be veiled so that she may attain to the figure itself (to the figure capable,
in figuring itself as such, of [re]presenting art in its spiritual destination), who
must be clothed and transformed (if not disguised) through some speculative
"Pygmalionism" into Pallas, into virgin Athena ("In the case of the Greek god-
desses what predominates is the maiden form which least of all permits the ap-

pearance of a woman's natural vocation"),[96] emerging all armed from the fore-head of Zeus because she is the daughter (and the promise) of the Spirit, and whose chlamys unveils, in fact, her spiritual belonging and filiation. – But another Aphrodite, about whom it doubtless matters little (desire, as we know, does not depend upon it) whether we see/know [(sa)voir] her to be veiled or unveiled; an Aphrodite who "slips" [se "dérobe"], so to speak, from the opposition of the sensuous and the spiritual, who does not belong to the Platonic division between the Pandemian and the Uranian: neither prostitute nor priestess, nor "sacred prostitute"–and, moreover, rather a Venus, a *Latin*, *Roman* Aphrodite who no longer speaks the language of the Spirit, even though she is not without "spirit." A figure figuring only the figure or its own plasticity and thereby, in fact, the tute-lary goddess of aesthetics, if it is true that the *ars fingendi* itself, in which the entire *veritas aesthetica* is gathered, is sustained by what Baumgarten calls the *ingenium venustum* (*ingenium venustum et elegans connatum*), or, as we are com-pelled to say, the *Venusian*[97] genius, gift, or nature (*phusis, natura, euphuia . . . dispositio naturalis animae totius . . . quacum nascitur*).

But, as we know, Hegel never names Baumgarten.[98] A silence even heavier, in the context of aesthetics, than the one surrounding *Lucinde*–and literature. A silence explained by the fact that the redressing of aesthetics (the surreptitious covering up of Aphrodite), whence precisely the "plot" against literature will be organized, can only be effected at this price–an exorbitant price, if we think about it (but then it seems that nothing is too expensive for the speculative). Properly speaking, there is here–the word is unavoidable–a *subornation*: the subornation (sub-ornation) of Aphrodite is the subornation of aesthetics, the buy-ing of its silence, the annulment or the diversion of its testimony in favor of, or to the advantage of, the Spirit. Just as it is generally indispensable not to let speak, to silence–to forbid–what does not work in the interests of the Spirit, that is, in sum–the category is unique–"the impudence of the understanding." What held true for *Lucinde* holds true a fortiori for aesthetics, which will never be for-given for allowing *Venustas* to be exhibited, even under "cover" of "elegance" and of "thinking beautifully."

Hence the violence of the accusation of shamelessness. Hence the ethical dis-tortion or drifting of the aesthetic objection. The ethical scandal has always been, in fact, an aesthetic scandal, *the scandal of the aesthetic*–which, like every scan-dal in the eyes of Knowledge and the Spirit, consists in having revealed that *there is nothing to unveil*. Or at least that there might be nothing to unveil. In unveiling the figure in its self-sufficiency, in *showing* Venus–in showing that Venus has nothing to hide, but that she shows herself quite simply (to show herself) and that this is sufficient for her beauty (that is, for beauty)–aesthetics will almost have definitively given the figural over to shamelessness, if indeed shamelessness is basically not otherwise defined than by the refusal to lend oneself or to give one-self to sublation. The woman who refuses herself–to *appropriation*–is always accused of shamelessness (or, to put it more brutally, is called a whore): this is a reaction considered specific to male "paranoia." It is, in any case, the reaction of speculative "absolutism." That the "sensuous" figure may give itself as an "end in itself" is, from the point of view of the speculative, something intolerable. That is to say, *unbearable*. The speculative cannot bear that anything nonspiritual be considered an "end in itself" — be, if you will, *cut off* [*coupé*] from the spiritual. The *abscission* [*coupure*] is intolerable. And Venus, no doubt, is the name of the abscission.

This is why everything that entails the risk of exhibiting the abscission — figure or *Witz*, metaphor or (subjective) "subject," irony, humor, mixture, etc. — must be *veiled*.

Beginning with literature, if it is true that literature is compelled to (re)present itself in the figure of "female instinctive nature." In the features, for instance, of Lucinde.

Translated by Claudette Sartiliot

A Note on Sources

La Fable: originally published in *Poétique* 1 (1970): 51–63. Collected in *Le Sujet de la philosophie: Typographies I* (Paris: Aubier-Flammarion, 1979), 7–30.

Le Détour: originally published in *Poétique* 5 (1971): 53–76. Collected in *Le Sujet de la philosophie: Typographies I* (Paris: Aubier-Flammarion, 1979), 31–74.

Nietzsche Apocryphe: originally published under the title "*La Dissimulation*" in *Nietzsche aujourd'hui?* (Paris: U.G.E., 1973), 2: 9–36. Collected in *Le Sujet de la philosophie: Typographies I* (Paris: Aubier-Flammarion, 1979), 75–109.

L'Oblitération: originally published as a review of Heidegger's *Nietzsche* in *Critique* 313 (June 1973): 487–513. Collected in *Le Sujet de la philosophie: Typographies I* (Paris: Aubier-Flammarion, 1979), 111–84.

La Scène est primitive: originally published under the title "*Note sur Freud et la représentation*" in *Digraphe* 3 (Fall 1974): 70–81. Collected in *Le Sujet de la philosophie: Typographies I* (Paris: Aubier-Flammarion, 1979), 185–216.

L'Imprésentable: originally published in *Poétique* 21 (1975): 53–95.

Notes

Editor's Preface

1. Philippe Lacoue-Labarthe, *Typography: Mimesis, Philosophy, Politics*, ed. Christopher Fynsk (Cambridge, Mass.: Harvard University Press, 1989); *L'Imitation des modernes: Typographies II* (Paris: Galilée, 1986); *Le Sujet de la philosophie: Typographies I* (Paris: Aubier-Flammarion, 1979). The essay "Typographie" was originally published in the collection *Mimesis: Des articulations* (Paris: Aubier-Flammarion, 1975), 165–270.

2. See the foreword to *Le Sujet de la philosophie* (5–6) and to *L'Imitation des modernes* (9–11). One advantage of including "The Unpresentable" here is that this essay pursues a major preoccupation of *Le Sujet de la philosophie*, namely, the relation between literature and philosophy, prolonging in this way the trajectory that would have led to *L'Avortement de la littérature*.

Foreword: Persistence

1. G. W. F. Hegel, *Lectures on the History of Philosophy*, trans. R. F. Brown and J. M. Stuart (Berkeley: University of California Press, 1990), 3: 131. I am paraphrasing somewhat; Hegel says: "Here [with Descartes], we may say, we are at home and, like the sailor after a long voyage, we can at last shout 'Land ho' ['*Land*' *rufen*]."

2. *Hegel's Phenomenology of Spirit*, trans. A. V. Miller (Oxford: Oxford University Press, 1977), 10.

3. See chapter 1, "The Fable," 8.

4. Ibid., 4.

5. I do not mean to slight the differential character of manifestation as it is defined in *Identity and Difference*; but neither can I discuss it at any length here. Again, I refer the reader to Lacoue-Labarthe's analysis in "Obliteration" (see, for example, p. 97–98). Concerning the terms *Ent-fernung* and *é-loignement*, see n. 18, p. 174.

6. Friedrich Nietzsche, *Werke in drei Bänden*, ed. Karl Schlechta (Munich: Hanser, 1956), 3: 862 (Nietzsche's emphasis). See *The Will to Power*, trans. Walter Kaufmann and R. J. Hollingdale

(New York: Random House, 1968), 283: *"We cease to think when we refuse to do so under the constraint of language*; we barely reach the doubt that sees this limitation as a limitation."

7. But probably in a different way. Whereas Lacoue-Labarthe shares a certain historical situation with Nietzsche, Freud, and Heidegger, he does not really share it with Hegel, for the simple reason that the situation itself can be legitimately characterized as post-Hegelian. In other words, in "The Unpresentable," Lacoue-Labarthe occupies alone (unless it is in conjunction with the German romantics) a position of metaphysical undecidability and historical belatedness *relative to* Hegel. Nevertheless, to the extent that he does justice to the ambivalences of Nietzschean, Freudian, and Heideggerian discourse as well as to those of Hegel's text, Lacoue-Labarthe must be given credit for resisting the temptation, strongly pronounced in his generation, to portray Hegel simply and simplistically as *the* figure *against whom* any subsequent self-respecting thought must react.

8. "The Fable," 9.

9. See chapter 4, "Obliteration," 72.

10. Ibid., 59–61, and n. 17, pp. 173–74.

11. Martin Heidegger, "Hölderlin and the Essence of Poetry," trans. Douglas Scott, in *Existence and Being*, ed. Werner Brock (South Bend: Gateway, 1949), 289.

12. "Obliteration," 97.

13. Ibid., 98.

14. Ibid.

15. See Jacques Derrida, *La Voix et le phénomène* (Paris: PUF, 1967), especially 98–99; *Speech and Phenomena*, trans. David B. Allison (Evanston: Northwestern University Press, 1973), 88–89.

16. *La Poésie comme expérience* (Paris: Bourgois, 1986), 30–31; but see also "The Fable," p. 12, where "experience" is already used in this sense.

17. "The Fable," 13.

18. See Jacques Derrida's introduction (entitled "Desistance") to Lacoue-Labarthe's *Typography: Mimesis, Philosophy, Politics*, ed. Christopher Fynsk (Cambridge, Mass.: Harvard University Press, 1989), 1–42. For exemplary instances of its use by Lacoue-Labarthe, see *Typography*, 116, 129, 141, 175, but also the more recent *Musica ficta (Figures de Wagner)* (Paris: Bourgois, 1991), 86. Finally, I would like to mention what I cannot possibly enlarge on here, namely, the implications of desistance for the thinking of gender: see, for example, both *Typography*, 127–29, and the discussion of Hegel and German romanticism in chapter 6, "The Unpresentable," especially 133ff., where desistance, while not yet a component of Lacoue-Labarthe's vocabulary, could arguably be intercalated somewhere—but this is, of course, precisely what would have to be determined—between the "insistence" of the female and the "existence" of the male.

19. *Typography*, 6.

＊

1. The Fable (Literature and Philosophy)

1. Ideology will be understood here as any metaphysics that is unaware of itself as such. But obviously, and for many reasons, this is only a tentative definition.

2. Friedrich Nietzsche, *The Will to Power*, trans. Walter Kaufmann and R. J. Hollingdale (New York: Random House, 1967), 291.

3. The first of these conditions governs the other three to such an extent that we will not be able to avoid referring to it. As for the second, a systematic inventory of the use of the *we* in Nietzsche's language would be required. Concerning the third, the text in its very brevity may be deceptive; the play of negativity is therein produced in a way that is apparently too simple: the negative formulation of Parmenidean identity followed by the affirmation of its reversal. But, on the one hand, one cannot speak of a pure and simple reversal as long as one does not know what Nietzsche means by fiction, and, on the other hand, supposing one does know what he means, if the dialectical appearance is

created by the rapid, laconic, elliptical nature of Nietzsche's style, it is to the general status of Nietzschean *affirmation* that we would have to refer.

4. That is, with the radicalization of the critique of science: all the concepts of metaphysics and science are lies or fictions, conventional fictions, etc. (see, for example, *Beyond Good and Evil*, trans. Walter Kaufmann [New York: Random House, 1966], Part I ["On the Prejudices of Philosophers"], 7–32). But this theme is already present in the notebooks from the years 1872–76.

5. Friedrich Nietzsche, " 'Reason' in Philosophy," §2, *Twilight of the Idols*, trans. Walter Kaufmann, in *The Portable Nietzsche* (New York: Viking, 1954), 480–81.

6. Nietzsche, *Twilight of the Idols*, 486.

7. Nevertheless, one would also have to say that Nietzsche is never altogether "naïvely" anti-Platonic or anti-Christian. As some illustrious examples have shown, the reestablishment of Nietzsche's "seriousness" may weaken a thought that doubtless sought, in the most brutal struggle against Platonism and Christianity, a decisive weapon—more decisive than one may think—against metaphysics itself, which is also to say *piety* in general, *belief.*

8. It is also, according to other texts one must consider, to "practice" appearance for its own sake and to lose oneself in it as in an eternal dream. (See, for example, §54 of Book I of *The Gay Science*, trans. Walter Kaufmann [New York: Random House, 1974], 116, entitled "The consciousness of appearance.")

9. Pierre Klossowski, "Nietzsche, le polythéisme et la parodie," in *Un si funeste désir* (Paris: Gallimard, 1963), 185–228.

10. Ibid., 194.

11. See also the text entitled "Forgetting and Anamnesis in the Experience of the Eternal Return of the Same," pp.107–14 of "Nietzsche's Experience of the Eternal Return," trans. Allen Weiss, in *The New Nietzsche: Contemporary Styles of Interpretation*, ed. David B. Allison (New York: Dell, 1977).

12. Martin Heidegger, *What Is Called Thinking?* trans. J. Glenn Gray (New York: Harper & Row, 1968), 10 (translation modified).

13. Missing, however, is the *murder* of God.

14. [Lacoue-Labarthe refers to Heidegger's use of *das Scheinen* instead of *die Erscheinung* in the second sentence of the passage just quoted: "Sagen ist für die Griechen: offenbar machen, erscheinen lassen, nämlich das Scheinen und das im Scheinen, in seiner Epiphanie, Wesende" (Martin Heidegger, *Was heißt Denken?* [Tübingen: Niemeyer, 1954], 6). This "ennoblement" is preserved in the French (*Qu'appelle-t-on penser?* trans. Aloys Becker and Gérard Granel [Paris: PUF, 1959], 29) through the use of *paraître* instead of *apparence*, and has here been restored to the English translation through the replacement of "appearance" by "appearing."—*Editor*]

15. The whole first part of *What Is Called Thinking?*, which is devoted to Nietzsche, seems to be dominated by this properly metaphysical interpretation, particularly (and Derrida's analysis could easily be applied here) where Heidegger emphasizes the opposition between scream and script ("Script easily smothers the scream," etc., 49) or where he acknowledges the unique "purity" of Socrates (17). These are themselves Nietzschean themes, but such a commentary makes them dull, fixed, and univocal. For example, to the well-known "Socrates, he who does not write" from the notes of 1870–72, Heidegger replies with this revealing text, which doubtless requires no commentary: "All through his life and right into his death, Socrates did nothing else than place himself into this draft, this current [the current toward that which withdraws and hence gives food for thought, etc.], and maintain himself in it. This is why he is the purest thinker of the West. This is why he wrote nothing. For anyone who begins to write out of thoughtfulness must inevitably be like those people who run to seek refuge from any draft too strong for them. An as yet hidden history still keeps the secret why all great Western thinkers after Socrates, with all their greatness, had to be such fugitives. Thinking entered into literature" (17–18, translation modified).

This is also one of the reasons why we have not wanted to follow here the path opened by Heidegger under the theme of poetry and thought. We would sooner be inclined to detect in the poetic, that is, no matter what anyone says, in the figurative, the surest indication of the metaphysical as such. Furthermore, Nietzsche himself thought of this (see the unpublished essay of 1873 "On Truth and Lying in an Extra-Moral Sense," trans. David J. Parent, in *Friedrich Nietzsche on Rhetoric and Language* [New York: Oxford University Press, 1989], 246–57). Surely, for this reason, one must also question the relation between *rhetoric* and *metaphysics*.

16. See the Aristotelian definition of philosophy (*Metaphysics*, Book IV, 1003, a21): *theorei to on e on kai ta touto huparchonta kath'auto,* which Heidegger translates: " 'it looks at what is (in appearance) present as such (thus present), and so (looks at) what already prevails in it (the phenomena in their appearance), from itself' " (*Hegel's Concept of Experience* [New York: Harper & Row, 1970], 134). The reduction of difference is indicated by the inevitable *as (e)* of ontological discourse, even if one speaks of *Differenz als Differenz* (see Martin Heidegger, *Identity and Difference*, trans. Joan Stambaugh [New York: Harper & Row, 1969]).

17. This assumes that the will, which is being in post-Cartesian metaphysics, including Hegel (where the Absolute *wants* to be near us) and the Nietzschean discourse on the will to power, derives from the Greek *eros* and does not fundamentally modify it.

18. Johann Wolfgang von Goethe, *Maxims and Reflections of Goethe*, trans. Bailey Saunders (New York: Macmillan, 1893), 97 (translation modified).

19. "On each side," "at the same time" are, of course, locutions that must be made to disappear.

20. See "Attempt at a Self-Criticism" (1886), in *The Birth of Tragedy*, trans. Walter Kaufmann (New York: Random House, 1967), 17–27, and "Why I Write Such Good Books," in *Ecce Homo*, trans. Walter Kaufmann (New York: Random House, 1967), 259–325, esp. 270–75.

21. *The Birth of Tragedy*, 89.

22. Ibid., 90.

23. Ibid., 90–91.

24. We should also point out the relation that Nietzsche establishes between "formal" constraint, aesthetic constraint, and thought. This relation explains why Sophocles and "the older art" are not so radically different from Plato and why they perhaps do not escape either from metaphysics. The myth of the pre-Socratics, in Nietzsche, is not so pure.

25. Gérard Genette, "Frontiers of Narrative," in *Figures of Literary Discourse*, trans. Alan Sheridan (New York: Columbia University Press, 1982), 127–44. Genette's whole analysis takes off from texts by Plato (*Republic*, III) and Aristotle (*Poetics*), that is, from the distinction between *diegesis* and *mimesis*.

26. René Girard, *Deceit, Desire and the Novel: Self and Other in Literary Structure*, trans. Yvonne Freccero (Baltimore: The Johns Hopkins University Press, 1965), and "From *The Divine Comedy* to the Sociology of the Novel," in Elizabeth and Tom Burns, eds., *Sociology of Literature and Drama* (Harmondsworth: Penguin, 1973), 101–8.

27. See Jacques Derrida, "Force and Signification," in *Writing and Difference*, trans. Alan Bass (Chicago: University of Chicago Press, 1978), 3–30.

2. The Detour

1. At the time of its first publication in *Poétique* 5 ("Rhétorique et philosophie"), this text preceded a collection of documents entitled "Nietzsche—Rhétorique et langage" (pp. 99–142), prepared in collaboration with Jean-Luc Nancy and introducing the first French translation of a group of notes and course fragments dating from the years 1872–75: the course on rhetoric of 1874 (§§1–7, the only ones published so far in the various German editions of the complete works), some passages from the course on the history of Greek eloquence, the introduction (devoted to the question of the origin of language) to a course on Latin grammar, etc. It is to this collection of texts that I refer here, as well as to *The Birth of Tragedy*, *Philosophy in the Tragic Age of the Greeks*, and *The Book of the*

Philosopher. The course on rhetoric has been abbreviated as *Rh*. [The reader is referred to "Rhéto-rique et langage" for complete bibliographical information pertaining to the various German editions of the texts under discussion. These editions will be cited where appropriate. — *Editor*]

2. I refer here to Jacques Derrida's "White Mythology," originally published in the same issue of *Poétique* and subsequently reprinted in *Marges de la philosophie* (Paris: Minuit, 1972). [*Margins of Philosophy*, trans. Alan Bass (Chicago: University of Chicago Press, 1982), 207-71.]

3. Nietzsche appears to remain faithful here to the classical tradition, which tends to conflate a reoriented rhetoric with grammar in general (see Gérard Genette, "Introduction," in Pierre Fontanier, *Les Figures du discours* [Paris: Flammarion, 1968], 7-8). One reads in Nietzsche's Course on Rheto-ric, for example: "Grammar in its entirety is the product of so-called *figurae sermonis*" (*Rh.* §3; *Gesammelte Werke* [Munich: Musarion, 1922], 5: 300; see "Description of Ancient Rhetoric," trans. Carole Blair, in *Friedrich Nietzsche on Rhetoric and Language*, henceforth *NRL* [New York: Oxford University Press, 1989], 25 [translation modified]).

4. A peremptory remark from the last outline of *The Book of the Philosopher* (fragment 193) seems finally to give notice, by brutally reinscribing rhetoric within the space of philosophy itself: "Often among the Greeks an *older* form is a superior form, for example, *dithyramb* and *tragedy*. The danger for the Greeks resided in their *virtuosity* in all genres; with Socrates begin the virtuosos of life, Socrates, the new dithyramb, the new tragedy, *the invention of the rhetor! The rhetor is a Greek invention of the late era.* They invented 'form in itself' (and also the philosopher to go along with it)." But this text is *also* ambiguous since it targets, after all, only a certain "institutionalization" of rhetoric and can still preserve a "natural" or "primitive" rhetoric of which Rhetoric itself would be the virtuoso repetition. [Section numbers cited by Lacoue-Labarthe refer to Friedrich Nietzsche, *Das Philoso-phenbuch/Le Livre du philosophe*, French trans. Angèle K. Marietti (Paris: Aubier-Flammarion, 1969); all further references to this work, henceforth abbreviated *Phb.*, will include the section num-ber of this bilingual edition as well as the appropriate page number from the *Gesammelte Werke* (Munich: Musarion, 1922), vol. 6. The passage quoted here is from p. 105. — *Editor*]

5. Precisely as of this period, Nietzsche violently stresses this "empiricism." He does so, for ex-ample, in the drafts for the preface or introduction to *Philosophy in the Tragic Age of the Greeks*. It is still a matter of simply reversing a certain interpretation of philosophy and its history: "philosoph-ical systems are wholly true for their founders only" (preface of 1874, in *Philosophy in the Tragic Age of the Greeks*, trans. Marianne Cowan [Washington, D.C.: Regnery Gateway, 1962], 23); "The only thing of interest in a refuted system is the personal element. It alone is what is forever irrefutable" (preface of 1879, ibid., 25). But this theme is tied rather clearly to the suspicion that philosophy is to be considered as a work of art, a "literary" work. Thus, in *The Book of the Philosopher* (I, §53; Musarion, 6: 20), where philosophy appears as a form of poetry [*Dichtkunst*] and where poetry, in its turn, presents itself as an "extension of the *mythic instinct*": "overcoming [*Überwindung*] of knowl-edge by *myth-creating* forces." This chain, which leads, through "literature," from "personality" to "myth," doubtless heralds the *textual* resumption that Nietzsche will ultimately attempt of his own life and of all philosophy. I refer the reader to the "biographical" analyses of Gilles Deleuze and Pierre Klossowski as well as to the reading of *Ecce Homo* and *The Antichrist* proposed by Dominique Tassel ("Le Texte et ses œuvres," in Nietzsche, *L'Antéchrist* [Paris: U.G.E., 1967], 123-82).

6. This is what Nietzsche, in *Ecce Homo*, calls an "accident": "whatever marks an epoch in [my life] came my way by accident, never through someone's recommendation" (*Ecce Homo*, trans. Walter Kaufmann [New York: Random House, 1967], 244). It is true that this concerns the reading of Stendhal. Nothing *philological* seems to have had, for Nietzsche, such importance: "Of course there are also my *philologica*. But this no longer interests either of us," states a letter to Brandes of April 1888 (in *Nietzsche Briefwechsel*, ed. Giorgio Colli and Mazzino Montinari [Berlin: de Gruyter, 1984], 3 [5]: 288). Even less so when it is only a matter of notes. The texts in question here are thus forgotten, buried; they belong to no recognized period. This is obviously their *fortune* [*chance*].

7. For example — and this is not the only one, although it is especially revealing — in this critique

of Florentine aesthetics as guilty of having given birth to opera: "Because [the man incapable of art] does not sense the Dionysian depth of music, he changes his musical taste into an appreciation of the understandable word-and-tone-rhetoric of the passions in the *stilo rappresentativo*, and into the voluptuousness of the arts of song" (Friedrich Nietzsche, *The Birth of Tragedy*, trans. Walter Kaufmann [New York: Random House, 1967], 116–17).

8. See Charles Andler (*Nietzsche, sa vie et sa pensée* [Paris: Gallimard, 1958], 1: 455ff. and 2: 75ff.), who abundantly exploits this vein but makes no mention whatsoever, in his commentary on *The Book of the Philosopher*, of the work on rhetoric (even less of its sources). It is true that the reading of Zöllner is decisive, as, moreover, Nietzsche's scientific readings always were. To be brief, Nietzsche found in Zöllner a kind of "Schopenhauerism" more critical and less idealistic (metaphysical in a loose sense) than in Schopenhauer himself: in this case, a psychophysiology and a sociology of the genesis of knowledge (of language, the concept, truth, etc.). It is this scientific inflection of Schopenhauer that Nietzsche begins by playing against the romantic and Wagnerian reading which is still, to a large extent, that of *The Birth of Tragedy*. And it is to a bit of this same strategy, but in an entirely different text, that Nietzsche will return in the years 1876–79 (*Human, All Too Human*). So that one might think that the detour through rhetoric, given its sources (through Gerber, it is in effect an entire legacy recaptured by romanticism that is transmitted to Nietzsche), marks a "critical retreat." It is doubtless nothing of the kind. To speak only of critical radicality, Gerber and the theme of rhetoric (in Nietzsche's use of them) are quite as important as Zöllner, whose hypothesis of a matter endowed with sensations, for example, risks obliterating representational separation in its entirety (see *Phb.*, I, §98; Musarion, 6: 40). Furthermore, the reading of Zöllner also marks the rhetorical theme or conspires with it (see the beginning of "On Truth and Lying in an Extra-Moral Sense" [1873], where Nietzsche manages to reconcile the two readings). All of this is, of course, very approximate. We would have to locate precisely Gerber's intrusion into this text (this reading) of the first draft of *The Book of the Philosopher*, in order to calculate its effects. Let us say quickly that the crux of the matter seems to be determined around fragment 130, even though the term *metaphor* appears earlier (fragment 90).

9. At least this: Nietzsche himself, in *Ecce Homo*, characterizes them as "thoroughly warlike." Of the four pieces that were alone completed and published, there is not one that could not be considered as a work of Wagnerian "propaganda." Yet we know that at the very time when he was writing them, Nietzsche was already thinking about something else entirely.

10. I refer here to the text of Maurice Blanchot, "Nietzsche et l'écriture fragmentaire," in *L'Entretien infini* (Paris: Gallimard, 1969), 227–55. We wish to oppose this fragmentation to *Darstellung* in the Hegelian sense of a "presentation of emerging [*apparaissant*] knowledge," and so also to the Book. This opposition is equally valid for dissertation in the sense, for example, of Kant's *Dissertation of 1770*. The Birth of Tragedy would still, according to this hypothesis, be a Book—in spite of some fractures, a certain running in place, and perhaps, already, a real inability to be one. It might be, ultimately, Nietzsche's only "Book," although this would have to be rigorously demonstrated.

11. In *The Birth of Tragedy*, the *fatum libellorum* designates the catastrophic history of Books, accidental fragmentation. The major models are the pre-Socratics and Pascal.

12. [There is no entirely satisfactory way to translate *désœuvrement*, whose semantic scope in both Blanchot and Lacoue-Labarthe is determined not only by a certain conception of the *œuvre* as totality or totalization, but also by an understanding of the prefix in terms other than those of (dialectical) negativity. In other words, *dés-œuvrement* is not just the absence of an *œuvre*, it is also the undoing or failure of work as an *activity*, of the labor of negation, and in this sense might also be translated as *inaction*. —Editor]

13. Nietzsche will speak of a *crisis* (*Ecce Homo* and the letter to Brandes already cited). He also speaks of a brutal realization, while denying that the break with Wagner had been decisive and even that there had been a "break." But one has to interpret attentively how this crisis, this awakening, this

false break are inscribed within a whole "family romance," or, as G. Durand says, a "mythic décor." For example, all of this *repeats* the illness and death of his father.

14. See *The Birth of Tragedy*, §18, and *The Book of the Philosopher*, I, §§37ff.; Musarion, 6: 11ff.

15. Musarion, 5: 3; "The History of Greek Eloquence," trans. David J. Parent, in *NRL*, 213.

16. Musarion, 5: 4-5; *NRL*, 214.

17. Musarion, 5: 3; *NRL*, 213. This theme recurs constantly beginning with the question of Greek tragedy, which we do not know because we only dispose of the scenarios (see the lecture of 1870 entitled "Greek Musical Drama," in Friedrich Nietzsche, *Werke Kritische Gesamtausgabe* [henceforth *KGW*], ed. Giorgio Colli and Mazzino Montinari [Berlin: de Gruyter, 1973], 3 [2]: 3-22). In the texts devoted to rhetoric, it is also a political theme (the decline of language is linked, for example, to journalism, which dominates public life since 1848). We must here postpone the analysis of this subject. We would also have to compare this "debasement" of writing with the "semanticism" governing the analysis of rhetoric, and, in particular, the massive reduction of rhetoric in general to trope (see *Rh.*, §3).

18. Musarion, 5: 4; *NRL*, 213.

19. *Nietzsche's Werke* (Leipzig: Naumann, 1903), 10: 330-31.

20. Immanuel Kant, *The Critique of Judgement*, trans. James Creed Meredith (New York: Oxford University Press, 1952), 184.

21. *Rh.* §1— Musarion, 5: 288; *NRL*, 3.

22. In his analysis of characteristic style, Nietzsche identifies the art of the orator with that of the actor: it is a direct art or a game—of substitution or imitation (*Rh.*, §4). In this way are extended certain analyses of *The Birth of Tragedy* (chapter 8, for example) that will be taken up again with regard to the philosopher (see *Phb.*, I, §58 [Musarion, 6: 23] and the chapter devoted to Thales in *Philosophy in the Tragic Age of the Greeks*). See also, on this subject, the fragment entitled "Cicero and Demosthenes" (in Naumann, 10: 485-86).

23. Course on Eloquence, Musarion, 5: 5; *NRL*, 214.

24. The *Theoretical Introduction* of 1873 (*Phb.*, III, §2; Musarion, 6: 88) states very clearly that "that drive to form metaphors, that fundamental desire in man, which cannot be discounted for one moment, because that would amount to ignoring man himself, is in truth not overcome and indeed hardly restrained by the fact that out of its diminished products, the concepts, a regular and rigid new world is built up for him as a prison fortress. It seeks a new province for its activities and a different riverbed and generally finds it in *myth* and in *art*" ("On Truth and Lying in an Extra-Moral Sense," trans. David J. Parent, in *NRL*, 254). This is one of the major motifs of romantic "linguistics." See Gérard Genette, *Mimologiques: Voyage en Cratylie* (Paris: Seuil, 1976), and Tzvetan Todorov, *Theories of the Symbol*, trans. Catherine Porter (Ithaca: Cornell University Press, 1984). I also refer the reader to A. W. Schlegel's "Leçons sur l'art et la littérature," in Philippe Lacoue-Labarthe and Jean-Luc Nancy, *L'Absolu littéraire* (Paris: Seuil, 1978); original in *Kritische Ausgabe der Vorlesungen* (Paderborn: Schöningh, 1989), vol. 1.

25. *Rh.* §3 Musarion, 5: 297 98; *NRL*, 21.

26. "On the Origin of Language," Musarion, 5: 467-70; *NRL*, 209-12. One can find analogous remarks elsewhere, particularly in the inaugural lecture at Basel ("Homer and Classical Philology"), where philology is also defined as a "science of nature." This is also a theme of romantic linguistics, which is not simply historical and comparative.

27. A good part of this third lecture is devoted to the presence of *poetry* "already in the simple material formation of languages" (Friedrich Wilhelm Joseph Schelling, *Philosophie der Mythologie* [Darmstadt: Wissenschaftliche Buchgesellschaft, 1986], 1: 52). We can discern here an analysis that Gerber (and therefore Nietzsche) will take up again and in which poetry is defined less through metaphor than through simple naming or the difference of genres (see Course on Rhetoric, §3, on synecdoche and metaphor, to which Gerber in fact linked genre; see also the *Introduction* of 1873, *Phb.*, III, §1). It is in the same passage that Schelling, in distinguishing the genres, points out that "we are

quite prepared thus to express spiritual notions through masculine and feminine deities." To which he adds this statement, which requires no comment: "One is almost tempted to say that language itself is only an anemic mythology [*verblichene Mythologie*], and that it has preserved only in an abstract and formal state what mythology contains in a living and concrete state." It is in this sense that Nietzsche can say, in *The Wanderer and His Shadow*, §11: "A philosophical mythology lies concealed in language which breaks out again every moment, however careful one may be otherwise" (*Human, All Too Human*, trans. R. J. Hollingdale [Cambridge: Cambridge University Press, 1986], 306). As for the metaphors of pallor, anemia, and death, used to designate an aged language, they reappear in all the texts on rhetoric.

28. *Rh.* §1—Musarion, 5: 291; *NRL*, 9.

29. *Phb.*, I, §130; Musarion, 6: 49.

30. *Rh.*, §3—Musarion, 5: 298; *NRL*, 21.

31. *Rh.*, §1—Musarion, 5: 287; *NRL*, 3.

32. *Rh.*, §3—Musarion, 5: 298; *NRL*, 23.

33. *Rh.*, §3—Musarion, 5: 298; *NRL*, 21 (translation modified).

34. *Rh.*, §3—Musarion, 5: 298; *NRL*, 23.

35. *Rh.*, §7—Musarion, 5: 316; *NRL*, 53.

36. *Phb.*, III, §1; Musarion, 6: 79; *NRL*, 248–49.

37. *Even* among the Greeks, although rhetoric, precisely, is the acceptance of what the fragment of 1874 ("Cicero and Demosthenes," in Naumann, 10: 485–86) calls *disloyalty*. It is in this sense, moreover, that "all art contains a degree of rhetoric."

38. See Derrida, "White Mythology."

39. See "Attempt at a Self-Criticism" (in *The Birth of Tragedy*, 17–27) and *Ecce Homo*. On Nietzsche's relation to the Hegelian dialectic, see Gilles Deleuze, *Nietzsche and Philosophy*, trans. Hugh Tomlinson (New York: Columbia University Press, 1983).

40. *KGW*, 3 (3): 45–46.

41. Jacques Derrida, *Of Grammatology*, trans. Gayatri Chakravorty Spivak (Baltimore: The Johns Hopkins University Press, 1974), 97ff. See also "The Theater of Cruelty and the Closure of Representation," in *Writing and Difference*, trans. Alan Bass (Chicago: University of Chicago Press, 1978), 232–50.

42. Naumann, 9: 214.

43. The last allusion to the problematic of music appears in fragment 111 of *The Book of the Philosopher*: "Music as a supplement [*Supplement*] to language" (Musarion, 6: 44).

44. This is why I resigned myself to rendering it, in the French translation of *The Birth of Tragedy*, by "substitut analogique." See "Note des traducteurs," in *La Naissance de la tragédie* (*Œuvres philosophiques complètes* [Paris: Gallimard, 1977], 1: 19).

45. *Rh.*, §7—Musarion, 5: 316; *NRL*, 55.

46. "The Dionysian Worldview," in Naumann, 9: 93; also *KGW*, 3 (2): 64.

47. Naumann, 9: 87; *KGW*, 3 (2): 59.

48. *KGW*, 3(3): 378; also Naumann, 9: 214. We designate by "Draft of 1871" the text entitled, in the Naumann edition (9: 212ff.), "Music and Tragedy."

49. Naumann, 9: 92; *KGW*, 3 (2): 67.

50. Naumann, 9: 95; *KGW*, 3 (2): 66.

51. One thinks of the celebrated text *Der Satz vom Grund* (Pfullingen: Neske, 1957), where Heidegger borrows from Angelus Silesius the "epithet" by which he designates Mozart ("the lute of God"—see chapter 9, p. 118). This is a text we would have to compare with another, from *Holzwege*, where Heidegger describes Nietzsche's struggle against Wagner as "the necessity of our history" (see *The Question Concerning Technology*, trans. William Lovitt [New York: Harper & Row, 1977], 143).

52. Naumann, 9: 96–97; *KGW*, 3 (2): 67–68.

53. *The Birth of Tragedy*, 100.

54. See "Rhétorique et langage," 102.

55. See fragment 1 of "Reading and Writing," in Naumann, 9: 329–31.

56. *KGW*, 3(3): 46.

57. *The Birth of Tragedy*, 53.

58. *Rh.*, §3—Musarion, 5: 297; *NRL*, 21.

59. See "Reading and Writing," §6. On this problematic of rhythm, Sarah Kofman offers some useful explanations in her *Nietzsche et la métaphore* (Paris: Payot, 1972) and corrects, in particular, those aspects of the analysis developed here which are, I confess, perhaps too rigid, but necessary to my argument.

60. "Tragedy and Free Spirits," Naumann, 9: 123.

61. *The Birth of Tragedy*, 40. My emphasis.

62. It is revealing that in "Cicero and Demosthenes," reiterating the "legend" according to which Empedocles was the inventor of rhetoric, Nietzsche defines the status of rhetoric precisely by this Empedoclean concept.

63. See Naumann, 9: 286.

64. *The Birth of Tragedy*, 104. My emphasis.

65. *Phb.*, III, §1; Musarion, 6: 85; *NRL*, 252 (translation modified).

66. *The Birth of Tragedy*, 49 (translation modified).

67. Musarion, 3: 343. My emphasis.

68. See draft of 1871.

69. See, for example, *The Gay Science*, trans. Walter Kaufmann (New York: Random House, 1974), Book II, §80: "Art and nature."

70. It is perhaps unnecessary to recall this statement: "I am afraid we are not rid of God because we still have faith in grammar" (*Twilight of the Idols*, trans. Walter Kaufmann, in *The Portable Nietzsche* [New York: Viking, 1954], 483).

71. Nietzsche himself speaks most often in terms of style, of literary writing. In 1886, he notes again that he should perhaps have written *The Birth of Tragedy* "as a poet," or, if not as a poet, then as a "philologist." But this whole preoccupation with style requires much closer study.

72. For a long time, Nietzsche respected certain watchwords of romanticism, particularly those which F. Schlegel divulged in *The Athenaeum* (see "Talk on Mythology," trans. Ernst Behler and Roman Struc, in *Dialogue on Poetry and Literary Aphorisms* [University Park: Pennsylvania State University Press, 1968], 81–93), but which are equally those of Hölderlin, Novalis, K. Ph. Moritz, and the early Schelling, and which obviously reappear in Wagner's major theoretical texts.

73. *The Birth of Tragedy*, 105.

74. See in particular the analysis of Plato that Nietzsche conducts, following Hirzel, in the first chapter of the Course on Rhetoric: "The *mythic* component in the dialogues is the rhetorical: the myth has the verisimilar for its content; and therefore not the aim of instruction, but one of inspiring a *doxa* in one's audience, thus to *peithein*" (Musarion, 5: 290; *NRL*, 7).

75. Eugen Fink, *Nietzsches Philosophie* (Stuttgart: Kohlhammer, 1960), 41–42. Analyzing the texts from 1873 to 1875, Fink "reproaches" Nietzsche for bringing an aesthetic interest to the Greek philosophers and for not recognizing "the ontological concept": "It is possible that in this refusal of the ontological concept [being according to Parmenides, which Nietzsche in fact sees as a metaphor], there resides the essential reason for which Nietzsche could not pursue beyond poetic metaphor his intuition that the world is the play of the Dionysian and the Apollinian." On the "ontological" interpretations of Nietzsche, see Sarah Kofman, "Généalogie, interprétation, texte," *Critique* 275 (April 1970), reprinted in *Nietzsche et la métaphore*, 173–206.

76. It would be more correct to say the figures of sacrilege and of parricide, since the Titans are responsible for the murder of the child Dionysus (Zagreus) whom they tore to pieces (see *The Birth of Tragedy*, §10).

77. See *The Birth of Tragedy*, §§9-10. "When after a forceful attempt to gaze on the sun we turn away blinded, we see dark-colored spots before our eyes, as a cure, as it were. Conversely, the bright image projections of the Sophoclean hero—in short, the Apollinian aspect of the mask—are necessary effects of a glance into the inside and terrors of nature; as it were, luminous spots to cure eyes damaged by gruesome night" (§9, p. 67). This is the way in which Nietzsche states that neither the sun nor death can be looked in the face; but it is also, as we know, a commentary on *Tristan*, which is a little like the "national anthem" of Nietzsche's love for Ariane-Cosima (Wagner).

78. See the plan for a drama entitled *Prometheus* (1874), which concludes with this declaration of the vulture: "I am a bird of misfortune, I have become a myth" (Naumann, 10: 489).

79. *The Birth of Tragedy*, 130.

80. See the draft of the drama entitled *Empedocles*, in Naumann, 9: 130-36.

81. This text had already been written when there appeared, aside from Sarah Kofman's work mentioned earlier, Joachim Goth's *Nietzsche und die Rhetorik* (Tübingen: Niemeyer, 1970) and Bernard Pautrat's *Versions du soleil* (Paris: Seuil, 1971), which, on the texts analyzed here, propose in their turn an indispensable demonstration.

3. Apocryphal Nietzsche

1. Originally a talk given at the conference on Nietzsche at Cerisy-la-Salle in July 1972.

2. [Lacoue-Labarthe's use of the term *démarque* is based here on at least two senses of the verb *(se) démarquer*: first, in sports—European football, for example—it means to free oneself or to escape (from a defender); and second, more generally, it means to take one's distance or to distinguish oneself.—*Editor*]

3. Martin Heidegger, *Nietzsche*, trans. David Farrell Krell (New York: Harper & Row, 1984), 2: 72-73. The English translation of the first volume of this work, quoted further on, was published in 1979.

4. *Nietzsche*, 2: 35.

5. Martin Heidegger, "The Origin of the Work of Art," in *Poetry, Language, Thought*, trans. Albert Hofstadter (New York: Harper & Row, 1971), 62. My emphasis.

6. [*Envoi* and *destination* here translate the German *Geschick* (destiny), itself derived from the verb *schicken*: to send, dispatch, transmit, but also, in the reflexive, to happen, come to pass, chance.—*Editor*]

7. *Nietzsche*, 2: 36.

8. Ibid.

9. Ibid., 1: 8.

10. Ibid., 1: 80.

11. See *Nietzsche*, 1: 103-4.

12. See *Nietzsche*, 1: 131.

13. See "The Origin of the Work of Art," Addendum of 1961, 87.

14. See *Nietzsche*, 1: 164. This analysis of the Heideggerian reading is taken up again and elaborated in "Typography," trans. Eduardo Cadava, in *Typography: Mimesis, Philosophy, Politics*, ed. Christopher Fynsk (Cambridge, Mass.: Harvard University Press, 1989), especially 71ff. Originally published in the collection *Mimesis: Des articulations* (Paris: Flammarion, 1975), 165-270.

15. See *Der Grosse Duden*, Band VII, *Etymologie*. The modern form goes back, through the Middle High German *tihten*, to the Old High German *dihton* and *tihton*: "to compose [*abfassen*], to conceive [*ersinnen*] in writing [*schriftlich*]," itself derived from the Latin *dictare*: to pronounce, to compose by pronouncing in order to have copied in writing.

16. *Nietzsche*, 1: 103.

17. See, for example, *Nietzsche*, 1: 59ff.

18. See *Nietzsche*, 1: 77ff., and "The Origin of the Work of Art," 79ff.

19. See *Hegel's Concept of Experience* (New York: Harper & Row, 1970) and *Identity and Difference*, trans. Joan Stambaugh (New York: Harper & Row, 1969).

20. See G. W. F. Hegel, *Aesthetics*, trans. T. M. Knox (Oxford: Clarendon, 1975), 2: 1001ff.

21. Friedrich Schelling, *The Ages of the World*, trans. Frederick de Wolfe Bolman, Jr. (New York: Columbia University Press, 1942), 84.

22. See chapter 6, "The Unpresentable," and, in collaboration with Jean-Luc Nancy, "Le Dialogue des genres," *Poétique* 21 ("Littérature et philosophie mêlées," 1975): 148-75. See also Philippe Lacoue-Labarthe and Jean-Luc Nancy, *The Literary Absolute: The Theory of Literature in German Romanticism*, trans. Philip Barnard and Cheryl Lester (Albany: SUNY Press, 1988).

23. See *Nietzsche's Werke* (Leipzig: Naumann, 1901), 12: 400: "Den Mythus der Zukunft dichten."

24. See Jean-Michel Rey, "Nietzsche et la théorie du discours philosophique," in *Nietzsche aujourd'hui?* (Paris: U.G.E., 1973), 1: 301-21.

25. Naumann, 9: 67. My emphasis.

26. Course of 1875-76, chapter 1; see Friedrich Nietzsche, *Gesammelte Werke* (Munich: Musarion, 1922), 5: 216.

27. Ibid., 5: 140.

28. Ibid., 5: 68.

29. Ibid., 5: 80.

30. Ibid., 5: 142.

31. Ibid., 5: 142ff.

32. Ibid., 5: 146.

33. Ibid., 5: 143.

34. Ibid., 5: 153.

35. See Jean-Luc Nancy, "La Thèse de Nietzsche sur la téléologie," in *Nietzsche aujourd'hui?* 1: 57-80.

36. Musarion, 5: 161-62.

37. See the famous fragment quoted by Heidegger (*Nietzsche*, 1: 120): "What it takes to be an artist is that one experience what all nonartists call 'form' as *content*, as 'the matter itself.' With that, of course, one is relegated to an *inverted world*. For from now on one takes content to be something merely formal — including one's own life."

38. *Ecce Homo*, trans. Walter Kaufmann (New York: Random House, 1967), 326.

39. Concerning the problematic so outlined of "philosophical madness," I take the liberty of referring the reader once again to "Typography."

4. Obliteration

1. From a lecture delivered by Heidegger on February 24, 1951 at Bühlerhöhe, published and translated as "La Parole dite" in *Revue de poésie* 90 (October 1964): 52-57.

2. Martin Heidegger, "Logos," in *Early Greek Thinking*, trans. David Farrell Krell and Frank A. Capuzzi (New York: Harper & Row, 1975), 78.

3. Martin Heidegger, *Nietzsche* (Pfullingen: Günther Neske Verlag, 1961), 2 vols. The French translation, by Pierre Klossowski, was published by Gallimard in 1971. [The English translation was published by Harper & Row in four volumes: vol. 1, *The Will to Power as Art*, trans. David Farrell Krell, 1979; vol. 2, *The Eternal Recurrence of the Same*, trans. David Farrell Krell, 1984; vol. 3, *The Will to Power as Knowledge and as Metaphysics*, trans. Joan Stambaugh, David Farrell Krell, and Frank A. Capuzzi, 1987; vol. 4, *Nihilism*, trans. Frank A. Capuzzi, 1982. Unless otherwise indicated, all further references are to this translation. — *Editor*]

4. As is the case, for example, with Eugen Fink's *La Philosophie de Nietzsche* (translated into French in 1965). For reasons that will become apparent in a moment — and aside from the fact that

it is entirely dominated by a Heideggerian type of problematic—the publication of this book in Germany one year before Heidegger's (1960) does not in any way affect matters.

5. I refer to the thesis of Jean Granier, *Le Problème de la vérité dans la philosophie de Nietzsche* (Paris: Seuil, 1966), and more precisely to the appendix (pp. 611-28). From a point of view one easily imagines completely diverging from Granier's, Jean Beaufret also examined very closely certain analyses from *Nietzsche* in his contribution to the Royaumont Colloquium in 1964 ("Heidegger et Nietzsche—le concept de valeur," Cahiers de Royaumont, Philosophie no. 6, *Nietzsche* [Paris: Minuit, 1967]), 245-64. As for Heidegger himself, certain of his texts, in *Nietzsche* or elsewhere, have occasionally looked like a kind of systematic recapitulation of earlier ones, for example, section VI of *Nietzsche* ("Nietzsche's Metaphysics") or "The Overcoming of Metaphysics" (notes from the years 1936-44 that "cover," in a certain way, the whole second volume of *Nietzsche*).

6. "Considered as a whole, the publication aims to provide a view of the path of thought I followed from 1930 to the 'Letter on Humanism' (1947). The two small lectures published just prior to the 'Letter,' 'Plato's Doctrine of Truth' (1942) and 'On the Essence of Truth' (1943), originated back in the years 1930-31. The book *Commentaries on Hölderlin's Poetry* (1951), which contains one essay and several lectures from the years between 1936 and 1943, sheds only indirect light on that path" (*Nietzsche*, 1: xl). The whole of this introductory statement requires commentary, as, more generally, a systematic reading is required of all the prefaces and postfaces, all the forewords, clarifications, etc., that accompany, without exception, *all* of Heidegger's texts. On the other hand, we must not forget that in 1961, the publication of *Nietzsche* could still respond to other preoccupations, "political" ones in particular, since in fact it was around 1960 that the most precise attacks multiplied. So it was perhaps not altogether useless, when publishing all the courses from the years 1936-41, which concerned precisely one of those "eponymous heroes" confiscated by the Nazis, to show what political reserve and withdrawal had followed upon the "mistake" of the rectorship. A few years ago, Maurice Blanchot spoke along these lines (*L'Entretien infini* [Paris: Gallimard, 1969], 208-10), without at all depreciating the character, "frightening in every respect," of the proclamations of 1933. It is not a question here of *precipitously* reopening a debate that precipitation itself—biting commentary or doubtful, apologetic "good will"—has until now, and on both sides, barely raised above the level of pure anecdote. But we must at least point out that a *political* reading of the debate with Nietzsche (and, in general, of the whole itinerary following the break [*cassure*] of *Sein und Zeit*) is necessary.

7. *Introduction à la métaphysique* (1958); *Essais et conférences* (1958); *Qu'appelle-t-on penser?* (1959). Only *Holzwege* (*Chemins qui ne mènent nulle part*) was translated later (1962).

8. See Michel Deguy, "En marge du *Nietzsche* de Heidegger," *Cahiers du chemin* 16 (October 1972): 88-94.

9. Here, however, is a whole trail one could follow. Because, first of all, Heidegger's "thought" (that is, if only in the most banal sense, his writing) can be regarded or even entirely gathered as a ceaseless labor of translation (see, in this respect, Gérard Granel's introduction to the translation of *Was heißt Denken?* [Martin Heidegger, *Qu'appelle-t-on penser?* trans. Aloys Becker and Gérard Granel (Paris: PUF, 1959), 1-19], and Jacques Derrida, "*Ousia* and *Gramme*," in *Margins of Philosophy*, trans. Alan Bass [Chicago: University of Chicago Press, 1982], 29-67). But also for this other (and twofold) reason that, on the one hand, Klossowski's writing is like the lining [*doublure*] of a practically uninterrupted labor of translation (in which Latin occupies what is perhaps a privileged place, unlike the preference for Greek exhibited by Heidegger), and, on the other, his theoretical work—if indeed we can separate the one from the other—appears to inscribe itself, in recent years, between the lines of the translation of *Nietzsche*, or rather, and although certainly not in a simple way, *against* Heidegger's interpretation. Testifying to this, aside from *Nietzsche et le cercle vicieux* (which is based on Nietzsche's "experience" of madness), would be a book such as *La Monnaie vivante*, which doubtless is only readable (but will not be read) as an *a contrario* proof of the *discredit*, so to speak, into which Heidegger has brought every problematic of value.

10. Granier, 625-26.

11. To be convinced of this, it is enough to read in the same text—in the "appendix" that assumes the form of a final justification and whose very position, from an economic point of view, is certainly not accidental—the paragraph immediately following the passage just quoted: "It is not our intention here to subject this interpretation to an exhaustive critique. For this would force us to repeat the arguments already developed, which would be tedious. We prefer to leave to the reader the task of directly comparing the explanations proposed by Heidegger and the analyses we have presented on our own account in the different chapters of this work. To focus the reader's attention, we will limit ourselves to emphasizing the essential points on which the interpretations diverge" (Granier, 626).

12. See Sarah Kofman's critique of Granier's book in "Généalogie, interprétation, texte," *Critique* 275 (April 1970): 359–81; reprinted in *Nietzsche et la métaphore* (Paris: Payot, 1972), 173–206.

13. Granier, 28–29: "In reference to the *origin*, an origin conceived by us as that radical "ontological experience" [the experience of transcendence as identical to *Selbstüberwindung*, to the "overcoming" of self] from which Nietzsche derives his major insights, all the Nietzschean themes—life, nihilism, will to power, Overman, eternal return, Dionysianism and Apollinianism—are organized in a totality that, for density, coherence, and magnitude, is second to none of the most solid constructs of classical philosophy." This "ontological experience" (the quotation marks here do not indicate reservation), which functions as origin and center, is borrowed from Jaspers (see Granier, 24–27), against whom, as Blanchot has very clearly pointed out in *L'Entretien infini* (211–12), Heidegger articulated the principles of a rigorous interpretation (see, for example, *Nietzsche*, 1: 21; and, in the German original, 2: 473ff., in the French translation, 2: 382ff. [this section not being included in the English translation]).

14. This refers us firstly and fundamentally to the Aristotelian sense, and, despite the subsequent changes (in particular, the abandonment, after *Sein und Zeit*, of the question bearing on the *meaning* of being in favor of the question—which the introduction to *What Is Metaphysics?* explicitly calls identical—bearing on the *truth* of being), to the *interpretation*, in *De Interpretatione*, 1–6, of *logos* as *apophansis* (of "discourse" insofar as that of which there is discourse, that which is spoken of, *reveals* [*fait voir*] on the basis of that of which there is discourse and comes from that on which it is discourse), on which is partly founded, at the beginning of *Sein und Zeit* (§7, b-c), the project of a fundamental ontology as the phenomenology, that is, as the *hermeneutics*, of *Dasein*. That this onto-phenomenology, as such, proved to be impossible, that it was unable to produce the destruction of the history of ontology it was supposed to precede and inaugurate in the program initially foreseen in *Sein und Zeit*, that it was necessary to take up "otherwise" the question of being (that is, to put it simply, to begin *Sein und Zeit* again by beginning with the second part and by abandoning, along with the hope of an ontology, the project of a hermeneutics of *Dasein*)—none of this prevents the same concept of hermeneutics from being at work in the subsequent reading of the history of metaphysics understood, as of *Sein und Zeit*, as the history of the oblivion of being (see the first paragraph as well as the opening subtitle, Martin Heidegger, *Being and Time*, trans. John Macquarrie and Edward Robinson [New York: Harper & Row, 1962], 21). The same concept of hermeneutics means, despite a growing analytical complexity, the same interpretation of *logos*, of *aletheia*, and of their relation. It is, moreover, because he passes over in silence this fundamental determination of hermeneutics that Granier, opposing to the Heideggerian "conception" of metaphysics the "metaphilosophical" concept of interpretation, submits to Heidegger's "jurisdiction," as we will soon have occasion to point out.

15. See "Nietzsche's So-called Major Work," in *Nietzsche*, 3: 10–14. We will come back to this.

16. Granier, 626: "Heidegger tacks *his* definition of metaphysics onto Nietzsche's philosophy without seeing that Nietzsche himself possesses an understanding of the essence of Metaphysics that shatters the framework of Heidegger's definition."

17. Granier, 609: "Metaphilosophy would be to traditional philosophy what Freudian metapsychology is to classical psychology. Just as, indeed, metapsychology locates and captures the unconscious source of the meanings and symbols that consciousness receives and cultivates, so metaphilosophy would clarify the origin of philosophical thought by trying to determine the status

of this metalanguage which conditions the possibility of all philosophical discourse in general." To which it is enough to oppose, without commentary, this text, for example: "The question What is philosophy? is not a question aiming to establish a kind of knowledge based on itself (a philosophy of philosophy)" *(Was ist das—die Philosophie?* [Pfullingen: Neske, 1956], 17-18).

18. [The French term *é-loignement*, which translates the German *Ent-fernung*, is retained here since there is no one English word capable of satisfactorily conveying the tensional nature of the movement designated, which is simultaneously that of a distancing and of a bringing nearer. This tensional nature is underscored by the isolation of the ambiguous prefix (*é-/Ent-*), which serves *both* as an intensive *and* as a sign of privation or opposition.—*Editor*]

19. This is the very overture to *Nietzsche*, the first sentence of the *Vorwort* (German, 1: 9; English, 1: xxxix).

20. Gérard Granel, *Traditionis traditio* (Paris: Gallimard, 1972), 114ff.

21. Thinking can in fact refer, as we shall see, to the philosophical itself (in particular in the expression, taken from Hegel, *die Sache des Denkens*, the subject, the affair, the cause, the matter of thought). For the moment, we refer to an (apparently) simple opposition between *philosophizing* and *thinking* as it appears, for example, in this statement from "Return to the Foundation of Metaphysics": "Metaphysics remains the first element [*das Erste*] of philosophy. It does not reach the first element of thought" *(Was ist Metaphysik?* [Frankfurt: Klostermann, 1955], 9).

22. As early as the text entitled "The Overcoming [*Überwindung*] of Metaphysics" (in *Vorträge und Aufsätze* [Pfullingen: Neske, 1954], §1, p. 71), and even more in *Zur Seinsfrage* (Frankfurt: Klostermann, 1956), Heidegger goes beyond the Nietzschean concept of *Überwindung* (surmounting, overcoming, transgression, domination) into that of *Verwindung*. In current usage, *Verwindung*—originally very close to *Überwindung* (identical root *winn*, cf. *gewinnen*)—also designates distortion, a deformative twisting (*Windung*). Yet Heidegger understands it in another way. Thus, in a note to André Préau's translation of the first lines of "The Overcoming of Metaphysics" (see *Essais et conférences* [Paris: Gallimard, 1958], p. 80, n. 3), Heidegger indicates that *verwinden* must be understood in the sense of "making a thing one's own by entering more deeply into it and by raising it to a higher level." It is thus not a question, in the project of an "overcoming" of metaphysics, of a repression (*Wegdrängen*) of metaphysics: "The overcoming of metaphysics takes place as an acceptance [*Verwindung*] of being. . . . Metaphysics, even when overcome, does not disappear. It returns in another form and retains its supremacy [*Herrschaft*] as the still valid difference between Being and beings" ("Überwindung der Metaphysik," 72). In *Zur Seinsfrage*, this *Verwindung* (which Granel translates as *Appropriation*) is the *Verwindung* of metaphysics itself, in which consists the "overcoming," the *Überwindung*, of nihilism.

23. We refer here, as our terminology indicates, to the introduction to "What Is Metaphysics?" ("Return to the Foundation of Metaphysics"), which Heidegger added to the fifth edition in 1949.

24. We are obliged here to harden somewhat Granel's text. Granel knows and says that thought (as it is understood by Heidegger) has no other "element" (if we may speak like Hegel, who never defines it, or even like Heidegger, who perhaps does not define it any more than Hegel) than writing itself. (See, for example, the whole introductory section of *Traditionis traditio*, or, in the text that interests us here, the "methodological" note [p. 138] that justifies his reading, based on the German text itself, of §14 of *Sein und Zeit*, "what is in question being each time the very tissue of writing.") This hardening is therefore limited. It is nevertheless already required by the project of disturbing a certain dissymmetry in what Granel calls "thoughtful writing [*écriture pensante*]," in which thought seems indeed always already to have won out.

25. *Traditionis traditio*, 114-15.

26. Martin Heidegger, *Identity and Difference*, trans. Joan Stambaugh (New York: Harper & Row, 1969), second part: "The Onto-theo-logical Constitution of Metaphysics."

27. Martin Heidegger, "The Anaximander Fragment," in *Early Greek Thinking*, trans. David Farrell Krell and Frank A. Capuzzi (New York: Harper & Row, 1975), 14.

28. By saying that everything is there, from the beginning, in the debate with Hegel, we do not mean to exclude (or minimize) the question of the debate with Husserl, such as Granel has raised it. The important thing here is that the debate with Hegel, which shows through as of the first lines of *Sein und Zeit*, supplanted the debate with Husserl. From one phenomenology to another, then. This is doubtless not an accident, since in each case, as Granel reminds us, phenomenology "inhabits . . . that limit of transcendental subjectivity called the absolute," fulfills the "modern meaning of being," of *Sein* as *Bewußtsein*, consciousness (*Traditionis traditio*, 100) and, correlatively, philosophy as science, that is, as "the Knowledge that knows itself as being" (181). And this despite the doubtless irreducible differences separating Husserl and Hegel. The fact remains that to place the emphasis or the whole emphasis on the debate with Husserl, as Granel is always tempted to do, is perhaps already to *propose* a certain reading of Heidegger, or, in other words, already to grant everything to Heidegger's *thought*. This is attested by the way in which Granel restricts to the "single" question of the *world* (but is there, in truth, any other?) the whole problematic of *Sein und Zeit*: "Heidegger's thinking begins with a meaning of being sometimes called 'world' and sometimes 'difference,' and at yet other times by its other names, but which is always 'older' than the metaphysical meaning" (115). "The question [of *Sein und Zeit*] consists of a 'thesis' on the meaning of being. . . . The thesis says a single thing in three ways: (1) being is World; (2) being is an unveiling of self in a 'there' (Da-sein) that we are and that, however, is not man but the being of man; (3) Da-sein is finitude—'finitude in man'—*as* understanding of being" (117). "It is, therefore, by a leap, and only by a leap, that we can try to approach here the threefold and unique thesis of *Sein und Zeit*. Still, it is not a question of claiming to better explain (or even simply to 'explain') what Heidegger has already said, but rather of discouraging the will to explain, to the extent that it always holds the difficulty or the obscurity to be apparent and endeavors to dissipate them. On the contrary, it is by going over the very features of the 'failure' of the question of being (or of its explicitation) that we have some chance of approaching what is essential in that question. This is what we will attempt to do for the 'phenomenon' that is at the center of all the others: the 'phenomenon of the world' " (129). While one can only subscribe to the intention of "discouraging the will to explain," the "reduction" of the threefold thesis to the single thesis of the world may give rise to certain difficulties. This is essentially so (although it would have to be shown) because this gesture tends to efface another difficulty that haunts the whole beginning of *Sein und Zeit* (and ends up governing the entire work until its break) and that is related to the *duplicity* of the text offered to hermeneutics with a view to the destruction of the history of ontology; or else, as Derrida says, the text of *Dasein* (see "The Ends of Man," in *Margins of Philosophy*, 109–36), or the text of philosophy itself (in which case everything should *begin* with the destruction and not with the attempt at a *fundamental ontology*—as will necessarily happen after the break). This difficulty involves the whole reading of the beginning (the opening) of *Sein und Zeit*. Either, as for Granel, *Sein und Zeit* begins with the first word of the first paragraph (see *Traditionis traditio*, 116), or else one calls into question the textual economy of the "beginning," and in this case one must take into account the subtitle (first page of German edition), where the question of being is explicitly rooted in the Platonic aporia concerning the meaning (*Bedeutung*) of the word *being* [*étant*]. Between these two beginnings, it is not only the whole question of the text of philosophy that is implicated, but also, in all probability, the question of *language* [*langue*] itself, in which, several years later, in the postface to "The Origin of the Work of Art," Heidegger will recognize the specific place of the formulation and of the difficulty of the question of being.

29. See, for example, *Aus der Erfahrung des Denkens* (Pfullingen: Neske, 1965), 15: "Three dangers threaten thought. / The good and salutary danger is the nearness of the poet who sings. / The most malignant and mordant danger is thought itself. It must think against itself, which it can only rarely do. / The bad danger, the bewildered [*wirr*] danger is philosophizing."

30. See *Sein und Zeit*, §5.

31. *Identity and Difference*, 45–46. But this text, like the ones that follow it, "defies translation," as Klossowski puts it. [Lacoue-Labarthe quotes but modifies André Préau's translation in *Questions*

1 (Paris: Gallimard, 1968), 281. In particular, he translates *Sache* as *cause* rather than *affaire* or *propos*; *Selbigkeit* as *mêmeté* rather than *identité*; and *Verschiedenheit* as *différence* rather than *diversité.*—*Editor*]

32. Ibid., 47–49 (translation modified).

33. Ibid., 73–74.

34. *Hegel's Concept of Experience* (New York: Harper & Row, 1970).

35. This is the word Heidegger used earlier in reference to Hegel.

36. *Identity and Difference*, 50 (translation modified).

37. See again, in this connection, Jacques Derrida's "The Ends of Man."

38. *Identity and Difference*, 52.

39. *Traditionis traditio*, 127.

40. "All questions that do justice to the subject are themselves bridges to their own answering. Essential answers are always but the last step in our questioning. The last step, however, cannot be taken without the long series of first and next steps. The essential answer gathers its motive power from the insistence [*Inständigkeit*] of the asking and is only the beginning of a responsibility where the asking arises with renewed originality. Hence even the most genuine [*echt*] question is never stilled [*aufgehoben*] by the answer found." Martin Heidegger, "What Is Metaphysics?" trans. R. F. C. Hull and Alan Crick, in *Existence and Being* (South Bend, Ind.: Gateway, 1949), 351–52 (translation modified).

41. *Identity and Difference*, 63–64.

42. "What Is Metaphysics?" 334ff.

43. *Identity and Difference*, 50.

44. Denounced as such as of §2 of *Sein und Zeit*.

45. *Identity and Difference*, 64–65. We should note here the way in which Heidegger "translates" *Differenz* by *Austrag*. In a passage from *Nietzsche*, he writes that "differentiation as 'difference' [*Unterscheidung als 'Differenz'*] means that a *settlement* [*Austrag*] between Being and beings exists [*besteht*]" (4: 155). In a note, Klossowski justifies the translation of *Austrag* by *différent* by saying: "After 'Differenz,' Heidegger uses the German term *Austrag: différent* (Lat. differens-differre, to carry apart) both in the sense of differing [*différend*] (which was first written with a 't') and in that of divergence, discrepancy, disagreement" (2: 167). *Austrag* would thus mean, *in German*, the same as *Differenz*. This is why, later on, in section X ("La Remémoration dans la métaphysique"), Klossowski translates *Austrag* as *dif-férence*: "the remembrance of the history of being thinks the historial event as the always distant arrival of a 'dif-ference' [*Austrag*] of the essence of truth, an essence in which Being itself comes initially into its own [*ereignet*]" (French trans., 2: 391). Dif-ference thus provokes the event (the coming-to-be, the advent, *Ereignis*) of Being, in which, as is known, must also be heard *Eigenheit*, property or properness, being-proper, propriation (see *Nietzsche*, French trans., 2: 391–92, n. 2, and Jacques Derrida, "The Ends of Man," in *Margins of Philosophy*, 129). What must therefore be thought in *Differenz als Austrag* is what is proper to being. Moreover, in the most current sense, *der Austrag* means the arrangement, the settlement, the solution of an affair (*zum Austrag bringen*: to settle a difference), although the verb *austragen* has conserved, among others, its first meaning in which difference is noticeable: *aus-tragen*, to put, to place outside. In *Austrag*, then, identity (sameness) wins out over difference. This is why, in a note added to André Préau's translation of *Identity and Difference* (*Questions 1*, 299), Heidegger sanctions the equivalence *Austrag/conciliation*, indicating that *Austrag* is understood as the *Versöhnung des Streites*, the (re)conciliation of conflict, of difference (*Versöhnung* is an item of religious vocabulary—capable of designating redemption or propitiation—which, incidentally, Nietzsche detested because of the use Wagner had made of it). [*Austrag* is here rendered, following Lacoue-Labarthe, as *conciliation* rather than, following the English translation, as *perdurance.*—*Editor*]

46. But they (laboring of syntax, dislocation of the semantic) are probably the same thing. This at least would be worth proving. And maybe it would then be necessary to find support in the famous

statement from the introduction to *Sein und Zeit* (§7): "It is one thing to give a report in which we tell about [*erzählend*] entities, but another to grasp entities in their *Being*. For the latter task we lack not only most of the words but, above all, the 'grammar' [*die 'Grammatik'*]" (63).

47. A return to presence with which, in spite of everything, Granel's text also concludes (see *Traditionis traditio*, 153).

48. *Nietzsche*, 1: 24; 3: 187.

49. See *Identity and Difference*, 47–48. Hegel essentially retains from Kant the theory of the originary synthesis of apperception, in other words, that by which—to the detriment of what Granel calls the ontology of the phenomenon—Kant remains within the limits of Cartesian ontology (see "Kant's Thesis About Being," trans. Ted E. Klein, Jr., and William E. Pohl, *Southwestern Journal of Philosophy* vol. 4, no. 3 [Fall 1973], 7–33).

50. As we shall see, *obliteration* can also mean, according to Littré, "the condition of a conduit that has been obstructed by a solid body or whose walls have adhered to each other (the obliteration of an artery, a vein)."

51. See "The Origin of the Work of Art," trans. Albert Hofstadter, in *Poetry, Language, Thought* (New York: Harper & Row, 1971), 71–78.

52. See chapter 3, "Apocryphal Nietzsche."

53. Martin Heidegger, *Introduction to Metaphysics*, trans. Ralph Manheim (Garden City, N.Y.: Doubleday, 1961), 29, 30–31. [The quotations from Nietzsche are to be found in *Twilight of the Idols*, trans. Walter Kaufmann, *The Portable Nietzsche* (New York: Viking, 1954), 481, 483.]

54. Ibid., 30.

55. See *Nietzsche*, 4: 200–201 ("Nihilism as Determined by the History of Being").

56. *Destruction*, in *Sein und Zeit*, is *Destruktion*. But at the Davos Colloquium (March 1929), *Destruktion* is "translated" as *Zerstörung*, by a word, then, from Nietzsche's vocabulary: "This position means: destruction [*Zerstörung*] of what has been until now the foundation of Western metaphysics (Spirit, Logos, Reason)" (in Ernst Cassirer and Martin Heidegger, *Débat sur le kantisme et la philosophie* [Paris: Beauchesne, 1972], 24).

57. *Nietzsche*, 3: 4.

58. Winter semester 1934–35. Lecture: Hölderlin's Hymns ("Der Rhein" and "Germanien"). Summer semester 1935: Introduction to Metaphysics. See W. J. Richardson, *Heidegger: Through Phenomenology to Thought* (The Hague: Nijhoff, 1963), 668.

59. Winter semester 1935–36: Kolloquium: Die Überwindung der Ästhetik in der Frage nach der Kunst (mit Bauch). See "The Origin of the Work of Art" (1935–36), where no reference is made to Nietzsche, but where, on the other hand, the Hegelian definition of tragedy ("the battle of the new gods against the old") is accepted and taken up as such ("The Origin of the Work of Art," 43).

60. "The Anaximander Fragment," 14.

61. See, among other texts, the prefaces to *Philosophy in the Tragic Age of the Greeks*, trans. Marianne Cowan (Washington, D.C.: Regnery Gateway, 1962), 23–25.

62. And Heidegger himself has read Schelling, for whom, as people tended to say in Jena in the 1800s, "all poetry is of the same spirit" (F. W. J. Schelling, *The Philosophy of Art*, trans. Douglas W. Stott [Minneapolis: University of Minnesota Press, 1989], 19).

63. See, for example, *Das Philosophenbuch/Le Livre du philosophe*, trans. Angèle K. Marietti (Paris: Aubier-Flammarion, 1969), I, §§48, 49, 53, 61, etc.; *Gesammelte Werke* (Munich: Musarion, 1922), 6: 17–18, 20, 24–25, etc.

64. Ibid.; see also *Philosophy in the Tragic Age of the Greeks* and chapter 2, "The Detour."

65. Martin Heidegger, *Die Kategorien- und Bedeutungslehre des Duns Scotus*, in *Gesamtausgabe* (Frankfurt: Klostermann, 1978), 1: 195–96.

66. *Nietzsche*, 3: 3–4.

67. Friedrich Nietzsche, *The Gay Science*, trans. Walter Kaufmann (New York: Random House, 1974), 33.

68. For all of this I refer the reader to "Typography," in *Typography: Mimesis, Philosophy, Politics*, ed. Christopher Fynsk (Cambridge, Mass.: Harvard University Press, 1989), 43–138.

69. The text quoted by Bataille is from *Ecce Homo*, trans. Walter Kaufmann (New York: Random House, 1967), 326 ("Why I am a Destiny").

70. I refer here to Jacques Derrida's analysis of Blanchot's texts concerning Artaud's and Hölderlin's madness ("La parole soufflée," in *Writing and Difference*, trans. Alan Bass [Chicago: University of Chicago Press, 1978], 169–95).

71. *Nietzsche* (Pfullingen: Neske, 1961), 2: 484–85. [This part of Heidegger's study, "Die Erinnerung in die Metaphysik," is not included in the English translation. – *Editor*]

72. Martin Heidegger, *What Is Called Thinking?* trans. J. Glenn Gray (New York: Harper & Row, 1968), 52–54.

73. As is known, this is ultimately the oldest and most widespread meaning of the verb *aufheben*.

74. It is true that in the passage to which we refer, Heidegger does quote a text from *Thus Spoke Zarathustra*, but this text is quoted in Nietzsche's *name* (following this format: "it is not for nothing that [Nietzsche] has Zarathustra say . . . " [53]).

75. See the now well-known text, quoted by Jacques Derrida in "From Restricted to General Economy: A Hegelianism without Reserve," *Writing and Difference*, p. 334, n. 3: "It is strange to perceive today what Kierkegaard could not know: that Hegel, like Kierkegaard, experienced the rejection of all subjectivity before the absolute idea. In principle, one would imagine – the rejection being Hegel's – that it was a question of a conceptual opposition; on the contrary. The fact is not deduced from a philosophical text, but from a letter to a friend to whom he confides that for two years he thought he would go mad. . . . In a sense, Hegel's rapid phrase perhaps has a force that Kierkegaard's long cry does not have. It is not any less within existence – which trembles and exceeds – than this cry." It is also to be noted that *aufheben*, as Hegel points out in an addition to the *Encyclopedia*, can also mean, in its positive sense, *bewahren*: to save. Further on, in connection with truth itself, we will again encounter this theme of the guard or the safeguard.

76. See *Nietzsche*, vol. 1, *The Will to Power as Art*.

77. *Nietzsche*, 3: 10.

78. Ibid., 10–11.

79. Ibid., 12.

80. Ibid., 12–14.

81. *What Is Called Thinking?* 48–49. See also 64–65: "The words of our statement, about what is most thought-provoking in our age, would then hark back to Nietzsche's words. Our statement would join with Nietzsche's words in a destiny to which, it seems, our whole earth is destined to its remotest corners. That destiny will above all shake the foundations of all of man's thinking, in dimensions of such magnitude that the demise we moderns are witnessing in only one sector, literature, is a mere episode by comparison."

82. Ibid., 17–18 (translation modified).

83. The role played by the "metaphor" of the way in Heidegger is well known, including in the titles: *Der Feldweg, Wegmarken, Holzwege, Mein Weg in die Phänomenologie, Unterwegs zur Sprache*, etc. We would need to apply ourselves to an analysis of all the "values" entailed by this "metaphor": earth, walking, furrow, trace, etc. It would not be a matter of confirming an already too obvious "thematism" but of trying to discover where such a series of signifiers, which are all related in one way or another to salvation, to guarding and safeguarding, might "lead." And this is perhaps the precise spot where it would be necessary to bring in Freud – but evidently for something other than a "diagnosis."

84. See "Who Is Nietzsche's Zarathustra?" trans. Bernd Magnus, in *The New Nietzsche: Contemporary Styles of Interpretation*, ed. David B. Allison (New York: Dell, 1977), 64–79.

85. *What Is Called Thinking?* 55.

86. *Nietzsche*, 4: 4, 203.

87. *What Is Called Thinking?* 75-76.

88. "Einleitung zu: 'Was ist Metaphysik?' (Der Ruckgang in den Grund der Metaphysik)," in *Gesamtausgabe*, 9: 379.

89. "The Word of Nietzsche: 'God is Dead,' " trans. William Lovitt, in *The Question Concerning Technology* (New York: Harper & Row, 1977), 111-12.

90. [Littré refers to John Palsgrave's *Lesclarcissement de langue francoyse* (1530). —*Editor*]

91. Jacques Derrida, *Of Grammatology*, trans. Gayatri Chakravorty Spivak (Baltimore: The Johns Hopkins University Press, 1974), 18-20.

92. *What Is Called Thinking?* 76.

93. "The Anaximander Fragment," 36 (translation modified).

94. See *Sein und Zeit*, §7. This is the text we quote in note 46. It would of course be necessary to compare it with the well-known statement from the *Letter on Humanism* concerning the break of *Sein und Zeit* (that is, as Granel writes, the impossibility of the break or "the impossibility of *assigning* the break with metaphysics regarding the meaning of being"): "The section in question [the third division of the first part, "Time and Being"] was held back because thinking failed in the adequate saying of this turning [*Kehre*] and did not succeed *with the help of the language of metaphysics*" (Martin Heidegger, "Letter on Humanism," trans. Frank A. Capuzzi and J. Glenn Gray, in *Basic Writings* [San Francisco: Harper, 1977], 208; my emphasis).

5. The Scene Is Primal

1. We know that this manuscript was given by Freud—on an unspecified date—to Max Graf, an historian and theoretician of music who for a long time belonged to the circle of friends and disciples surrounding Freud. Graf published it for the first time in 1942 in *Psychoanalytic Quarterly*, vol. 11, no. 4 (October), translated into English by H. A. Bunker under the title "Psychopathic Characters on the Stage." The version in vol. 7 of the Standard Edition is by James Strachey. As for the original, it was published in 1962 (*Neue Rundschau*, vol. 73) before appearing in volume 10 (*Bildende Kunst und Literatur*, 1970) of the *Studienausgabe* published by Fischer in Frankfurt. It is not included in the *Gesammelte Werke* from the same publisher. Although Graf believed the text to have been composed in 1904, today it is generally thought that it was written in 1905, or, at the latest, at the very beginning of 1906. It may be considered roughly contemporaneous with the *Drei Abhandlungen zur Sexualtheorie*, the *Witz* [*Jokes and Their Relation to the Unconscious*], and perhaps even the *Gradiva* [*Delusion and Dreams in Jensen's 'Gradiva'*]. On the other hand, Freud's reasons for giving this text to Graf, without making the slightest move to publish or even simply correct it, are unknown. An earlier version of the present essay accompanied the first French translation of Freud's text, undertaken in collaboration with Jean-Luc Nancy. ["Psychopathische Personen auf der Bühne" can now be found in the *Nachtragsband* of the *Gesammelte Werke* (Frankfurt: Fischer, 1987), 655-61.—*Editor*]

2. See especially René Girard, *Violence and the Sacred*, trans. Patrick Gregory (Baltimore: The Johns Hopkins University Press, 1977).

3. Jean Starobinski, "Hamlet et Freud" (preface to the French translation of Ernest Jones, *Hamlet et Œdipe* [Paris: Gallimard, 1967]); André Green, *Un Œil en trop: Le Complexe d'Œdipe dans la tragédie* (Paris: Minuit, 1969) and "Shakespeare, Freud et le parricide" (in *La Nef* 31 [July-October 1967]: 64-82). For readings of "Psychopathic Characters on the Stage," see also O. Mannoni, *Clefs pour l'imaginaire ou l'Autre scène* (Paris: Seuil, 1969), and Sarah Kofman, *L'Enfance de l'art* (Paris: Payot, 1970).

4. [Lacoue-Labarthe is here appealing to the derivation of *sollicitation* from the Latin *sollicitare*, to thoroughly disturb, agitate, from *sollus*, whole, entire, and *ciere*, to put in motion, move. —*Editor*]

5. See in particular Jacques Derrida's two nearly contemporaneous texts (1966) in *Writing and Difference*, trans. Alan Bass (Chicago: University of Chicago Press, 1978): "The Theatre of Cruelty and the Closure of Representation" (232-50) and "Freud and the Scene of Writing" (196-231).

6. Jean-François Lyotard, "Beyond Representation," preface to the French translation of Anton Ehrenzweig's *L'Ordre caché de l'art* (Paris: Gallimard, 1974), trans. Jonathan Culler in *The Lyotard Reader*, ed. Andrew Benjamin (Oxford: Blackwell, 1989), 156–57. We are quoting from this text only those passages which are directly relevant to "Psychopathic Characters on the Stage," but it goes without saying that one ought not to lose sight of Lyotard's whole critical treatment of Freudian aesthetics, which, aside from this preface, also includes (though with different degrees of critical radicality) such texts as "Jewish Oedipus," trans. Susan Hanson, in *Driftworks* (New York: Semiotext(e), 1984), 35–53, and "The Psychoanalytical Approach," in Mikel Dufrenne, ed., *Main Trends in Aesthetics and the Sciences of Art* (New York: Holmes and Meier, 1978), 134–50, as well as "Freud selon Cézanne," in *Des Dispositifs pulsionnels* (Paris: U.G.E., 1973; Paris: Bourgois, 1980), 67–88.

7. Freud doubtless *never* goes beyond comparing. The model here is the famous formula: "the Oedipus tragedy unfolds *like* an analysis." But if Lyotard is thus able to "literalize" this figure, it is because he previously interpreted the text as deducing psychopathy (neurosis)—and then psychopathology itself as well as psychoanalysis—from Greek tragedy. But Freud simply says that the tragic scene, at a specific moment and for specific reasons, becomes the site of a neurotic type of conflict. And this is not quite the same thing: theater enters the space of neurosis; it does not produce it, any more than tragedy produces the Oedipus complex, even though the form of the Oedipus complex is *necessarily* dramatic, or even though the scene, in general, is *necessarily* Oedipal.

8. Lyotard, "Beyond Representation," 157: "According to Freud's thesis the incentive bonus functions in the same way as *sleep* does in the theory of dreams: the latter also has the role of lowering defences and thus conspires with the process of secondary elaboration" (translation modified).

9. Sigmund Freud, "Psychopathic Characters on the Stage," in *The Complete Psychological Works of Sigmund Freud* [henceforth Standard Edition], trans. and ed. James Strachey (London: Hogarth, 1953), 7: 305. All further references will be to this edition.

10. Friedrich Nietzsche, *The Birth of Tragedy*, trans. Walter Kaufmann (New York: Random House, 1967), 132–33.

11. This is the *classical* mistranslation par excellence, to which, virtually without exception, the whole seventeenth century in France fell victim. [Lacoue-Labarthe refers to the mistranslation of Aristotle originating in sixteenth-century Italy and subsequently perpetuated by Racine, and according to which tragedy purges the passions *in general*, rather than just terror and compassion.—*Editor*]

12. To put it yet another way, Freud in every respect upholds the Aristotelian thesis of an "accompaniment of pleasure" doubling (and constituting) catharsis, that is, the thesis of *kouphisis meth edones*, of soothing or relief with pleasure (see *Politics*, VIII, 1342a).

13. One finds this again, for example (to give quickly just a few of the more obvious references), in "Der Dichter und das Phantasieren" (1908) and in §6 of the "Formulierungen über die zwei Prinzipien des psychischen Geschehens" of 1911.

14. See Jean Starobinski, "Hamlet et Freud," p. ix. This is clearly what makes possible the analytical "verification" of the paradigmatic nature of *Oedipus Rex* in Aristotle's *Poetics* and—in keeping with the function of theatricality as a matrix for analysis—the resulting elevation of the Oedipus complex in general to the rank of absolute paradigm. We know that "beyond the pleasure principle," even primary identification (despite the practically insurmountable difficulties it poses, particularly in the articulation of chapters 6 and 7 and in the Postscript, B of *Group Psychology and the Analysis of the Ego*), in spite of everything remains officially Oedipal.

15. See particularly, in chapters 21–24 of *The Birth of Tragedy*, Nietzsche's analysis of the tragic effect developed from the point of view of the "artist spectator" and focused primarily upon the *exemplary* function of tragic myth. In this analysis, we find the seeds of a theory of identification whose place in Nietzschean "typology" is well known.

16. "Psychopathic Characters," 305–6.

17. "But the suffering represented is soon restricted to *mental* suffering; for no one wants *physical* suffering who knows how quickly all mental enjoyment is brought to an end by the changes in somatic

feeling that physical suffering brings about. If we are sick we have one wish only: to be well again and to be quit of our present state. We call for the doctor and medicine, and for the removal of the inhibition on the play of phantasy which has pampered us into deriving enjoyment even from our own sufferings. If a spectator puts himself in the place of someone who is physically ill he finds himself without any capacity for enjoyment or psychical activity. Consequently a person who is physically ill can only figure on the stage as a piece of stage-property and not as a hero, unless, indeed, some peculiar physical aspects of his illness make psychical activity possible—such, for instance, as the sick man's forlorn state in the *Philoctetes* or the hopelessness of the sufferers in the class of plays that centre round consumptives" ("Psychopathic Characters," 307).

18. "In general, it may perhaps be said that the neurotic instability of the public and the dramatist's skill in avoiding resistances and offering forepleasure [*Vorlust*] can alone determine the limits set upon the employment of abnormal characters on the stage" ("Psychopathic Characters," 310). See *Drei Abhandlungen zur Sexualtheorie*, III, 1 (*Gesammelte Werke*, 5: 109-14; Standard Edition, 7: 208-12) and the *Witz*, B, 4 and 5 (*GW*, 6: 131-77; SE, 8: 117-58). The whole problem with this text derives from the fact that the forepleasure that should normally allow one to *avoid* unbearable tensions at least partly conceals another "specific" pleasure (having, according to Freud, its own mechanism) that is linked, in sexuality, to the deferral of the discharge and that ultimately conspires with a "surplus tension" sought for its own sake. Here we find, in a nutshell, the entire (future) problem of masochism. Hence the reading that we venture here and that tends to aggravate rather than resolve the problem.

19. See "Der Dichter und das Phantasieren" (1908), in *Gesammelte Werke*, 7: 213-23; "Creative Writers and Day-Dreaming," in Standard Edition, 9: 141-53.

20. "Psychopathic Characters," 305 (translation modified).

21. "Psychopathic Characters," 307. The problem of masochism is, in short, "resolved" *for* Freud at this time by the distinction between mental and physical suffering—between "unstable" neurosis and constituted neurosis or insanity itself. In which case *Vorlust* is ultimately able to "compensate" for suffering—though "just barely."

22. The heroic and mythic figure here invoked as emblematic of tragedy (in a way somewhat analogous to what happens in *Totem and Taboo* [chapter 4, §7]) is that of Prometheus: "The fact that drama originated out of sacrificial rites (cf. the goat and scapegoat) in the cult of the gods cannot be unrelated to this meaning of drama. It appeases, as it were, a rising rebellion against the divine regulation of the universe, which is responsible for the existence of suffering. Heroes are first and foremost rebels against God or against something divine. . . . Here we have a mood like that of Prometheus" ("Psychopathic Characters," 306). But just as the sacrificial origin of drama is inscribed, in *Totem and Taboo*, within the Oedipal matrix (revised, as it were, by Nietzsche: Dionysus ripped to shreds as a reminder of the originary murder), so here it is the Oedipus complex that governs the whole genealogy of drama and that makes it possible, above all, to give an account of psychopathological drama (in accordance with the Oedipal version of *Hamlet* proposed in the *Traumdeutung*).

23. *Traumdeutung*, V, IV, §2 [*The Interpretation of Dreams*, trans. James Strachey (New York: Avon, 1965), 298.] If one were here to follow the trail of Freud's interpretation of *Hamlet*, the place occupied by "Psychopathic Characters" in the dossier assembled by Starobinski (who, it seems, was unaware of this text) would be somewhere between the *Traumdeutung* and the *Introduction to Psychoanalysis* (the *Vorlesungen* of 1916). On the interpretation of the *hidden conflict* in *Hamlet* ("the conflict in *Hamlet* is so effectively concealed that at first I had to guess it" ["Psychopathic Characters," 310; translation modified]), see also Lyotard's "Jewish Oedipus," and especially everything concerning the "*unaccomplishment*" of the paternal word as modernity's difference from the Greek world" (39).

24. "Psychopathic Characters," 308-9.

25. "The first of these modern dramas is *Hamlet*. It has as its subject the way in which a man who has so far been normal becomes neurotic owing to the peculiar nature of the task by which he is faced, a man, that is, in whom an impulse that has hitherto been successfully suppressed endeavors

to make its way into action. *Hamlet* is distinguished by three characteristics which seem important in connection with our present discussion. (1) The hero is not psychopathic, but only *becomes* psychopathic in the course of the action of the play. (2) The repressed impulse is one of those which are similarly repressed in all of us, and the repression of which is part and parcel of the foundations of our personal evolution. . . . As a result of these two characteristics it is easy for us to recognize ourselves in the hero. . . . (3) It appears as a necessary precondition of this form of art that the impulse that is struggling into consciousness, however clearly it is recognizable, is never given a definite name; so that in the spectator too the process is carried through with his attention averted, and he is in the grip of his emotions instead of taking stock of what is happening. A certain amount of resistance is no doubt saved in this way, just as, in an analytic treatment, we find derivatives of the repressed material reaching consciousness, owing to a lower resistance, while the repressed material itself is unable to do so" ("Psychopathic Characters," 309-10).

26. Chapter 2, *in fine*.

27. *Beyond the Pleasure Principle*, trans. James Strachey (New York: Norton, 1961), 11. See Aristotle's *Poetics*, in *The Complete Works of Aristotle*, ed. Jonathan Barnes (Princeton: Princeton University Press, 1984), 2: 2318 (1448b): "Imitation is natural to man from childhood," etc. As for the "undecidable" nature of play, Freud points it out at least twice in the course of his argument — which makes problematic at the very least Lyotard's assertion that an analysis of the *fort/da* game would attest to "the continuing power of the theatrical schema in Freud's unconscious epistemological assumptions" ("Beyond Representation," 159).

28. "Psychopathic Characters," 306.

29. See *Group Psychology and the Analysis of the Ego*, Postscript, B (Standard Edition, 18: 135-37).

30. Might this explain its having been "forgotten"?

31. "Our Attitude Towards Death," Part II of *Thoughts for the Times on War and Death*, in Standard Edition, 14: 289. [More literally, the first sentence reads: "The fact is that our own death is unrepresentable (*unvorstellbar*) and every time we seek to represent it . . . " —*Editor*]

32. "Das Medusenhaupt" once again — but that is inevitable (see "Medusa's Head," in Standard Edition, 18: 273-74). Let us merely add that in following certain of Erwin Rohde's indications in *Psyche* (*Psyche: Seelencult und Unsterblichkeitsglaube der Griechen* [Freiburg: J. C. B. Mohr, 1894]; *Psyche: The Cult of Souls and Belief in Immortality among the Greeks*, trans. W. B. Hillis [New York: Harcourt Brace, 1925]), particularly concerning the catharsis of defilement or the conjunction of *apotropaïon* and catharsis, we would still need to examine, within the larger question of the relation between death (and suffering) and catharsis, that of the relation between catharsis and femininity.

33. "Our Attitude Towards Death," 291.

34. This is what always makes possible the "Jungian" slippage that Freud denounces, for example, in chapter 6 of *Das Unbehagen in der Kultur*. In other words, it is always possible to reduce drives to libido alone, a tendency apparent in all of Lyotard's most recent work (especially *Economie libidinale* [Paris: Minuit, 1975]).

35. Jacques Lacan, *Ecrits* (Paris: Seuil, 1966). On this subject see also my essay "The Caesura of the Speculative," in *Typography*, ed. Christopher Fynsk (Cambridge, Mass.: Harvard University Press, 1989), 208-35.

36. In "The Psychoanalytical Approach," Lyotard, "carrying out" the interpretation that Blanchot has proposed of the Orpheus allegory, writes the following: "But the legendary tale goes on: Orpheus turns around. His desire to *see* the figure overcomes his desire to bring it to the light. Orpheus wants to see in the night, to see night. By trying to see Eurydice he loses all hope of making her be seen: the figure is that which has no face, it kills the one that looks at it because it fills him with its own night. . . . It was *for the sake of this looking upon* that Orpheus went to fetch Eurydice, and not to create a work of art; the artist did not plunge into the night to put himself in a condition to compose a harmonious song, to reconcile night and day, to become renowned for his art. He went in search

of the figural instance, the other of his *very work*, to see the invisible, to see death. The artist is someone in whom the desire to see death even at the price of dying is stronger than his desire to create" (141–42, translation modified). This does not really make sense unless one considers death as essentially a "figure" and the artist's descent into Hell, as it is often portrayed in modern (that is, romantic) art, as itself, "biographically," a "work of art." But basically the equivocation we are challenging here was sanctioned as early as *Discours, Figure* (Paris: Klincksieck, 1971), where Lyotard employed a terminology we find reemerging in this text from the moment that "figure," Lyotard's *figural*, is used, contrary to all expectations, to designate what does not belong to the order of manifestation (and also from the moment that *writing* designates the order of constituted discourse). Therein, no doubt, lies the whole root of the conflict.

37. [I.e., royal, from the Greek *basileus*, king. – *Editor*]

38. See Luce Irigaray, "Les philosophes par-derrière," a talk delivered to the Groupe de recherches sur les théories du signe et du texte of the University of Strasbourg-II.

39. Sigmund Freud, *Civilization and Its Discontents*, trans. James Strachey (New York: Norton, 1962), 91.

40. "Beyond Representation," 156. My emphasis.

41. *The Birth of Tragedy*, 39.

42. "Vergänglichkeit," in *Gesammelte Werke*, 10: 358–61; "On Transience," in Standard Edition, 14: 305–7.

6. The Unpresentable

1. Maurice Blanchot, *L'Entretien infini* (Paris: Gallimard, 1969), 515–27.

2. See *Friedrich Schlegel's "Lucinde" and the Fragments*, trans. Peter Firchow (Minneapolis: University of Minnesota Press, 1971), 175.

3. *L'Entretien infini*, 522.

4. We are publishing here the first part of this work—the first part, which can be considered as an introduction to the (a) "reading of *Lucinde*."

a) References to *Lucinde* and the *Athenaeum* and *Lyceum Fragments* are to the previously cited edition and translation by Peter Firchow, *Friedrich Schlegel's "Lucinde" and the Fragments*.

b) References to Hegel's *Aesthetics* are to the translation by T. M. Knox (Oxford: Clarendon Press, 1975), a translation that will occasionally be modified.

5. *Aesthetics*, 1: 517.

6. There is only, *stricto sensu*, one dissolution, if we take into account the fact that, despite his desire (or the necessity) for speculative *Triplizität*, there is, for Hegel, strictly speaking—and whatever the letter of numerous passages of the *Aesthetics*—no dissolution of symbolic art. Probably because symbolic art is not really an art (as we are explicitly reminded by the *Philosophy of Religion*, trans. R. F. Brown, P. C. Hodgson, and J. M. Stewart [Berkeley: University of California Press, 1987], vol. 2 [*Determinate Religion*], pp. 357–81 ["Transition from Nature Religion to Spiritual Religion: The Religion of the Enigma (Egyptian Religion)"], especially pp. 375–76; but see also pp. 634–37) to the extent that "the essence of art lies not in the dissociation but in the identification of meaning and shape" (*Aesthetics*, 1: 422). For dissociation and identification are actually indissociable. But in symbolic art, the "kinship" and "analogy" (but not the identification as such) between form and meaning tend to cover up the dissociation. For this reason, the transition from symbolic to classical art rather takes the shape of a war, of a brutal conflict: classical art arises in a sort of historical rent (figured, as we know, by tragedy), as if it were necessary that some traumatism introduce, from the outside, difference or dissociation into the ahistorical and quasi-immobile reign, into the analogical "torpor" of symbolic art. As for the final dissolution of romantic art, Hegel defines it explicitly as the repetition of the dissolution of classical art (for example, 1: 593–94: "The last matter with which we now still have to deal in more detail is the point at which romanticism, already *implicitly* the principle

of the dissolution of the classical ideal, now makes this dissolution appear clearly in fact as dissolution"). This is why, most of the time, Hegel uses the simple designation "art" (or *die schöne Kunst*) exclusively for Greek classical art.

7. *Aesthetics*, 1: 504.

8. We should settle here the question of the status of tragedy, a status that, at least as much as the repetition of satire, disturbs the whole historical-systematic organization of the *Aesthetics* and that, in particular, marks Hegel's constant "hesitation" as to the determination of the essence of art (a "hesitation" already perceptible in the notable differences separating the chapter on "Aesthetic Religion" from the *Phenomenology* and from the *Aesthetics* itself). Of the theomachy through which (Greek) art establishes itself, tragedy is, in fact, more precisely the (re)presentation, the *Darstellung*: the reflective or reflexive (and thus abyssal) sublation, in other words, of symbolic "art." Indeed, because it has no other content (nor even any other definition) than the "battle between the old gods and the new," because it (re)presents the sublation, insured by art, of the symbolic—of all the dangerously fleeting and *elusive* forms of kinship and analogy that have to be "broken" in favor of the dialectizable and dialectizing unity of dissociation and identification—because, in other words, it "makes" the statues of classical art "speak" (signify) and gives Logos to stone or to the meaning emerging from stone, tragedy is perhaps *unassignable* since it may not belong, in the last instance, to art itself, but rather determines and *destines* philosophy as such (its dialogism and its dialectics).

9. *Aesthetics*, 1: 506. My emphasis.

10. Ibid., 1: 508.

11. [This is chapter III(B) in the German original, chapter 7 in the English translation.—*Editor*]

12. Ibid., 1: 61. Essentially, for Kant, the reconciliation between the sensuous and the concept, "apparently perfect . . . is still supposed . . . at the last to be only subjective." This is why the Kantian critique could constitute "the starting point for the true comprehension of the beauty of art, yet only by overcoming Kant's deficiencies could this comprehension assert itself as the higher grasp of the true unity of necessity and freedom, particular and universal, sense and reason" (1: 60–61).

13. We must read the whole text of this homage. Predictably, we shall see recurring here the motif of the *era*: "It has to be admitted that the artistic sense of a profound and philosophic mind has demanded, and expressed, totality and reconciliation (*earlier than philosophy as such had recognized them*) as against that abstract endlessness of ratiocination, that duty for duty's sake, that formless intellectualism, which apprehends nature and actuality, sense and feeling, as just a barrier, just contradicting it and hostile. It is *Schiller* who must be given great credit for breaking through [*durchbrechen*] the Kantian subjectivity and abstraction of thinking and for venturing on an attempt to get beyond this by intellectually grasping unity and reconciliation as the truth and by actualizing them in artistic production. For Schiller in his aesthetic writings has not merely taken good note of art and its interest, without any regard for its relation to philosophy proper, but he has also compared his interest in the beauty of art with philosophical principles, and only by starting from them and with their aid did he penetrate into the deeper nature and concept of the beautiful. Even so, one feels that at one period of his work he busied himself with thought more even than was advantageous for the naïve beauty of his works of art. Deliberate concentration on abstract reflections and even an interest in the philosophical Concept is noticeable in many of his poems. For this he has been reproached, and especially blamed and depreciated in comparison with Goethe's objectivity and his invariable naïveté, steadily undisturbed by the Concept. But in this respect Schiller as, a poet, only paid *the debt of his time*, and what was to blame was a perplexity which turned out only to the honour of this sublime soul and profound mind and only *to the advantage of science and knowledge*" (1: 61 [my emphasis]).

14. "The *unity* of universal and particular, freedom and necessity, spirit and nature, which Schiller grasped scientifically as the principle and essence of art and which he laboured unremittingly to call into actual life by art and aesthetic education, has now, as the *Idea itself*, been made the principle of knowledge and existence, and the Idea has become recognized as that which alone is true and actual" (1: 62–63).

15. The novel is thus a nongenre (or a unique "genre"), that is, *literature* itself, or *romantic art*, or even *transcendental poetry*: all these terms are *more or less* equivalent, and it is furthermore precisely this (divine) (terminological, conceptual) "confusion" that, because it largely eludes the grasp of theoretical unification, could not fail to embarrass and irritate Hegel. Basically, Schlegel's (or the Schlegels') theory—and that of others; we must take *symphilosophy* into account—the theory of "Schlegel," then, is *undecidable*, as massively systematic as it is not systematic at all, of an intolerable "irony," if irony has indeed anything to do with what is "fatal" in the fact of having (or not having) a system (*Athenaeum*, frag. 53) and, in the last instance, with a ("paradoxical"—*Lyceum*, frag. 48) refusal of the system: "Philosophy is the real homeland of irony, which one would like to define as logical beauty: for wherever philosophy appears in oral or written dialogues—and is not simply confined into rigid systems ["A dialogue is a chain or garland of fragments"-*Athenaeum*, frag. 77]— there irony should be asked for and provided" (*Lyceum*, frag. 42). We shall come back to this motif of "logical beauty." Whatever we are to make of this "transcendental buffoonery" (*Lyceum*, frag. 42), up to a certain point—but only up to a certain point—a certain continuous theoretical thread is detectable in the setting up of *literature* as literary theory or theoretical *Dichtung*, "beyond" poetry itself and beyond the poetics of genre, whose conditions of possibility—*transcendantal oblige*—it determines.

For example—we could follow many other threads:

We know that a novel is quite simply *a romantic book* (*Athenaeum*, "Letter about the Novel," in Friedrich Schlegel, *Dialogue on Poetry and Literary Aphorisms*, trans. Ernst Behler and Roman Struc [University Park: Pennsylvania State University Press, 1968], 94-105). Among other consequences, a major one is that a novel must also be, indissociably, a *theory of the novel*: "A *theory of the novel* . . . would be a theory in the original sense of the word; a spiritual viewing of the subject with calm and serene feeling [*Gemüt*]. . . . Such a theory of the novel would have to be itself a novel which would reflect imaginatively every eternal tone of the imagination [*Phantasie*] and would again confound the chaos of the world of the knights" (ibid., 102-3). This theory of the novel or this *philosophy of the novel* ("the rough outlines of which are contained in Plato's political theory") would be, in turn, the "keystone" of a "real aesthetic theory of poetry"—that is, a *philosophy of poetry*, which "would waver between the union and the division of philosophy and poetry, between poetry and practice, poetry as such and the genres and kinds of poetry; and it would conclude with their complete union," after having provided "the principles of pure poetics" and "the theory of the particular . . . types of poetry" (*Athenaeum*, frag. 252). This does not fail to bring us back to *satire*, analogically at least, if satire is at the same time the genre of chaos, mixture, arabesque (assuming therefore that kind of reflexive irony which is "the clear consciousness . . . of an infinitely teeming chaos"—*Ideas*, frag. 69), and, like the novel ("the Socratic dialogues of our time"—*Lyceum*, frag. 26), the refuge of *liberality*: after declaring that "all the classical poetical genres have now become ridiculous in their rigid purity" (*Lyceum*, frag. 60), Schlegel writes (*Lyceum*, frag. 117): "Poetry can only be criticized by way of poetry. A critical judgment of an artistic production has no civil rights in the realm of art if it isn't itself a work of art, either in its substance . . . or in the beauty of its form and open tone, like that of the old Roman satires." This is also why, in the *Athenaeum*, "Schlegel" can write that "there is a kind of poetry whose essence lies in the relation between ideal and real, and which therefore, by analogy to philosophical jargon, should be called transcendental poetry. It begins as satire in the absolute difference of ideal and real, hovers in between as elegy, and ends as idyll with the absolute identity of the two" (*Athenaeum*, frag. 238).

To which "he" adds—and it is probably not totally useless to quote him here: "But just as we wouldn't think much of an uncritical transcendental philosophy that does not represent the producer along with the product and contain at the same time within the system of transcendental thoughts a description of transcendental thinking: so too this sort of poetry should unite the transcendental raw materials and preliminaries of a theory of poetic creativity—often met with in modern poets—with the artistic reflection and beautiful self-mirroring that is present in Pindar, in the lyric fragments of the Greeks, in the classical elegy, and, among the Moderns, in Goethe. In all its descriptions, this poetry should describe itself [*in jeder ihrer Darstellungen sich selbst darstellen*] and always be simultaneously poetry and the poetry of poetry" (*Athenaeum*, frag. 238). But, in its turn, satire itself—which is "the classic universal poetry" of the Romans and colors all of "Roman literature" just as "the novel colors all of modern poetry" (*Athenaeum*, frag. 146) must still (with, consequently, the novel as the *genre* of the Moderns) *be dissolved* (this is the word that "Schlegel" almost always uses) in and as what is "properly" *romantic art*. This comes from the fact that romantic poetry is *dissolution* itself: "Just as one should search in mythology for the common source and the origin of all the kinds of poetizing [*Dichten*] and shaping [*Bilden*], so poetry is the highest summit of the totality, in whose blossoming each art and each science ultimately dissolves itself [*sich . . . endlich auflöst*] as it perfects itself [*sich vollendet*]" ("Vom Wesen der Kritik," in *Kritische Friedrich-Schlegel-Ausgabe* [Munich: Schöningh, 1975], 3: 55).

For all these reasons, romanticism actually transgresses every theory. As Blanchot suspects, this is perhaps the fate of *writing* "itself." In any case, this is why the *romantic program* is ultimately *impossible* in its very absoluteness. The famous Fragment 116 of the *Athenaeum*, which Blanchot quotes in part, gives evidence of this in an impressive way: "The aim of romantic poetry . . . isn't merely to reunite all the separate species of poetry and put poetry in touch with philosophy and rhetoric. It tries to and should mix and fuse poetry and prose, inspiration and criticism, the poetry of art and the poetry of nature; and make poetry lively and sociable, and life and society poetical; poeticize wit and fill and saturate the forms of art with every kind of good, solid matter for instruction, and animate them with the pulsations of humor. It embraces everything that is purely poetic, from the greatest systems of art, containing within themselves still further systems, to the sigh, the kiss that the poetizing child breathes forth in artless song. . . . Other kinds of poetry are finished and are now capable of being fully analyzed. The romantic kind of poetry is still in the state of becoming; that, in fact, is its real essence: that it should forever be becoming and never be perfected. It can be exhausted by no theory and only a divinatory criticism would dare try to characterize its ideal. It alone is infinite, just as it alone is free; and it recognizes as its first commandment that the will of the poet can tolerate no law above itself. The romantic kind of poetry is the only one that is more than a kind, that is, as it were, poetry itself: for in a certain sense all poetry is or should be romantic."

This is only one possible itinerary or *montage* among others. In a study translated and published in *Critique* 250 (March 1968) entitled "La théorie des genres poétiques chez Friedrich Schlegel" (pp. 264–92), Peter Szondi attempted, relying especially on the posthumous (philosophical and critical) fragments collected in the *Kritische Friedrich-Schlegel-Ausgabe* and on the *Literary Notebooks* edited by Hans Eichner, to reconstruct a "system" of Schlegelian poetics wavering between a "critique of poetic reason" and a sort of "pre-Hegelian" synthesis (in particular, in the handling of the categories of the *subjective* and the *objective*) and having as its axis the theory of the novel. But it is true that Szondi's analysis "concludes" with the recognition of Schlegel's contradictions and with a paraphrase of Fragment 116. What remains to be done is a study of what Schelling, and then Hegel, *owe* to "Schlegel." For in the theory of transcendental poetry, of romantic art, of dissolution, etc., in the systematization of the poetics of genre, what is being prepared and starting to function (*but while displacing itself*, and this is the whole "question") is already a logic of sublation—which does not only come from Fichte and denotes a certain "gift" for the speculative. Witness, among others, Fragment 121 of the *Athenaeum*, whose starting point—apart from the ironic drifting—is quasi-Hegelian and which, without detracting from Schiller's greatness, touches closely on the "authentic" determination of the ideal of art: "An idea is a concept perfected to the point of irony, an absolute synthesis of absolute antitheses, the continual self-creating interchange of two conflicting thoughts. An ideal is at once idea and fact. If ideals do not have as much individuality for the thinker as the gods of antiquity do for the artist, then any concern with ideas is no more than a boring and laborious game of dice with hollow phrases. . . . Nothing is more wretched and contemptible than this sentimental speculation without any object. But one shouldn't call this mysticism, since this beautiful old word is so very useful and indispensable for absolute philosophy, from whose perspective the spirit regards everything as a mystery and a wonder, while from other points of view it would appear theoretically and practically normal."

16. See *Aesthetics*, 1: 590–92.

17. Ibid., 1: 592–93.

18. Ibid., 1: 594.

19. Ibid., 1: 595.

20. The essence of satire is to oppose (in an insoluble and dissolving way) to an "abstract, finite, unsatisfied subject" an "equally finite reality," "a godless one"—a "corrupt existence." Then, "a noble spirit, a virtuous heart always deprived of the actualization of its convictions in a world of vice and folly, turns with passionate indignation or keener wit and colder bitterness against the reality confronting it, and is enraged with or scoffs at the world which directly contradicts its abstract idea of virtue and truth" (ibid., 1: 513; see also 1: 515). We must stress here that this "essence" of satire is, in the eyes of Hegel (who, on this point again, repeats or, more exactly, *copies* [*dé-marque*] "Schlegel"), what constitutes satire as a *non-genre* or as a simple "transitional form of the classical Ideal" (ibid., 1: 514).

21. That which *does not pass* for Hegel is always the *heterogeneous* (we know this very well since Bataille) and its consequences: mixture or blurring (also, for example, in Jean Paul; see *Aesthetics*, 1: 295); or even a certain condensation (as in *Witz*). This, of course, also applies to *fragmentation* (which is doubtless more than a simple consequence of the heterogeneous). In his frenetic "homogenization" of romanticism, Hegel "drops" ["laisse tomber"] (does not "sublate" [*ne "relève" pas*]) *worklessness* [*désœuvrement*], whatever the take nevertheless offered now and then (but not always) by the "theory of the fragment"—as in the famous statement: "A fragment, like a miniature work of art, has to be entirely isolated from the surrounding world and be complete in itself like a porcupine" (*Athenaeum*, frag. 206). But it is true—and we shall come back to this—that "*Witz* is . . . fragmentary genius" (*Lyceum*, frag. 9) and it is the fragmentary linked both to subjectivity ("I cannot give of myself, of my whole personality any other sample than a system of fragments, because I myself am something of the kind" [see Friedrich Schlegel, *Literary Notebooks: 1797–1801*, ed. Hans Eichner (London: Athlone, 1957), 17]) and to dissolution ("Many of the works of the ancients have become fragments. Many modern works are fragments as soon as they are written"—*Athenaeum*, frag. 24). This because, among other surprising but already more contradictory reasons, fragments ("You say that fragments are the real form of universal philosophy") are *fermenta cognitionis* (*Athenaeum*, frag, 259), or, as Novalis puts it, germs or "literary seeds" (*Pollen and Fragments: Selected Poetry and Prose of Novalis*, trans. Arthur Versluis [Grand Rapids, Mich.: Phanes Press, 1989], 39).

22. *Aesthetics*, 1: 66.

23. As we know, this is a constant and fundamental requirement of romanticism—and probably of the whole of modern art, *stricto sensu*—indissociable from the repatriation (or the deportation) of art into the space of subjectivity. And consequently into the space of the novel: "Many of the very best novels are compendia, encyclopedias of the whole spiritual life of a brilliant individual. . . . And every human being who is cultivated and who cultivates himself contains a novel within himself. But it isn't necessary for him to express it and write it out" (*Lyceum*, frag. 78). See Novalis: "A novel is a *life* considered as a book. Every life has an epigraph, a title, a publisher, a foreword, an introduction, text, *notes*, etc."; "One should, in order to learn to know life and to know oneself, always write a novel on the side"; "The novel deals with life—it (re)presents *life* [*stellt* Leben *dar*]"; "Nothing is more romantic than what is commonly called the world and destiny. We live in a huge novel (on a *large* and a *small* scale)" (*Schriften*, ed. Paul Kluckhohn and Richard Samuel [Stuttgart: Kohlhammer, 1960], 2: 599, 544, 570; 3: 434), etc. Hence the importance, in romanticism, of biography and autobiography. We shall come back to this point.

24. See *Aesthetics*, 1: 65.

25. All of these quotations are from *Aesthetics*, 1: 66–67.

26. Ibid., 1: 67.

188 NOTES TO PAGES 130-34

27. See *Grundlinien der Philosophie des Rechts*, ed. Hoffmeister (Hamburg: F. Meiner, "Phil. Bibliothek," 1955), 423; *Elements of the Philosophy of Right* [henceforth simply *Philosophy of Right*], trans. H. B. Nisbet (Cambridge: Cambridge University Press, 1991), 205-6.

28. *Philosophy of Right*, 204-5.

29. See on this point Hans Eichner's introduction to volume 5 (*Dichtungen*) of the *Kritische Friedrich-Schlegel-Ausgabe* (Munich: Schöningh, 1962), lii-liii; see also Otto Pöggeler, *Hegels Kritik der Romantik* (Bonn: Rheinische Friedrich-Wilhelms Universität, 1956), 196ff.

30. We know that, according to Schlegel, *Lucinde* is *ein religiöses Buch* (we shall return to this): it in part narrates, with a totally "Rousseauistic" complacency and honesty in confession and erotic-intellectual autobiography, the encounter (and then the cohabitation) of Schlegel and Dorothea Mendelssohn (see in particular chapters 1: "Confessions of a Blunderer"; 2: "A Dithyrambic Fantasy on the Loveliest Situation in the World"; 7: "Apprenticeship for Manhood"). A liaison already "scandalous" in itself for the time (as was the "communal living" of the Jena group) and whose scandalous character could only be enhanced by the publication of *Lucinde*—which was, moreover, received, for that reason, with some reticence by the members of the group themselves (Dorothea, Caroline, and A. W. Schlegel) and defended only with difficulty by Schleiermacher (see the *Vertraute Briefe über Schlegels Lucinde*). Fichte, alone among his contemporaries, saw in *Lucinde* (which, besides, owed a lot to him, as did all of Jena romanticism—at least for its terminology) a "work of genius" (see Eichner, op. cit., xlviff. and J.-J. Anstett's introduction to the Aubier edition, 37ff.). As to the scandal, we might be able to judge what could have shocked Hegel by reading this statement of Schlegel's in the *Athenaeum*: "Almost all marriages are simply concubinages, liaisons, or rather provisional experiments and distant approximations of a true marriage whose real essence, judged not according to the paradoxes of any old system but according to all spiritual and worldly laws, consists of the fusion of a number of persons into one person. A nice idea, but one fraught with a great many serious difficulties. For this reason, if for no other, the will should be given as much free rein as possible, since after all the will has some say in any decision of whether an individual is to remain independent or become only an integral part of a common personality. It's hard to imagine what basic objection there could be to a marriage *à quatre*. But when the State tries to keep even unsuccessful trial-marriages together by force, then, in so doing, it impedes the possibility of marriage itself, which might be helped by means of new and possibly more successful experiments" (*Athenaeum*, frag. 34).

31. *Philosophy of Right*, 206.

32. See, of course, Jacques Derrida, whose work will constantly guide us here (see, in particular, "Tympan," in *Margins of Philosophy*, trans. Alan Bass [Chicago: University of Chicago Press, 1982], ix-xxix; *Spurs: Nietzsche's Styles*, trans. Barbara Harlow [Chicago: University of Chicago Press, 1979] ; *Glas*, trans. John P. Leavey, Jr., and Richard Rand [Lincoln: University of Nebraska Press, 1990]).

33. We may be guided by a concept—deemed "general" by Hegel—of symbolism introduced, in the first part of the *Aesthetics*, to settle the question of the opposition between the ideal of art and nature: "The existing natural forms [*die vorhandenen Naturformen*] . . . are in fact to be regarded as symbolic in the general sense that they have no immediate value in themselves; on the contrary, they are an appearance of the inner and spiritual life which they express" (1: 172).

34. We propose this (double) *protrusion*—which will become triple when the question of *Witz* arises—as a doubling of the *relief* "picked up" ["relevé"] by Jean-Luc Nancy in his reading of the Hegelian *Aufhebung* (see *La Remarque spéculative* [Paris: Galilée, 1973], especially chapter 5: "Le Mot, le spéculatif ").

35. See *Philosophy of Right*, §166 (pp. 206-7), Remark: "In one of the most sublime presentations of piety—the *Antigone* of Sophocles—this quality is therefore declared to be primarily the law of woman, and it is presented as the law of emotive and subjective substantiality, of inwardness which has not yet been fully actualized, as the law of the ancient gods and of the chthonic realm, as an eternal law of which no one knows whence it came, and in opposition to the public law, the law of the state—

an opposition of the highest order in ethics and therefore in tragedy, and one which is individualized in femininity [*Weiblichkeit*] and masculinity in the same play."

36. *Aesthetics*, 1: 62.

37. G. W. F. Hegel, *Phänomenologie des Geistes, Werke in zwanzig Bänden* (Frankfurt: Suhrkamp, 1970), 3: 55; *Hegel's Phenomenology of Spirit*, trans. A. V. Miller (Oxford: Oxford University Press, 1977), 35. Hegel always rejected what, for instance, never ceased to haunt Schelling (see Philippe Lacoue-Labarthe and Jean-Luc Nancy, "Le Dialogue des genres," *Poétique* 21 [1975], 148-75). Nothing is more revealing in this respect than a note from *Kritische Xenien* (the *Wastebook*) of 1803-6: "The *fundamental principle* of a system of philosophy is its *result*. Just as we read the last scene of a play, the last page of a novel, or as Sancho thought it preferable to state in advance the solution of an enigma, so the beginning of a philosophy is certainly also its end, which is not the case in the aforementioned examples. For nobody will be content with the end or the solution of the enigma; on the contrary, the *movement* through which the end is produced will be deemed essential" (*Werke in zwanzig Bänden*, 2: 550).

38. Friedrich Nietzsche, *Beyond Good and Evil*, trans. Walter Kaufmann (New York: Random House, 1966), 169-70.

39. *Phenomenology of Spirit*, 455.

40. *Aesthetics*, 1: 62.

41. *The Will to Power*, frag. 811; quoted by Heidegger in *Nietzsche*, trans. David Farrell Krell (New York: Harper & Row, 1979), 1: 70. My emphasis.

42. *Aesthetics*, 2: 742.

43. Ibid., 1: 433-34.

44. Ibid., 2: 745, 739.

45. Ibid., 1: 434.

46. We are coming closest here to what, in Hegelian discourse—and in Hegelian discourse as reread by Heidegger—inscribes itself in psychoanalysis (that is, in Freud reread by Lacan). Mostly, we have in mind (its trace is now visible) a text such as "The Signification of the Phallus" (whose original title is, however, as we know, "Die Bedeutung des Phallus"), in which, on the question of (so-called) sexual difference, the themes of signification (of the Phallus), of Logos, of *Aufhebung*, and of *aletheia*—that is, correlatively, of the veil, the ornament, the fetish, etc.—are woven into a complex fabric impossible to untangle here. Let us say provisionally (we shall return to this elsewhere) that when one reads the Hegelian text, the text of Lacan also offers itself to be read. And particularly this: "The phallus is the privileged signifier of that mark in which the role of the Logos is joined with the advent of desire. / It can be said that this signifier is chosen because it is the most tangible element in the realm of sexual copulation, and also the most symbolic in the literal (typographical) sense of the term, since it is equivalent there to the (logical) copula. . . . / All these propositions merely conceal the fact that it can play its role only when veiled, that is to say, as itself a sign of the latency with which any signifiable is struck, when it is raised (*aufgehoben*) to the function of signifier. / The phallus is the signifier of this *Aufhebung* itself, which it inaugurates (initiates) by its disappearance. This is why the demon of *Aidos* (*Scham*) [the demon of shame] arises at the very moment when, in the ancient mysteries, the phallus is unveiled (see the famous painting in the Villa di Pompei)" (*Ecrits*, trans. Alan Sheridan [New York: Norton, 1977], 287-88).

47. *Aesthetics*, 2: 742-43.

48. It goes without saying that one could take the confrontation with Freud very far—up to the question, in fact, of the relation between *sublimation* and *sublation* (a question that still awaits its formulation). We only bring in repression or (especially) suppression here in order to indicate all that which, in this chapter of the *Aesthetics* (including the previous paragraphs on stature and attitude—the standing position, the face, the place of the nose in the [speculative] Greek profile, the eye and the gaze), invites this or that note in, for example, *Civilization and Its Discontents* (trans. James Strachey [New York: Norton, 1961], 37ff. and 52-54), among others, just as all that is said here about female

modesty invites, in large part, the fifth of the *New Introductory Lectures* ("Femininity," in Standard Edition, 22: 112–35).

49. *Aesthetics*, 2: 745.

50. Ibid., 2: 744.

51. Ibid., 2: 745.

52. This might explain why Socrates, the son of a sculptor and himself formerly a sculptor, may, at the very moment of the sublation of Greek art in and as philosophy (of consciousness) which he embodies, be like "one of those great plastic natures consistent through and through, such as we often see in those times — resembling a perfect classical work of art which has brought itself to this height of perfection" (*Lectures on the History of Philosophy*, trans. E. S. Haldane [New York: Humanities, 1955], 1: 393). A self-constituting and self-erecting figure: this is the last moment of the figure — not only the figure speaking, as in tragedy, but the figure enclosing (and only supported by) the "genius of inward conviction" (ibid., 1: 394).

53. See *The Philosophy of History*, trans. J. Sibree (New York: Dover, 1956), "Transition to the Greek World": "That the Spirit of the Egyptians presented itself to their consciousness in the form of a *problem*, is evident from the celebrated inscription in the sanctuary of the Goddess Neith at Saïs: '*I am that which is, that which was, and that which will be; no one has lifted my veil.*' This inscription indicates the principle of the Egyptian Spirit; though the opinion has often been entertained, that its purport applies to all times. Proclus supplies the addition: '*The fruit which I have produced is Helios.*' That which is clear to itself is, therefore, the result of, and the solution of, the problem in question. This lucidity is Spirit — the Son of Neith the concealed night-loving divinity. In the Egyptian Neith, Truth is still a problem. The Greek Apollo is its solution; his utterance is: '*Man, know thyself.*' In this dictum is not intended a self-recognition that regards the specialities of one's own weaknesses and defects: it is not the individual that is admonished to become acquainted with his idiosyncrasy, but humanity *in general* is summoned to self-knowledge. . . . Wonderfully, then, must the Greek legend surprise us, which relates that the Sphinx — the great Egyptian symbol — appeared in Thebes, uttering the words: 'What is that which in the morning goes on four legs, at midday on two, and in the evening on three?' Oedipus, giving the solution, *Man*, precipitated the Sphinx from the rock. The solution and liberation of that Oriental Spirit, which in Egypt had advanced so far as to propose the problem, is certainly this: that the Inner Being [the Essence] of Nature is Thought, which has its existence only in human consciousness" (220; see *Philosophy of Religion*, 2: 638–39). We must note that if this (speculative) allegorical interpretation of the myth of Saïs deliberately deviates from Kant (for he is indeed one of those who had "the opinion that . . . its purport applies to all times" [see *Critique of Judgement*, trans. James Creed Meredith (Oxford: Clarendon, 1952), 179, note: "Perhaps there has never been a more sublime utterance, or a thought more sublimely expressed, than the well-known inscription upon the Temple of *Isis* (Mother *Nature*): 'I am all that is, and that was, and that shall be, and no mortal hath raised the veil from before my face' "]), even if it deviates from Schiller ("The Veiled Image of Saïs" ends with the death of the seer), it is probably not unrelated (taking into account the differences, which are obviously abyssal) to a certain speculative *will* at work in *The Novices at Saïs* by Novalis (see, for example: "If it is true that no mortal succeeds in lifting the veil, as the inscription that I see there indicates, we shall therefore have to try to become immortal; whoever renounces lifting up the veil is not a real novice of Saïs" [*Schriften*, 1: 82]). The chain of these interpretations covers a whole history of the relation between philosophy and poetry. We are coming to this point.

54. *Phänomenologie des Geistes*, 589; *Phenomenology of Spirit*, 491 (translation modified).

55. *Aesthetics*, 1: 8.

56. Namely, that of romanticism itself as, for instance, it was defined by the "oldest systematic program of German idealism," to (the establishment of) which, as we know, Hegel was not a total stranger, or as Schelling had, with a certain obstinacy, tried to put it into practice (see our dossier in *Poétique* 21). Concerning the criticism of the historical and linguistic implications or presuppositions of this "return," I refer the reader to the introduction to *Reason in History: A General Introduc-*

tion to the Philosophy of History, "Reason in History," trans. Robert S. Hartman (New York: Macmillan, 1985), 72ff.

57. *Introduction to the Lectures on the History of Philosophy*, trans. T. M. Knox and A. V. Miller (Oxford: Clarendon, 1985), 156-59 (translation modified).

58. *Aesthetics*, 2: 960-61.

59. Ibid., 2: 968.

60. Ibid., 2: 971.

61. Ibid., 2: 973-74.

62. Ibid., 2: 976.

63. Ibid., 2: 973.

64. Ibid., 2: 976. This is why Hegel had to distinguish, in passing, between "a primitive poetry composed before ordinary prose had been skillfully developed and a poetic diction and mode of treatment developed within a period when prosaic expression had already been completely elaborated" (ibid., 2: 974).

65. See the *Republic*, II, 377ff. We have chosen here to transpose the *plastic* into *fictioning* in order to attempt, as it were, to pass between *Gestalt* and *Dichtung*, between *Bildung* and *Figur*.

66. *Aesthetics*, 2: 972.

67. *Theoretical fiction* would sooner be philosophical poetry (that is, Goethe, for instance, and especially Schiller). Not didactic poetry, which "is not to be numbered amongst the proper forms of art" and which is satisfied with merely "dressing up" a "content [that] has already been completely characterized prosaically" (*Aesthetics*, 1: 423). Besides, didactic poetry, unlike philosophical poetry, marks a "moment," which is that of the disappearance (*das Verschwinden*) of symbolic art and the birth of "primitive" (Greek) philosophy, of which Hesiod is the paragon (Lucretius, Virgil, and . . . Delille its epigones). Philosophical poetry, on the contrary, derives from Homer and the tragic writers, that is, in fact, from an era antecedent to the distinction (due to the understanding) between prose and poetry. It is not the "speculative kind" of poetry, but "primitive poetry," which "did not begin originally with a separation between the prose of thought (abstract thought) and poetry, i.e. thought's expression" (*Introduction to the Lectures on the History of Philosophy*, 157). Thus, philosophical poetry has nothing to do with horticulture, which "is for the most part just an external arrangement of a site already given by nature and not in itself beautiful," or with architectural decoration, which "makes pleasant the utility of premises devoted to prosaic circumstances and affairs" (*Aesthetics*, 1: 423), any more than with "mythical philosophizing," where, most of the time, it is as if "[philosophers] had the thought first and then have looked for the image" or as if one had "clothe[d] the thought in order to explain it" (*Introduction to the Lectures on the History of Philosophy*, 157). Philosophical poetry is poetry that, like religion (and "especially Greek religion"), "also contains thoughts and general ideas": "Poetry (i.e. the art which has language as its element) has got to the point of expressing thoughts, and we find in the poets too some profound and general thoughts. Such thoughts, e.g. about fate in Homer and the Greek tragedians, about living and dying, being and ceasing to be, birth and death, are indeed abstract and important thoughts, often presented in imagery, e.g. in Indian poetry" (ibid., 159). In other words, the difference between the "didactic" and the "philosophical" goes through the difference between abstract exteriority ("*belated*" ornamentation, bad rhetoric, the search for pleasure and elegance, etc.) and the (intimate) union of the figural and the spiritual. This is why, even if, in the *Darstellung* of the history of philosophy, one cannot include philosophical poetry (for the thoughts it contains have not reached "their proper form," that is, "the form of thought"), one must nevertheless acknowledge that "we could indeed talk of a philosophy of Aeschylus, Euripides, Schiller, Goethe, etc." (ibid.).

All of this brings us back, of course, to the *position of Schiller*, to the extent that Schiller—who never falls into didactic poetry—is the one who was able exemplarily to maintain, in speculative or philosophical poetry (in poetry as such, that is, as art), the balance between the theoretical and the fictional, the speculative and the figurative (see *Aesthetics*, 2: 1128 and 1146). Hence the position he occupies, beyond a poetics of genres (ibid., 2: 1146) and in the greatest proximity to the speculative, *reinscribing* [*remarquant*] in his poetry the very essence of poetry or the ideal (of beauty) in its concept—its figure. (See the *Aesthetics*, 1: 156, where Hegel comments in this way on "The Ideal and Life.") Basically, it is Schiller who produced "the poetry of poetry." What was needed was his "quiet control" (which Goethe did not have)—that control which he reveals even in his prose, itself exemplary, and hence akin to the great (historical and philosophical) prose of the Greeks, "the infinite . . . suppleness of their language" (see *Aesthetics*, 1: 408). Schiller has thus always been a *stylistic* model, for poetry (of the poetic essays of the "young Hegel," we know at least "Eleusis," sent to Hölderlin in 1796—Hölderlin, about whom the whole of the *Aesthetics* is impressively silent [see Hölderlin's *Correspondence*]) as, no doubt, for prose (which is attested—but one would have to examine this closely—by the *Phenomenology of Spirit*).

For all these reasons, if "theoretical fiction" designates rather appropriately philosophical poetry so understood, *fictional theory*—which one cannot equate, even though they are related, with didactic poetry (between them comes the whole pejorative weight of *fiction* in the banal sense)—would rather be the type of "poetry" embodied by Schlegel. Hegel, however, never goes so far as to say so. But this might be what Schlegel (by some dangerous *turn* that brings us back, but in a different way, to "theoretical fiction") had begun to perceive when, as a reader of the third *Critique* and in a quasi-Nietzschean way, he referred to a "logical fantasy [*Fantasie*]," or, even more radically, to a "logical fiction" ("The principle of contradiction itself and that of sufficient reason is a logical fiction, that is, the fiction of finality or of infinite connection"—Posthumous Philosophical Fragments, *Kritische Ausgabe*, 4: 1348; see also 1: 910). As we shall attempt to show, it is this (Kantian) (re)turn of fiction that the Hegelian valorization of philosophical poetry (of a particular species of "theoretical fiction") is trying to contain. And this with a view toward a rigorous separation of the philosophical and the poetic announced long before: "Of course, the *perfected* is always only *one*, but in particular in art, grandeur: the unwillingness to put colors on statues, to unite the lyrical element of the chorus with the dramatic element of the characters—or *philosophizing* and *poetizing*—in general, the determination of a necessary and strictly maintained dissociation" (*Wastebook*, 1803-6, p. 556).

68. *Aesthetics*, 2: 1001.

69. Ibid., 2: 1000.

70. Ibid., 2: 1001.

71. We are here at the very boundary of the problematic of *Witz*, which Hegel, precisely, never fails to *avoid* (at least in reference to romanticism). Concerning the Hegelian treatment of *Witz*, see Nancy, *La Remarque spéculative*, in particular the "epilogue." But we know that, here as elsewhere, what is always first condemned, as far as the use of language is concerned, is gratuity, insubordination (to the spiritual): the witticism for its own sake, in other words (as, to some extent, in Jean Paul; see *Aesthetics*, 1: 601), or—the proximity is not at all arbitrary—the figure for itself. Hence, for example, the condemnation of the romantic overuse of metaphors, which practically retraces that of *Witz* (see *Aesthetics*, 2: 1004 and 1012-13).

72. See Jacques Derrida, "White Mythology," in *Margins of Philosophy*, 207-71.

73. We could, in fact, relate all of this, not directly to the opposition between Kant and Hegel, but more strictly to the opposition between Kant *read by Nietzsche* (in Schopenhauer) and Hegel—in other words, to the opposition between a "philosophy of the *as if*" (of the *als ob*) and a philosophy of the *as such* (of the *als solche*)—assuming one does not make too serious a mistake by tracing negatively, in the thematics of the *as if*, the sign of a sort of muffled irruption of *aletheia* and of a displacement of the problematic of truth. Thus, a philosophy of the *as if*, with all it entails, that is, with the radical conclusion Nietzsche drew from "Kant"—but confronted with which Kant himself had basically retreated—namely, that philosophy itself is artistic (or fake [*artificieuse*], *künstlich* after all, as well as *künstlerich*) in essence, and that it is worth exactly what art is worth (and for the depreciation of which philosophy will have to pay). I refer the reader interested in this to *Philosophy in the Tragic Age of the Greeks* and *The Book of the Philosopher*, among other texts.

74. See, among others, Eric Auerbach, "Figura," in *Gesammelte Aufsätze zur romanischen Philologie* (Bern: Francke, 1967); J. Pépin, *Mythe et allégorie* (Paris: Aubier, 1958) and *Dante et la tradition de l'allégorie* (Paris: Vrin, 1970).

75. See *New Essays on Human Understanding*, trans. and ed. Peter Remnant and Jonathan Bennett (Cambridge: Cambridge University Press, 1981), III, X, §34 (p. 350).

76. [Lacoue-Labarthe alludes here to Jean Starobinski's monumental study *Jean-Jacques Rousseau: la transparence et l'obstacle* (Paris: Plon, 1957). —*Editor*]

77. *Republic*, II, 377c: "We must begin, then, it seems, by a censorship over our storymakers, and what they do well we must pass [*enkrinein*] and what not, reject [*apokrinein*]" (trans. Paul Shorey, in *Plato: The Collected Dialogues*, ed. Edith Hamilton and Huntington Cairns [Princeton: Princeton University Press, 1961], 624).

78. [One of the most important senses of *revenir* to which Lacoue-Labarthe alludes here is legal: the whole falls to, goes to, is the prerogative of, philosophy. —*Editor*]

79. See *Aesthetics*, 1, Introduction, 2 (1): "The Empirical Method" (14-21).

80. Aesthetics as science of sensuous knowledge is *gnoseologia inferior* (see Alexander Gottlieb Baumgarten, *Aesthetica* [Traiecti cis Viadrum: Kleyb, 1750], *Prolegomena*, §1 [p. 1]).

81. See Alfred Bäumler, *Kants Kritik der Urteilskraft, Ihre Geschichte und Systematik* (Halle: Niemeyer, 1923).

82. *Reflections on Poetry: Alexander Gottlieb Baumgarten's 'Meditationes philosophicae de nonnullis ad poema pertinentibus'* [henceforth *Meditationes*], translated with original text by Karl Aschenbrenner and William B. Holther (Berkeley: University of California Press, 1954), §9 (p. 7): *Oratio sensitiva perfecta est poema.*

83. *Meditationes*, §115 (p. 39), *Philosophia poetica est per scientia ad perfectionem dirigens orationem sensitivam.*

84. *Meditationes*, §117 (p. 40), *Rhetorica generalis scientia de imperfecte repraesentationes sensitivas proponendo in genere . . . Poetica generalis scientia de perfecte proponendo repraesentationes sensitivas in genere.*

85. [Lacoue-Labarthe alludes here (and below, p. 154) to Part VII ("Fundamental Problems of Aesthetics") of Ernst Cassirer's *The Philosophy of the Enlightenment*, trans. Fritz C. A. Koelln and James P. Pettegrove (Princeton: Princeton University Press, 1951). —*Editor*]

86. *Aesthetica, Prolegomena*, §1 (p. 1) —*Aesthetica (theoria liberalium artium, gnoseologia inferior, ars pulcre cogitandi, ars analogi rationis), est scientia cognitionis sensitivae.* —We should note here, however, if only in order to correct somewhat the effect that this analysis might produce, that the motif of the *analogon rationis*, whose determining character is obvious, has its origin in rhetoric and, more precisely, as Bäumler indicates, in the Aristotelian theory of the rhetorical paradigm, of analogical induction (see *Rhetoric*, II, 20). This is why one of the major concepts of the *Meditationes* is that of the *exemplum*, an instrument and milieu of comparison and a privileged mode of sensuous exposition. We shall come back to this point elsewhere.

87. *Aesthetica*, §483 (p. 309): *Est . . . veritas aesthetica . . . dicta VERISIMILITUDO.* —That fiction is the proper instrument of "probable knowledge" ["connaissance vraisemblable"] is confirmed by the treatment, in the heuristic of theoretical aesthetics, of *verisimilitudo* as *veritas aesthetica speciatim*, which, once again *speciatim*, comprises (historical and poetic, or extracosmic) fictions on the one hand, and fables on the other. In this distribution, "by far the greatest part of beautiful thinking" is said to belong to fiction (ibid., §505 [p. 325]).

88. See *Poetics*, 1459a.

89. *Aesthetica*, §28 (pp. 11 12).

90. *Aesthetica*, §31 (p. 13): *dispositio poetica* is the *facultas fingendi* —which is to "be referred" to *phantasia*. —See Novalis, "Theory of imagination [*Fantasie*]. It is the power to *make plastic* [*Sie ist das Vermögen des* Plastisierens]," *Schriften*, 3: 401.

91. *Aesthetica*, §25 (p. 10).

92. *Aesthetica*, §26 (p. 10): *Pars cognitionis, in qua peculiaris detegitur elegantia, est* FIGURA (*schema*).

93. See *Aesthetica*, §§505-38 (pp. 325-46).

94. *Aesthetica*, §6 (p. 3).

95. See *Meditationes*, §14 (p. 9).

96. *Aesthetics*, 2: 759.

97. *Aesthetica*, §§28-31 (pp. 11-13).

98. In all of Hegel, Baumgarten is apparently mentioned only once, in *The History of Philosophy*, as one of those who—along with Crusius and Mendelssohn—reworked (or exploited—*bearbeiten*) Wolfian philosophy. He does not appear anywhere in the *Aesthetics*, especially not in the chapter devoted to the "empirical method."

Select Chronological Bibliography of Works by Philippe Lacoue-Labarthe

Books

Le Titre de la lettre (with Jean-Luc Nancy). Paris: Galilée, 1972.

L'Absolu littéraire (with Jean-Luc Nancy). Paris: Le Seuil, 1978.

Portrait de l'artiste, en général. Paris: Bourgois, 1979.

Le Sujet de la philosophie (Typographies I). Paris: Aubier-Flammarion, 1979.

Retrait de l'artiste, en deux personnes (with François Martin). Lyon: MEM/Arte Facts, 1985.

L'Imitation des modernes (Typographies II). Paris: Galilée, 1986.

La Poésie comme expérience. Paris: Bourgois, 1986.

La Fiction du politique. Paris: Bourgois, 1987.

Musica ficta (Figures de Wagner). Paris: Bourgois, 1991.

Le Mythe nazi (with Jean-Luc Nancy). La Tour d'Aigues: Editions de l'Aube, 1991.

Uncollected Articles

"Le Dialogue des genres" (with Jean-Luc Nancy). *Poétique* 21 (1975): 148–75.

"Typographie." In *Mimesis: Des articulations*, 165–270. Paris: Aubier-Flammarion, 1975.

"Lettre (c'est une lettre)." In *Misère de la littérature*, 53–72. Paris: Bourgois, 1978.

"Le Retrait du politique" (with Jean-Luc Nancy). In *Le Retrait du politique*, 183–98. Paris: Galilée, 1983.

"La Vérité sublime." In *Du Sublime*, 97–147. Paris: Belin, 1988.

Edition

Les Fins de l'homme: A partir du travail de Jacques Derrida (with Jean-Luc Nancy). Paris: Galilée, 1981.

Miscellaneous

"Phrase" and "Clarification." In *Haine de la poésie*, 77–91. Paris: Bourgois, 1979.

"Ouverture" (with Jean-Luc Nancy). In *Les Fins de l'homme: A partir du travail de Jacques Derrida*, 9–21. Paris: Galilée, 1981.

"Ouverture" (with Jean-Luc Nancy). In *Rejouer le politique*, 11–28. Paris: Galilée, 1981.

Letter-postface to Michel Deutsch, *El Sisisi*, 119–25. Paris: Bourgois, 1986.

Foreword to *Théâtre des réalités*, 6–9 (English translation by Christine Decruppe, 114–16). Metz: Metz pour la photographie, 1986.

Foreword to Roger Laporte, *Lettre à personne*, 11–18. Paris: Plon, 1989.

Translations

F. Nietzsche. *La Naissance de la tragédie*. In *Œuvres philosophiques complètes*, vol. 1. Paris: Gallimard, 1977.

F. Hölderlin. *L'Antigone de Sophocle*. Paris: Bourgois, 1978.

W. Benjamin. *Le Concept de critique esthétique dans le romantisme allemand* (with Anne-Marie Lang). Paris: Flammarion, 1986.

V. J. Foix. *Gertrudis*, followed by *Krtu* (with Ana Domenech). Paris: Bourgois, 1987.

F. Nietzsche. *Fragments posthumes 1874-1876* (with Jean-Luc Nancy). In *Œuvres philosophiques complètes*, vol. 2(2). Paris: Gallimard, 1988.

In English

The Literary Absolute (with Jean-Luc Nancy). Translated by Philip Barnard and Cheryl Lester. Albany: State University of New York Press, 1988.

Typography: Mimesis, Philosophy, Politics. Edited by Christopher Fynsk. Cambridge, Mass.: Harvard University Press, 1989.

Heidegger, Art and Politics. Translated by Chris Turner. Oxford: Blackwell, 1990.

The Subject of Philosophy. Edited by Thomas Trezise. Minneapolis: University of Minnesota Press, 1993.

Index

Compiled by Hassan Melehy

Theory and History of Literature

Philippe Lacoue-Labarthe teaches at the University of Strasbourg and the University of California, Berkeley, and is currently Directeur de Programme at the Collège International de Philosophie in Paris. He is the author of numerous books, including *Typography: Mimesis, Philosophy, Politics*; *Heidegger, Art and Politics*; and, with Jean-Luc Nancy, *The Literary Absolute*.

Thomas Trezise teaches in the Department of Romance Languages and Literatures at Princeton University. He is the author of *Into the Breach: Samuel Beckett and the Ends of Literature*.

Linda Brooks is an assistant professor of comparative literature at the University of Georgia in Athens.